IMAGES
of America

WESTMONT

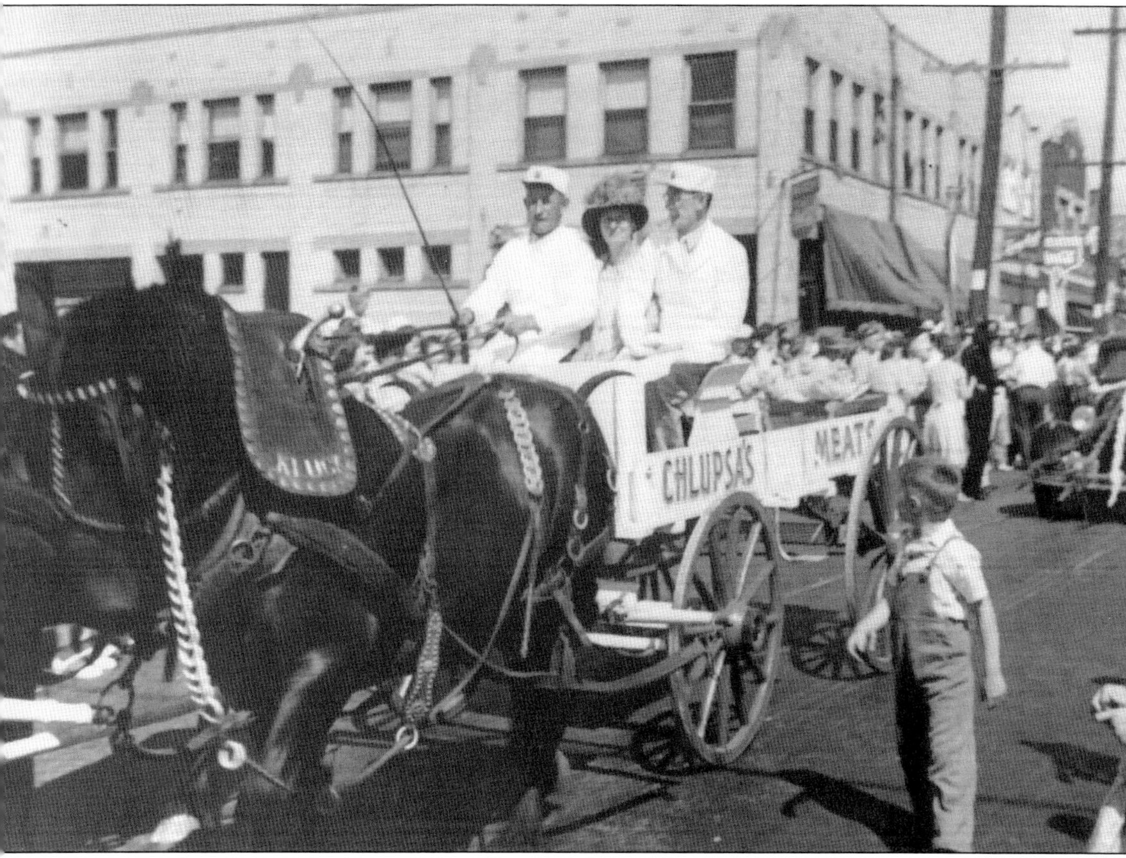

Some of Westmont's early residents take part in a parade. Horse-drawn buggies would have been common among area farmers and were easier to navigate on the unpaved streets of the village. The present-day Westmont Pharmacy building can be seen in the background. (Courtesy of the Westmont Area Historical Society.)

On the Cover: Three of Westmont's young residents participate in a soapbox derby. The race would have been held on Westmont's lighted baseball field just north of the Chicago, Burlington & Quincy Railroad (CB&Q) tracks. (Courtesy of the Westmont Area Historical Society.)

IMAGES
of America

WESTMONT

Maggie South with the
Westmont Area Historical Society

ARCADIA
PUBLISHING

ISBN 978-1-4671-0584-2

Published by Arcadia Publishing
Charleston, South Carolina

Printed in the United States of America

Library of Congress Control Number: 2020939661

For all general information, please contact Arcadia Publishing:
Telephone 843-853-2070
Fax 843-853-0044
E-mail sales@arcadiapublishing.com
For customer service and orders:
Toll-Free 1-888-313-2665

Visit us on the Internet at www.arcadiapublishing.com

For my grandparents.

Contents

ACKNOWLEDGMENTS

If it takes a village to raise a child, it takes a village, two historical societies, a park district, and a supporting cast of various friends and family to write a book.

First, my gratitude is given to the Westmont Area Historical Society, the Westmont Park District, and Alice Krampits. This book would not have been possible without the Sundays we spent poring over photographs in the museum and your office.

Second, a thank-you goes to the Village of Westmont, especially Mayor Ron Gunter, the board of trustees, and the anniversary committee.

Special thanks to Larry McIntyre, Jenny Babyar, and the Hinsdale Historical Society for their help with this project.

Finally, to the lovely group of people who have supported me during this process, my family and friends—*merci mille fois. Je vous aime.*

FOREWORD

While attending George Williams College in Downers Grove, one of my instructors was Joe Schultz, the director of the Westmont Park District. There was a position opening in Westmont, and Joe asked me to interview. I was hired and started my professional career as the Westmont Park District superintendent of recreation on May 15, 1977. When Joe Schultz left in 1980, I was promoted to director and served in that role until my retirement in 2016.

I attended my first park board meeting in a three-piece suit. Everyone else at the meeting was dressed casually in jeans, shorts, polos, and T-shirts. After the meeting, the commissioners took me with them to the Uptown. They put me at ease and let me know that I could just be myself. I never wore a three-piece suit to another meeting for the rest of my career.

From the very beginning, Westmont has been a perfect fit for me. The people are hardworking and have a great deal of pride. And they are equally generous and caring. Westmont has always been a community that cares about its people.

My wife, Toni, and I were married in 1978. We bought our first house, which was two blocks north of the railroad tracks, in 1980. We moved to East Dallas Street in 1984 and still live there today. Our son Brad was born in 1982, and daughter Natalie was born in 1985. They attended South School and then Westmont Jr. High and High School. When we started our family, Toni decided to be a stay-at-home mom. She devoted herself to our family and got involved as a religious education teacher, homeroom parent, and school fundraising volunteer—anything to do with our children and the school was her priority.

Being involved in the community became a way of life. I joined the Lions Club in 1979 and the Rotary Club in 1982. I became a member of the Knights of Columbus. I cochaired Pow Wow Days for many years with my friend and mentor, former mayor Jim Addington. I was a member of the Promote Westmont Commission and the 75th anniversary committee. I was a cochair for the Project 2000 celebration, which hosted the dedication of Westmont Centre on New Year's Eve at the turn of the 21st century. For me, the blend of personal life and community involvement was seamless.

Westmont has grown quite a bit since I first moved to town. In 1983, the park district purchased the Easy Acres private golf course, which was renamed Twin Lakes Golf Course. In 1991, the park acquired the Westmont Handball & Racquetball Club and then added a full gymnasium to the facility, which was renamed the Westmont Health Core and later became the Westmont Fitness Center. Also in 1991, the park acquired the land that became Twin Lakes Woods, which has since been renamed in honor of longtime park board commissioner Sandra Smith. An open area of land known as the Blackhorse property was acquired by the park district in 1991 and was later named after longtime park board commissioner and two-term Westmont mayor Frank Bellerive. In 1993, the park purchased the former Westmont Public Library facility at 55 East Richmond Street and transformed it into the park district's administration building and Westmont Senior Center.

In the late 1990s, we began conversations with Ty Inc., the company responsible for the international phenomenon of Beanie Babies. Ty built its corporate headquarters in Westmont adjacent to a 40-acre parcel of open land. The property was zoned for commercial development, but we were able to work with Ty and the Village of Westmont to transform this vacant land into the beautiful, award-winning Ty Warner Park. The park was opened on July 4, 2000, and has been the site of our annual fireworks ever since.

Westmont has been blessed for many years with community leaders who work cooperatively for the best interests of the entire community. Egos and differences are put aside so that we can do what we have been tasked to do—serve the community. I am very grateful for my time with the Westmont Park District working with several commissioners who each volunteered 30-plus years for the community—Bob Bernas, Frank Bellerive, Diane Main, Sandra Smith, and Jim Long. I could not be more proud to be involved in a community where our taxing bodies, public agencies, community organizations, businesses, and residents work together to ensure that Westmont is a great place to live, work, play, raise a family, go to work, buy a car, and dine.

The best thing about Westmont is the people. Year after year, I continue to be amazed by the number of people who step up and get involved in our community to make Westmont what it is. I've said it many times—Westmont has the best volunteers anywhere. Westmont is well-known for its many community events, none of which would be possible without our wonderful volunteers. These events include the Taste of Westmont, Westmont Cruisin' Nights and Street Fair, Independence Day celebration, Red, White & BBQ Festival, Wicked West Fest, Westmont Holly Days, and more. At one point, Westmont earned Governor's Hometown Awards, which recognize volunteerism and community involvement, for 10 consecutive years.

As my career with the park district was coming to a close, I thought about how I wanted to continue my life of community service. At the park district, I always wanted to be behind the scenes—I've always wanted to be more about the work itself and not the focus of attention personally. In fact, for most of my park district career, I rarely allowed my photograph to be taken whenever we had a special event or ceremony. So the idea of running for a village board position and entering politics was unsettling. But I was approached by people in the community who encouraged me to run for village board, and when I received the support of several board members who were planning to not run for reelection, I decided to give it a try. I've been lucky to run unopposed, and I am now completing my second term as mayor of Westmont and look forward to a third term.

As mayor, my eyes were opened to the details of our municipal government, and I've been impressed with our staff and their dedication to service. In the last eight years, our community has launched a number of new and successful initiatives including the approval of a community referendum that earmarks money for stormwater and infrastructure improvements; the creation of a new and wonderful sister city program; the accreditation of both our fire and police departments; the development of the incredible FMC Natatorium project, which is projected to bring in thousands of guests to Westmont each year; the revitalization of our South Westmont Business District at Cass Avenue and Sixty-Third Street; and much more. And by the fall of 2020, when we begin our yearlong celebration of our 100th anniversary of incorporation, we will open our new public works facility.

When we look back at the year 2020, we will be amazed that we battled a global pandemic in addition to international social unrest, and yet our people and community pushed forward toward a brighter future without hesitation. I've lived a blessed life. I've been lucky in so many ways. It's been my honor to serve the residents of this community, which I proudly call home. And yes, of course, I absolutely do love Westmont!

—Ronald J. Gunter, Mayor

Introduction

On the surface of things, Westmont, Illinois, looks like an average suburban town. There is one major artery through the downtown area, which is dotted with restaurants, bars, and insurance brokers. Everyone knows everyone. Case in point, my dad and aunt grew up in Westmont in the 1970s and 1980s. When I started my first job out of college with the Westmont Park District, I was working with people who had gone to high school with them.

I grew up in the unincorporated area of Westmont called Liberty Park and remember snatches of village history from my childhood. I very clearly remember the construction of Westmont Centre, and my sister and I were on the front page of the local paper playing in the fountain next to the train station. I obviously played with Beanie Babies when I was a kid. What child of the 1990s did not? But I did not realize Westmont's connection to the international phenomenon.

When I was researching this book, I came across a newspaper article wondering what made Westmont so special. It is, after all, a town like so many others in the western suburbs—tiny, close-knit, and blue-collar. As one starts to dig a little deeper, though, Westmont becomes much more fascinating. There is a rich history present here if you only know where to look. For such a sleepy small town, the village's history reads like a catalog of the Chicago area's greatest hits: speakeasies, the Chicago Cubs, Muddy Waters, Hollywood movies, and Beanie Babies. We have it all, even a tie to Eric Clapton and the Rolling Stones.

As I dug through the records in the Gregg House archives with Alice Krampits, who is the museum's curator, I was shocked by how much I did not know about this town. For example, our connection to Eric Clapton, who attended Muddy Waters's wedding while he lived in town. The Rolling Stones take their name from a Muddy Waters track and have (supposedly) visited town as well.

This town got its start as a little settlement in the middle of a sprawling swath of prairie. In just 100 years, it has grown to a thriving, busy commuter suburb with a population of approximately 25,000. The Westmont Park District maintains a huge amount of green space for residents to use for recreation. Its proximity to the city of Chicago, Fermilab, and Argonne National Laboratory make it a desirable place to live with an international presence—Westmont has a sister city relationship with Hsinchu County, Taiwan, and is home to Chicago's Taiwanese Cultural Center.

Over the course of its history, Westmont has faced what seem to be insurmountable problems like depressions and recessions. We always emerge from these challenges as a stronger, better community. We are so lucky to be a town of volunteers who will tirelessly give time making the village a better place to live, whether by donating food to the People's Resource Center or helping to park cars during Cruisin' Nights. Mr. Rogers always told us to look for the helpers, and I think that is what makes Westmont special. We are the helpers, and we all have the capacity to be helpers. The year 2020 has been a roller coaster, but the community has come together in unprecedented ways to help each other by sewing or donating masks and other protective equipment, offering to go to the store for neighbors who may not be able to, and in a million other small but important ways.

Growing up, I never imagined that I would be writing a book, let alone a book about the local history of my hometown. The town has been gifted with leadership that values its community history and preserving it. One of the struggles while working on this project was that so much of our recorded history is word-of-mouth rumor (like the Rolling Stones), and difficult to confirm. Hopefully, this book will serve as a definitive history of the first 100 years of the village. While writing this, I thought there was no way I would have enough information to fill 128 pages—I never anticipated that I would need to cut pages. Therefore, some information had to be left on the cutting-room floor. Any omissions are solely my fault, and I am very sorry for anything left out. All errors are also my own, and I apologize for them.

I do not know what the future will bring, but I know Westmont and its helpers will be here to face it with open hearts and hopeful spirits. Its history tells us we will.

One

Prairie to Progress

Preincorporation

The area that would become Westmont was originally inhabited by Potawatomi Native Americans, who vacated the land in 1833 for a small monetary settlement under coercion from the US government. Soon after, farmers began to stake their claims on the prairie. The Bush brothers from New York, who operated an early vegetable and livestock farm in the area, gave the settlement one of its earliest names—Bushville. Other early settlers, like Victor Fredenhagen, began to buy up swaths of the prairie to establish their dairy farms. The presence of the Chicago, Burlington & Quincy railroad allowed for Bushville's farmers to send their goods to and from the city with ease.

After the Great Chicago Fire of 1871, brick manufacturers began looking at the settlements around the city for materials they could use in the rebuilding efforts. One of these manufacturers was William L. Gregg, proprietor of the Excelsior Press Brick Manufacturing Company of Chicago, who chose Bushville as the home of his manufacturing operation in 1872. Excelsior had the capacity to employ up to 120 people and produce 70,000 bricks a day, although there is some debate as to how successful Excelsior was. Even though Gregg only stayed in the area for about two years, his presence continued to be felt for long after he went back to Philadelphia. The CB&Q station in town was called Gregg's Milk Station, later shortened to Gregg's. Cass Avenue was also called Gregg's Road for a time.

Slow but steady growth continued for the next several decades. European immigrants began to settle in what was now called Gregg's. City dwellers who had grown weary of urban living were attracted by the natural beauty of the land—south of what is now Fifty-Fifth Street was largely farmland, and to the north was an expansive prairie. These early settlers lived in small homes without paved streets, sidewalks, electricity, gas, sewers, or water mains. They often worked in Chicago at industrial jobs, bringing a more blue-collar group of people to the largely farming-based community.

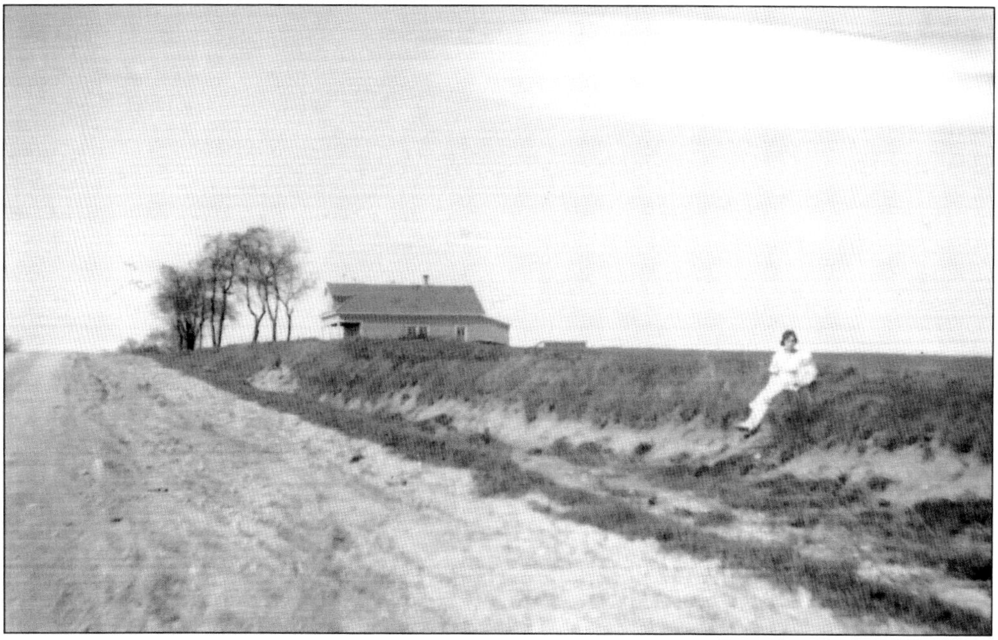

Lillian Misek and Frank Misek Jr. pose in this photograph. Many of Westmont's early residents lived on acres of rolling farmland and prairie, which provided a welcome respite from the crowded urban conditions of Chicago. The road seen here was unpaved until 1927. (Courtesy of the Westmont Area Historical Society.)

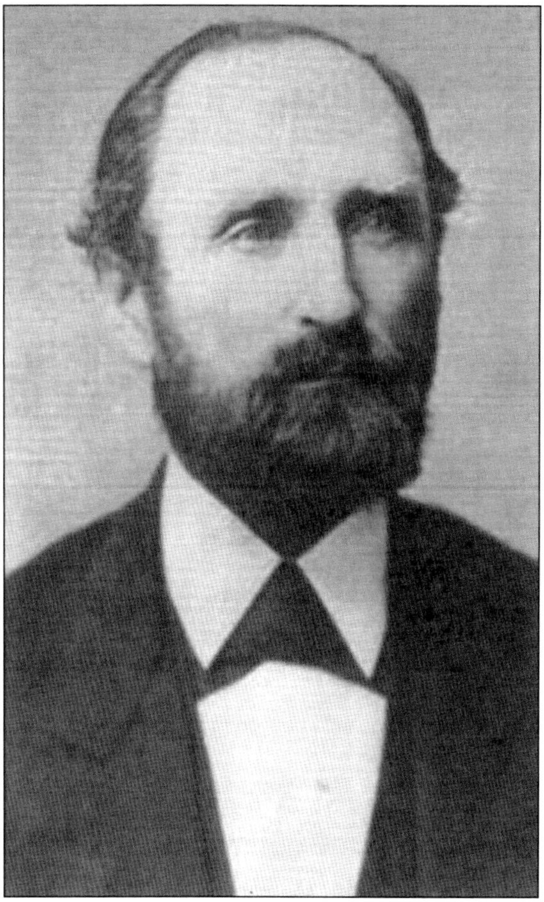

Victor Fredenhagen arrived in the area in 1855. He purchased approximately 1,200 acres of farmland to the south of what is today Fifty-Fifth Street and west of what would become Cass Avenue. He later donated part of this land for the establishment of the Maercker School. (Courtesy of the Westmont Area Historical Society.)

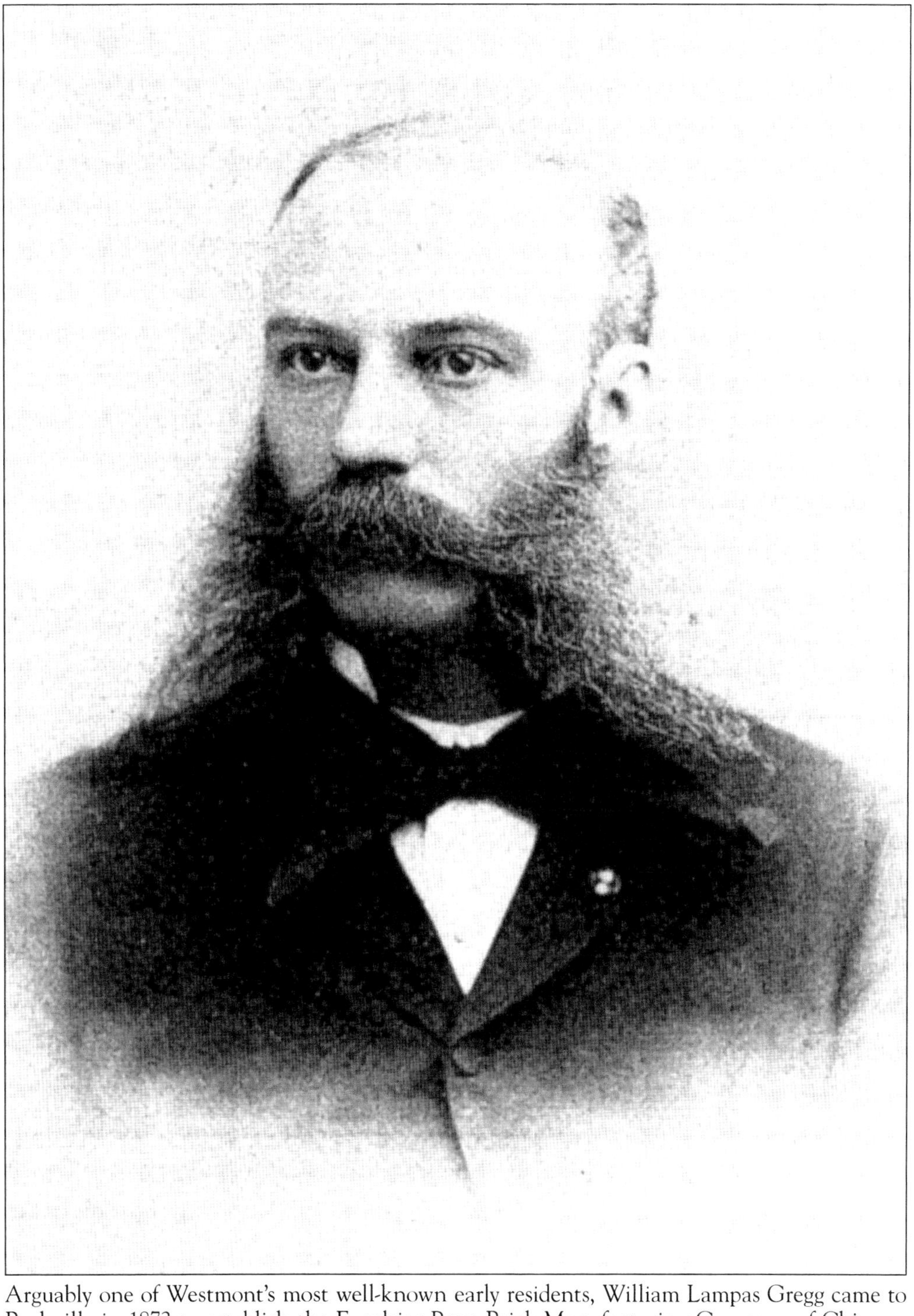

Arguably one of Westmont's most well-known early residents, William Lampas Gregg came to Bushville in 1872 to establish the Excelsior Press Brick Manufacturing Company of Chicago. Although Gregg left the area by 1875 to pursue other opportunities, he left an indelible mark on the community. (Courtesy of the Military Order of the Loyal Legion of the United States and the Union League Legacy Foundation.)

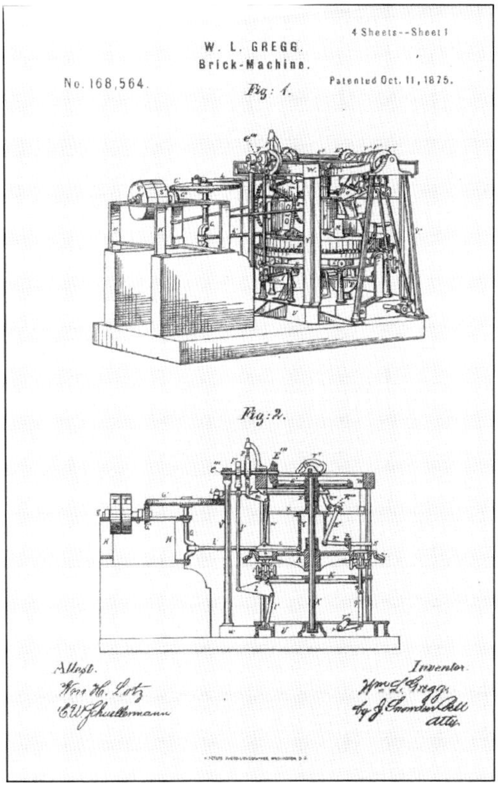

Among other things, William L. Gregg was an avid inventor who filed many patents. The patent pictured here dates from 1875 and is for his triple-pressure brick machine. Gregg alleged that this invention produced bricks that could withstand 100,000 pounds of pressure without cracking. (Courtesy of the Westmont Area Historical Society.)

Thomas A. Biddle purchased 100 shares of capital stock in the Excelsior Press Brick Manufacturing Company in 1873. Excelsior encountered financial difficulties by late 1875, despite an initial investment of $250,000 and William Gregg's technological advancements in the brick manufacturing process. (Courtesy of the Westmont Area Historical Society.)

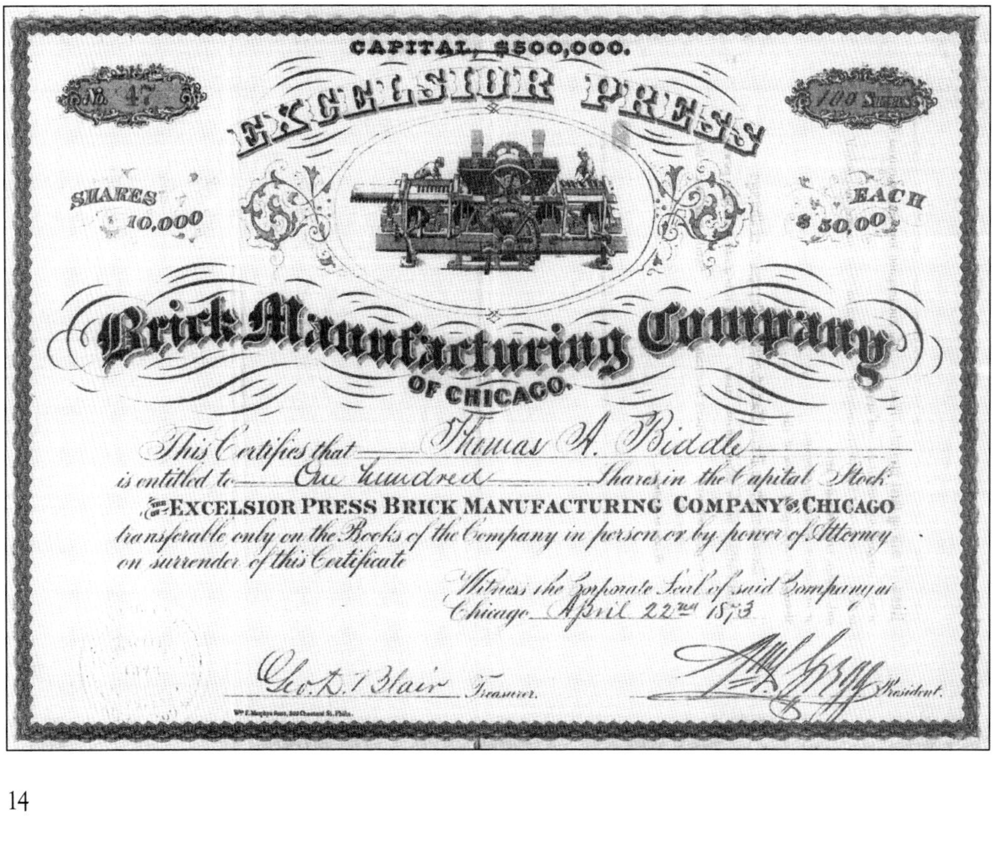

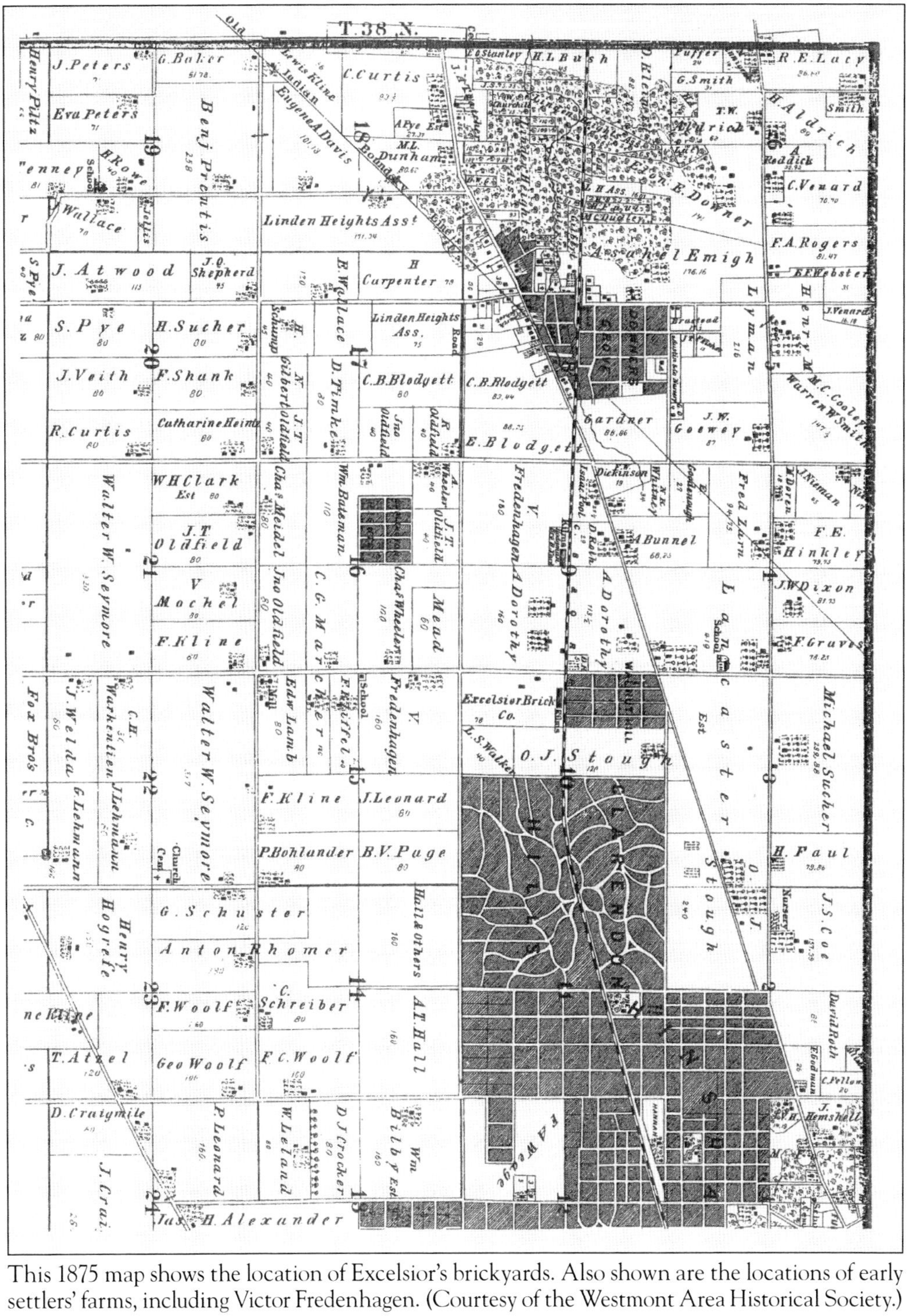

This 1875 map shows the location of Excelsior's brickyards. Also shown are the locations of early settlers' farms, including Victor Fredenhagen. (Courtesy of the Westmont Area Historical Society.)

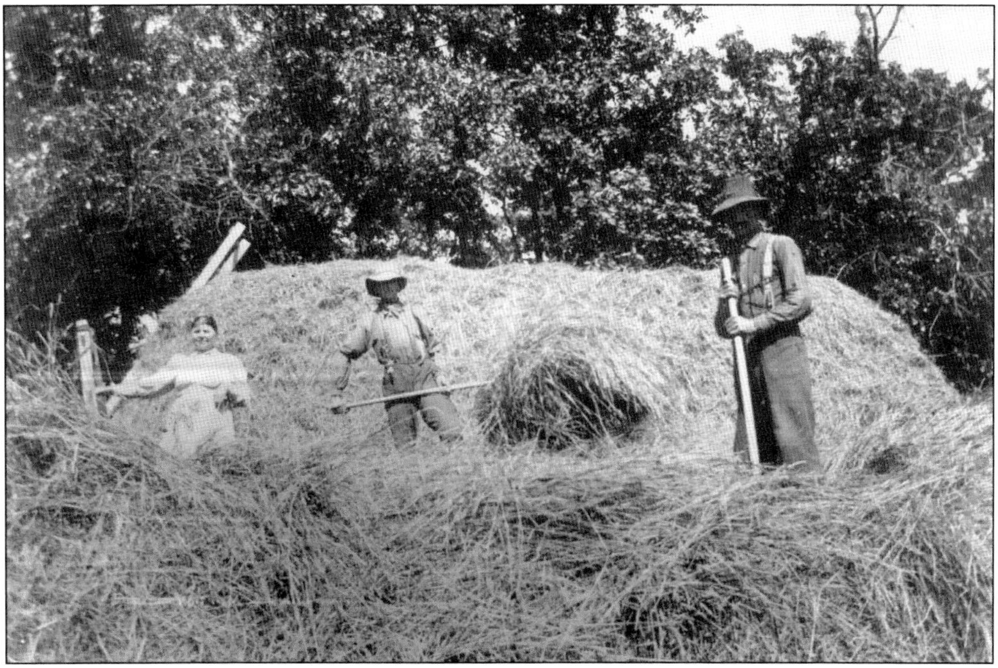

The Oestmann family operated a dairy farm on Sixty-Third Street in Westmont. Every August, Louis Oestmann and his family would invite other local farmers to participate in threshing bees to help harvest the grain that grew on the farm. Corn-shredding events took place in December. The Oestmann farmhouse still stands on Sixty-Third Street, just east of Cass Avenue. (Courtesy of the Westmont Area Historical Society.)

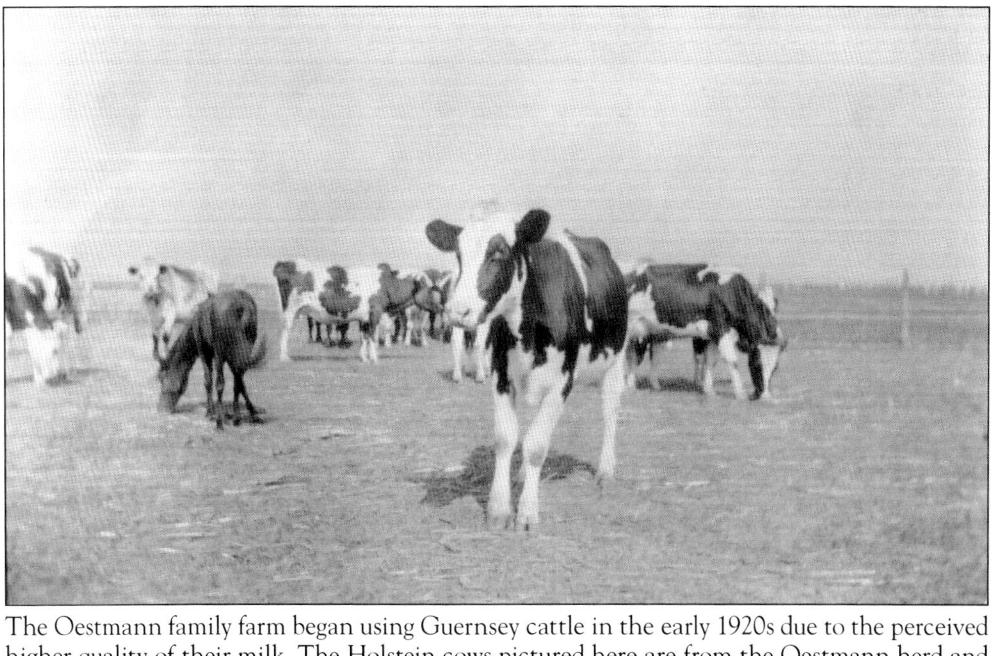

The Oestmann family farm began using Guernsey cattle in the early 1920s due to the perceived higher quality of their milk. The Holstein cows pictured here are from the Oestmann herd and would have grazed near Cass Avenue and Sixty-Third Street. (Courtesy of the Westmont Area Historical Society.)

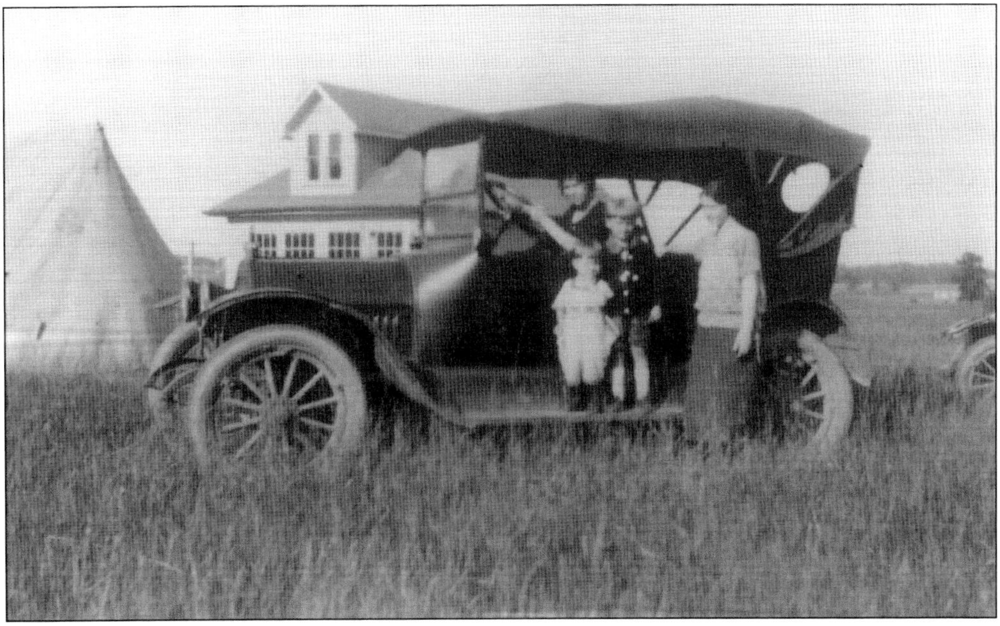

As new families arrived on the prairie, they often went without permanent lodgings. Some, like the Misek family, had to make do living in tents while they built their homes. (Courtesy of the Westmont Area Historical Society.)

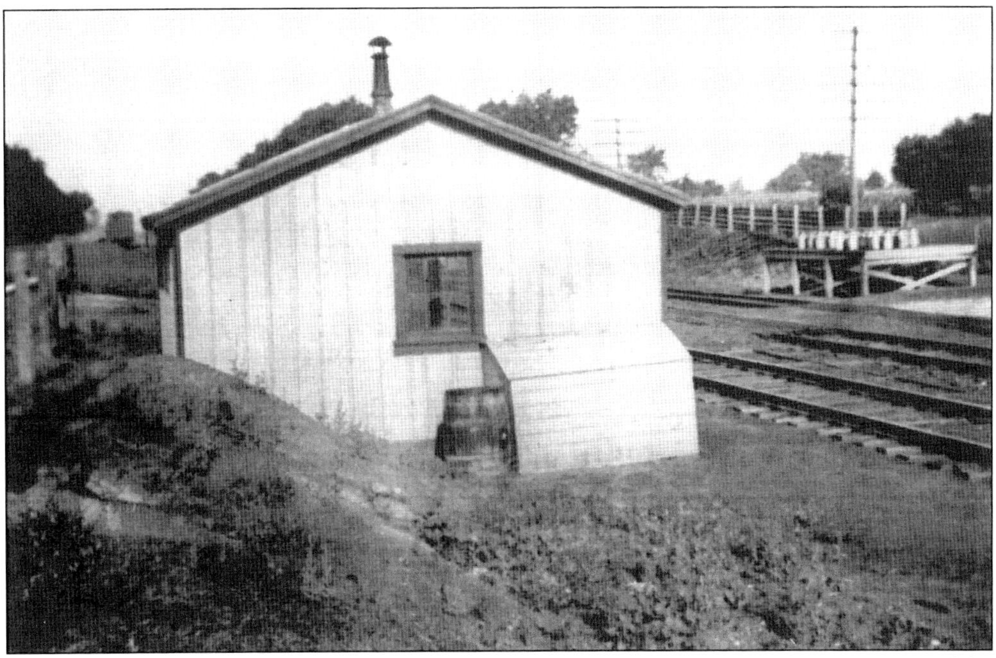

The most important development for the future growth of Westmont was the construction of the Chicago-to-Aurora branch of the Chicago, Burlington & Quincy railroad. Construction of this line was completed in 1864 and made commerce and travel more convenient for residents of the developing suburbs of Chicago. Dairy farmers sent their full milk cans into the city in the morning and retrieved the empty cans at night. In this 1919 photograph of Gregg's Milk Station, the empty milk cans can be seen on the north platform. (Courtesy of the Westmont Area Historical Society.)

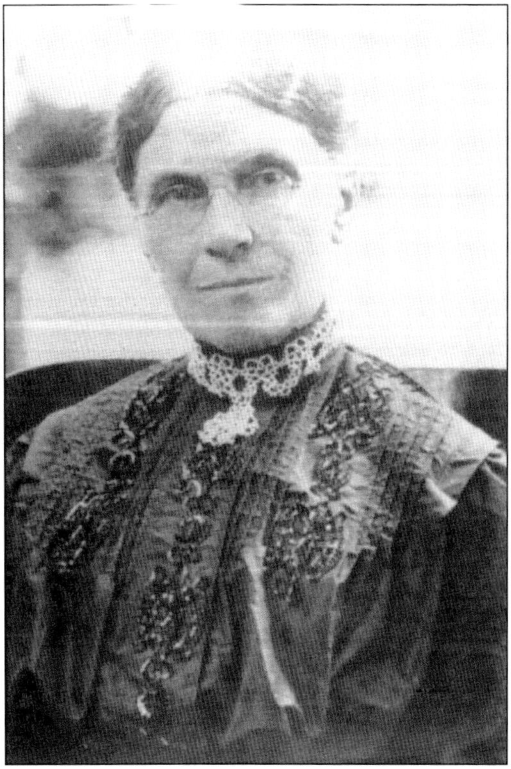

Anna Oldfield was born in England in 1842 and immigrated to the United States at the age of four. At 17, she married Charles Maercker, and they settled on a farm only a few hundred yards from Westmont's first school. In 1925, the parent-teacher association voted to name the school Maercker School to honor Anna's many years of work with the school and its students. (Courtesy of the Westmont Area Historical Society.)

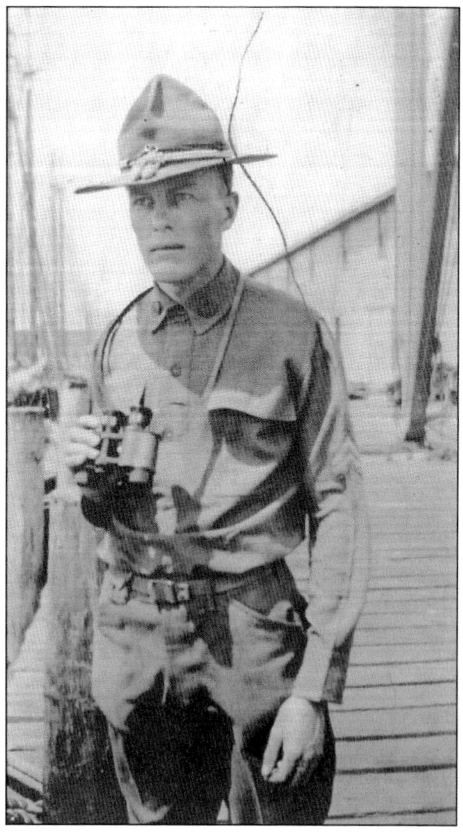

Claude Webster owned and operated Westmont's first pharmacy, originally located on North Cass Avenue. He enlisted in the Army in 1917 and was honorably discharged in 1919. He returned to Westmont and reopened Webster's Pharmacy, this time on Quincy Street, just south of the train tracks. Today, the building is home to commercial businesses and still stands at 19 West Quincy Street. (Courtesy of the Westmont Area Historical Society.)

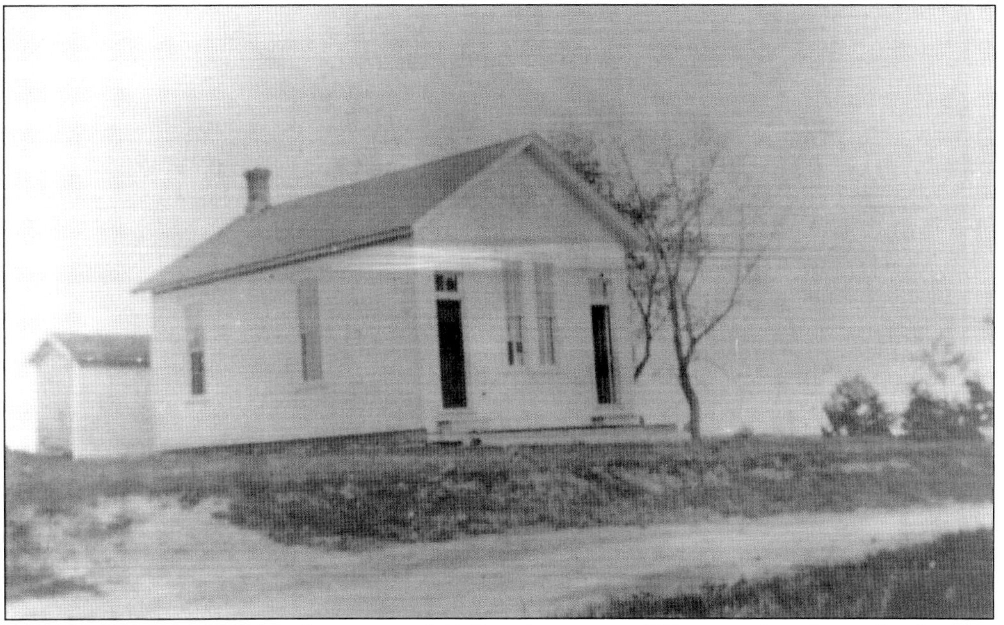

Maercker School opened its doors around 1857 and was one of Westmont's earliest schools. Also informally known as "South Gregg School" in the late 1800s, the wooden building stood on the site until the 1950s and consisted of a single room with a potbelly stove, pine benches, a granite wash basin and steel pail containing that day's water, and large wooden tables for desks. (Courtesy of the Westmont Area Historical Society.)

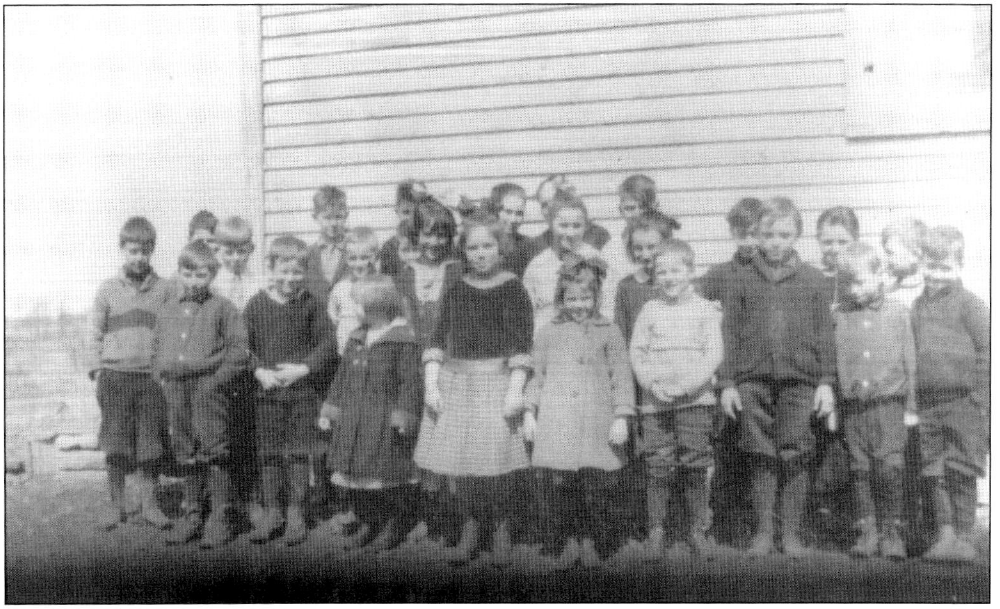

The class of Maercker School poses for a picture in 1918. Although boys and girls had to enter through separate doors, classes in the one-room schoolhouse were coeducational. (Courtesy of the Westmont Area Historical Society.)

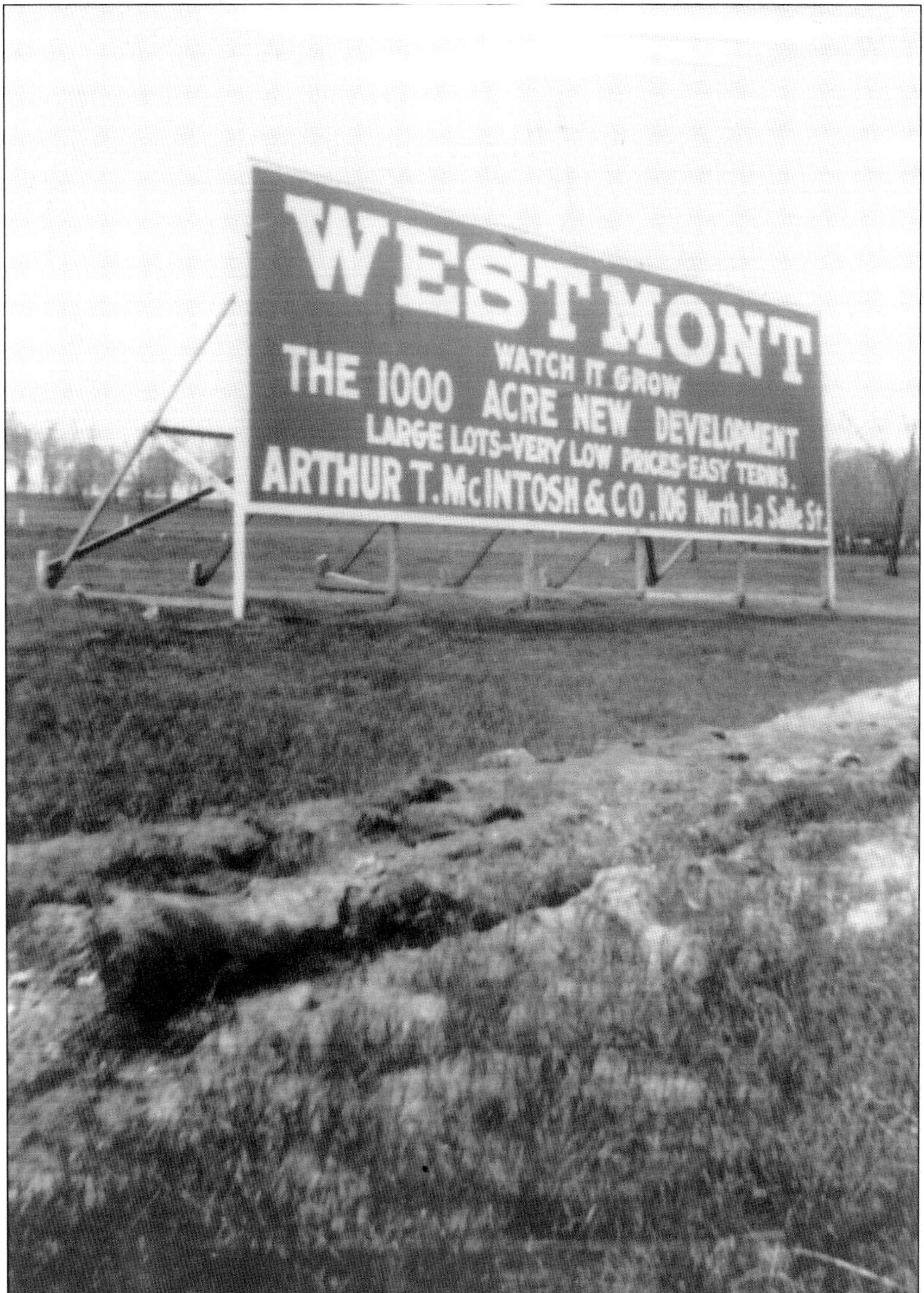

In the 1920s, Arthur T. McIntosh began selling houses and lots in Westmont. Lots were sold for $5 down with monthly payments, and homes could be purchased for $2,500 to $3,500. McIntosh also developed plans for early infrastructure, including paved streets and sidewalks, in order to attract residents. (Courtesy of the Westmont Area Historical Society.)

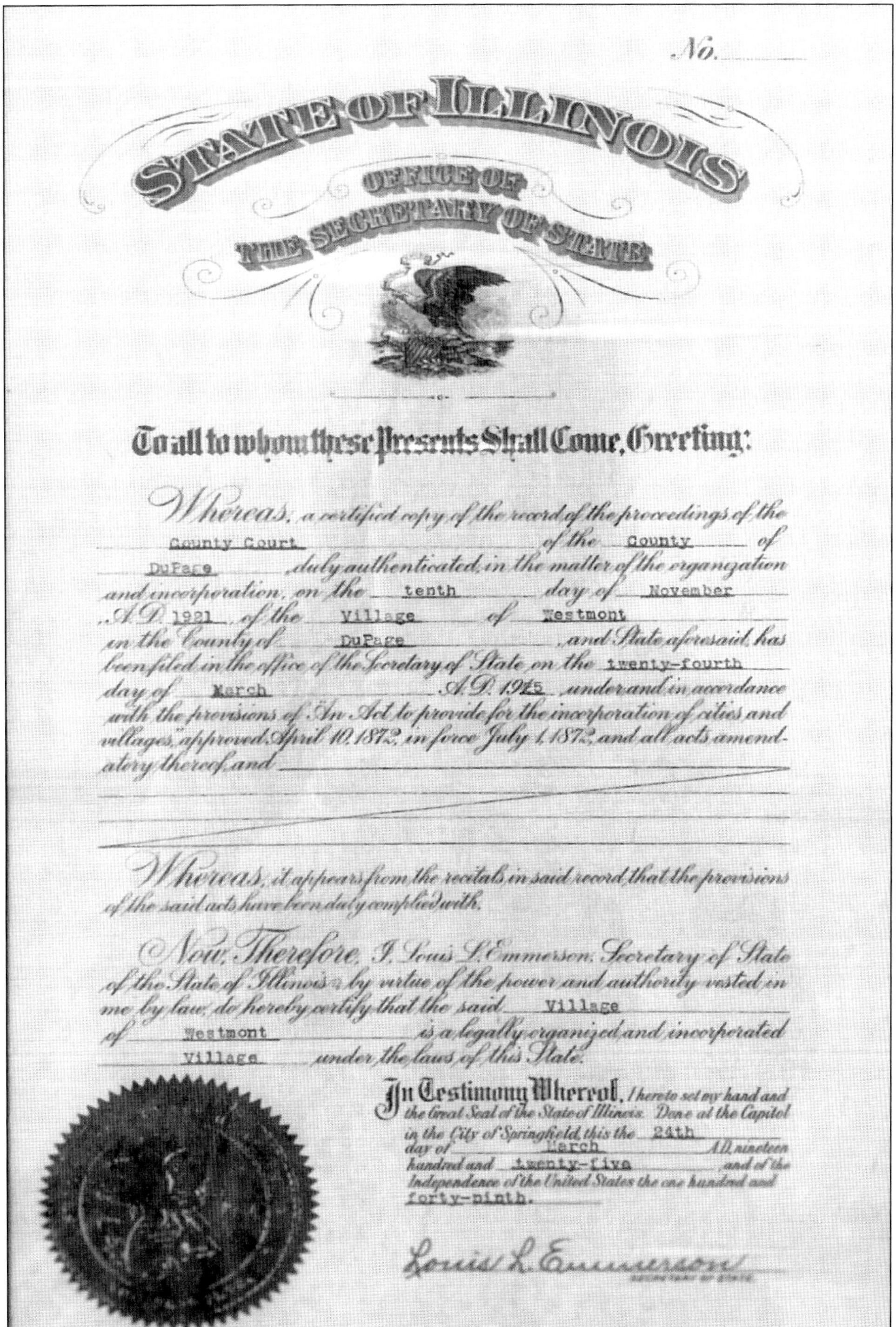

No.

STATE OF ILLINOIS
OFFICE OF
THE SECRETARY OF STATE

To all to whom these Presents Shall Come, Greeting:

Whereas, a certified copy of the record of the proceedings of the County Court of the County of DuPage duly authenticated, in the matter of the organization and incorporation, on the tenth day of November A.D. 1921, of the Village of Westmont in the County of DuPage, and State aforesaid, has been filed in the office of the Secretary of State on the twenty-fourth day of March A.D. 1925, under and in accordance with the provisions of "An Act to provide for the incorporation of cities and villages," approved April 10, 1872, in force July 1, 1872, and all acts amendatory thereof, and

Whereas, it appears from the recitals in said record that the provisions of the said acts have been duly complied with,

Now, Therefore, I, Louis L. Emmerson, Secretary of State of the State of Illinois, by virtue of the power and authority vested in me by law, do hereby certify that the said Village of Westmont is a legally organized and incorporated Village under the laws of this State.

In Testimony Whereof, I hereto set my hand and the Great Seal of the State of Illinois. Done at the Capitol in the City of Springfield, this the 24th day of March A.D. nineteen hundred and twenty-five, and of the Independence of the United States the one hundred and forty-ninth.

Louis L. Emmerson
Secretary of State

In November 1921, village residents voted 41-28 in favor of incorporation. The new village was named Westmont, alluding to its status as the highest point of elevation along the CB&Q west of Chicago. (Courtesy of the Village of Westmont.)

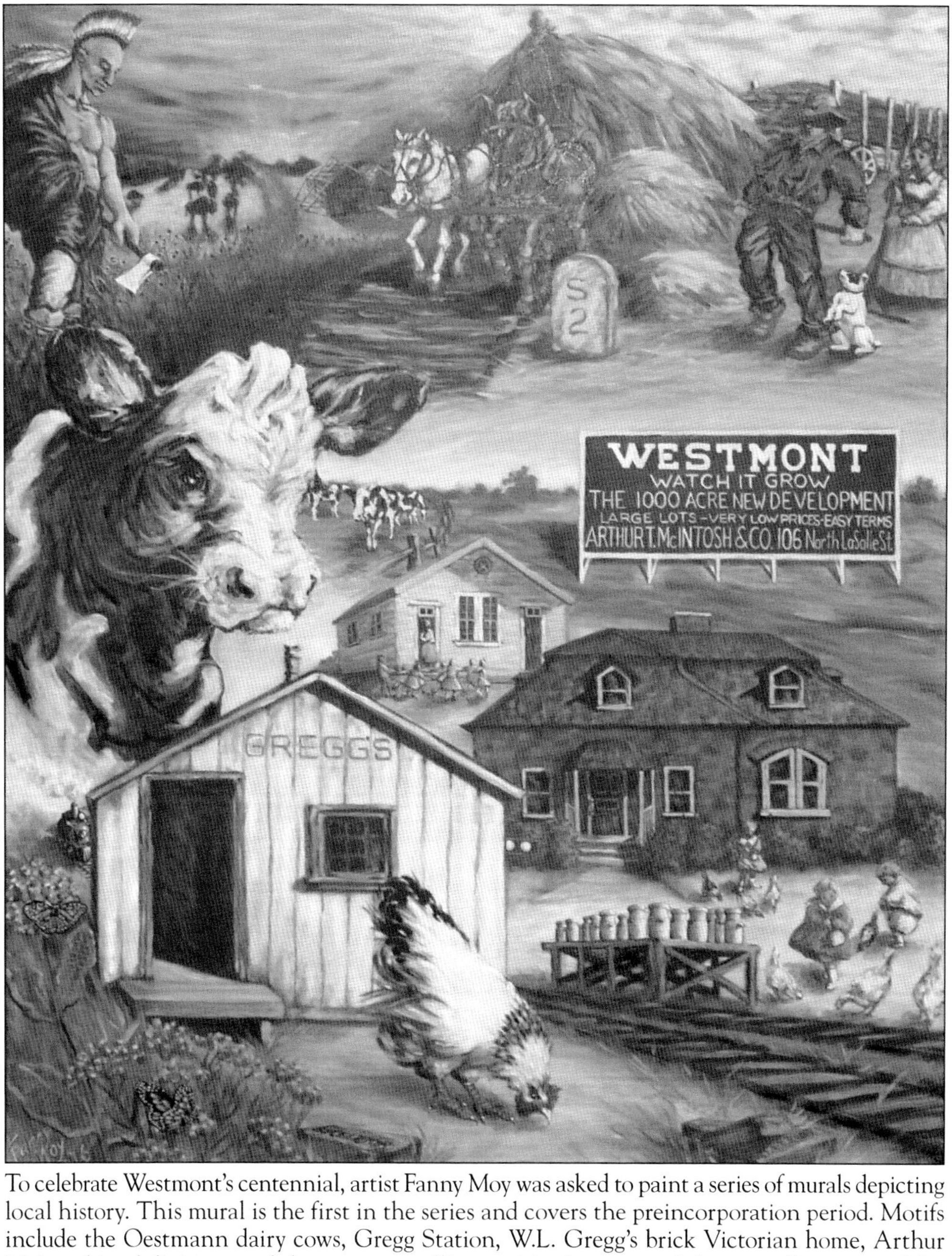

To celebrate Westmont's centennial, artist Fanny Moy was asked to paint a series of murals depicting local history. This mural is the first in the series and covers the preincorporation period. Motifs include the Oestmann dairy cows, Gregg Station, W.L. Gregg's brick Victorian home, Arthur McIntosh's subdivision, and the gorgeous rolling prairie that covered the area. (Courtesy of the Village of Westmont.)

Two

A Progressive Village 1920s to 1940s

In the 1920s, land developer Arthur McIntosh began to sell homes and lots in the community, as well as lay out streets and sidewalks for the new settlers. These new residents often worked blue-collar manufacturing jobs for Western Electric, International Harvester, or the Chicago, Burlington & Quincy Railroad and were drawn to the community for its more rural lifestyle.

In November 1921, the village was incorporated. Vince Pastor was selected as the first mayor. By 1924, the village boasted a fire department with one fire engine, as well as a library and community newspaper.

During the Great Depression, Westmont's growth came to a halt. The industries that had initially employed many of the village's early residents began to lay off workers en masse, and many families were receiving some type of federal relief. Between 1930 and 1940, the population only grew by about 300. During World War II, though, Chicago manufacturing plants began hiring workers to fulfill their defense contracts, lessening the financial burden on the village's residents. Finally, the village could resume its growth.

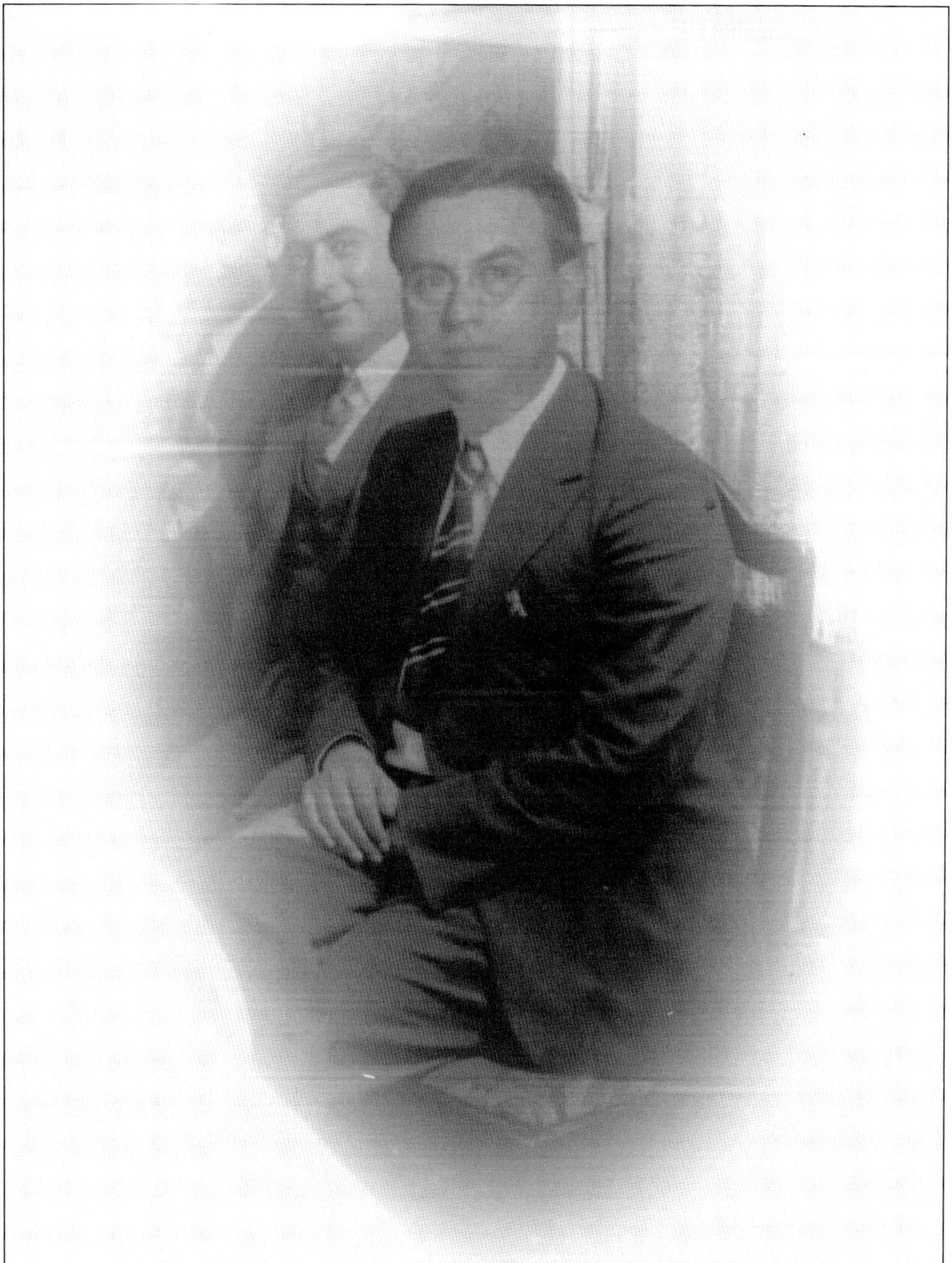

Following the village's incorporation in 1921, Vince Pastor was selected as the first mayor. He held the position for four years. (Courtesy of the Westmont Area Historical Society.)

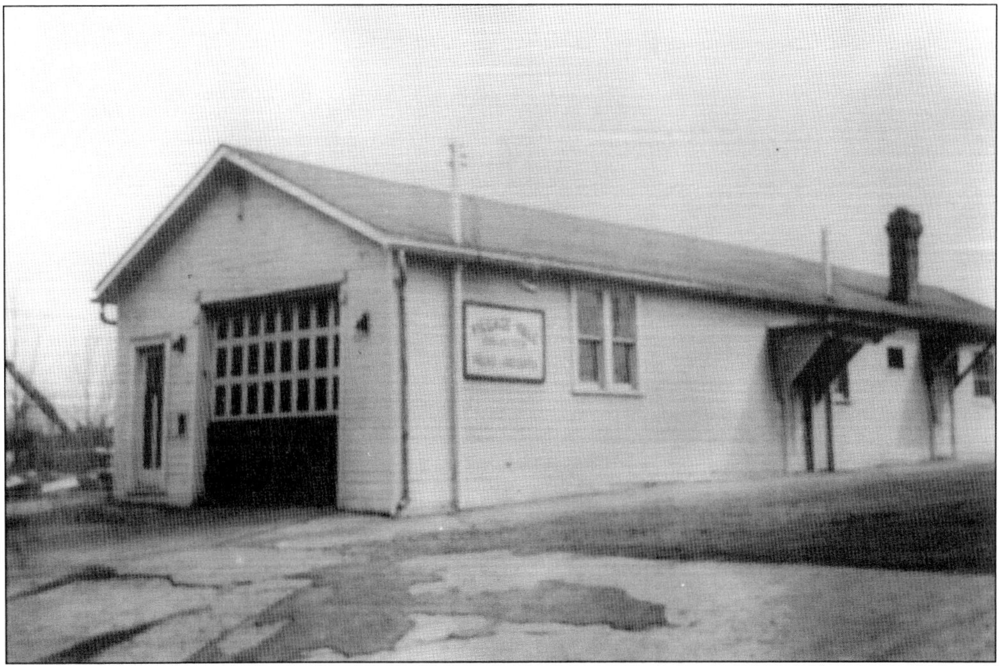

Westmont's earliest municipal buildings were on Burlington Avenue, just off Cass Avenue. Here, residents could find the village clerk's office, police department with its single holding cell, and the fire department. (Both, courtesy of the Westmont Area Historical Society.)

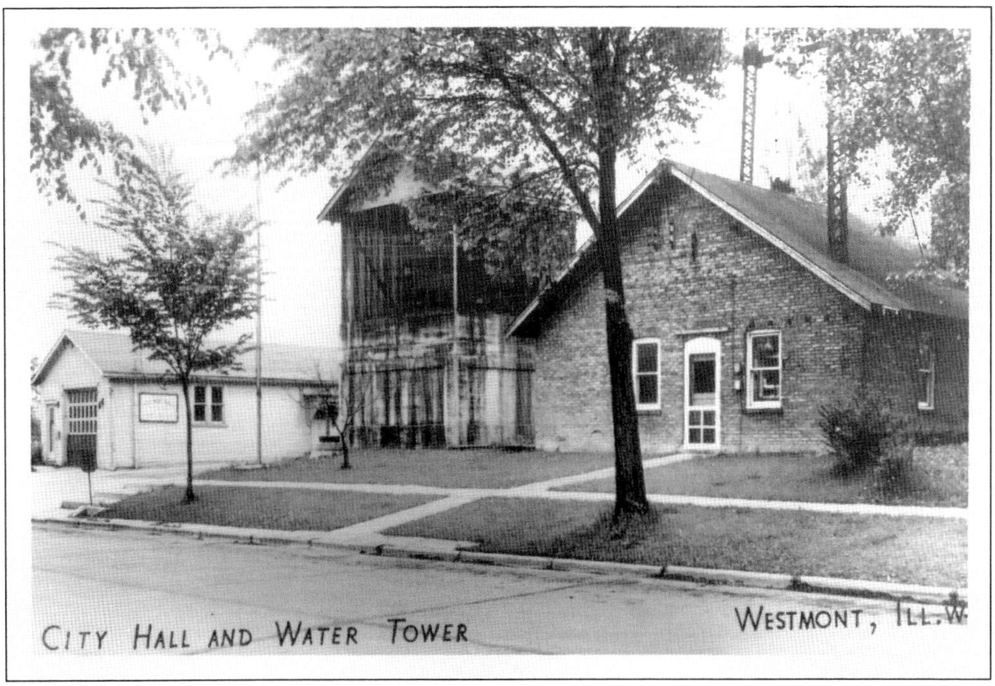

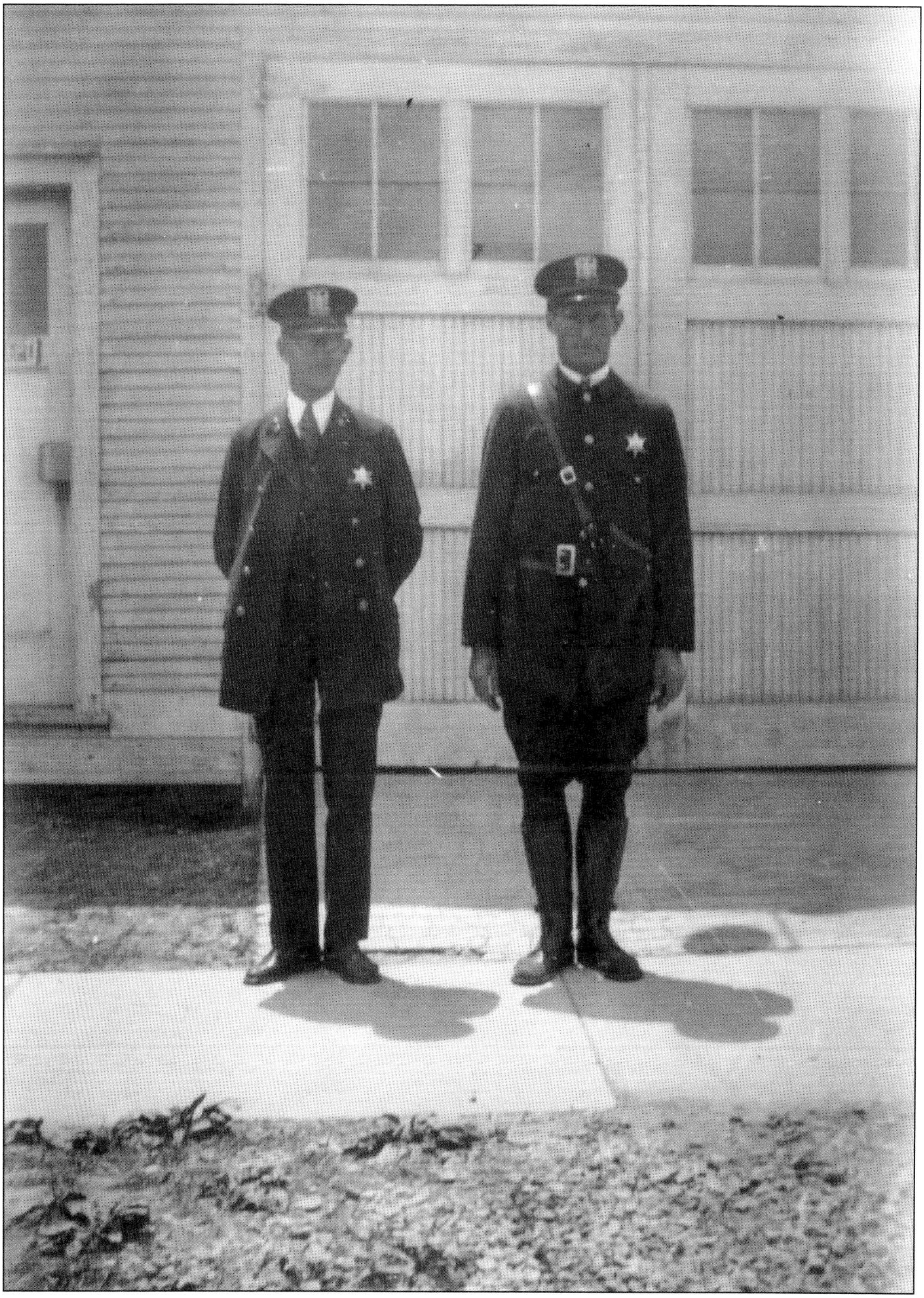

Following incorporation, Westmont could only boast two policemen. One worked the day shift, and the other worked nights. To signal that a policeman was needed, a 100-watt bulb at the top of the village's water tower was lit. The lack of policemen made it easy for the liquor trade in town to flourish in the face of Prohibition, leading some to later call the village "Wetmont" or "Whiskey Hill." (Courtesy of the Westmont Area Historical Society.)

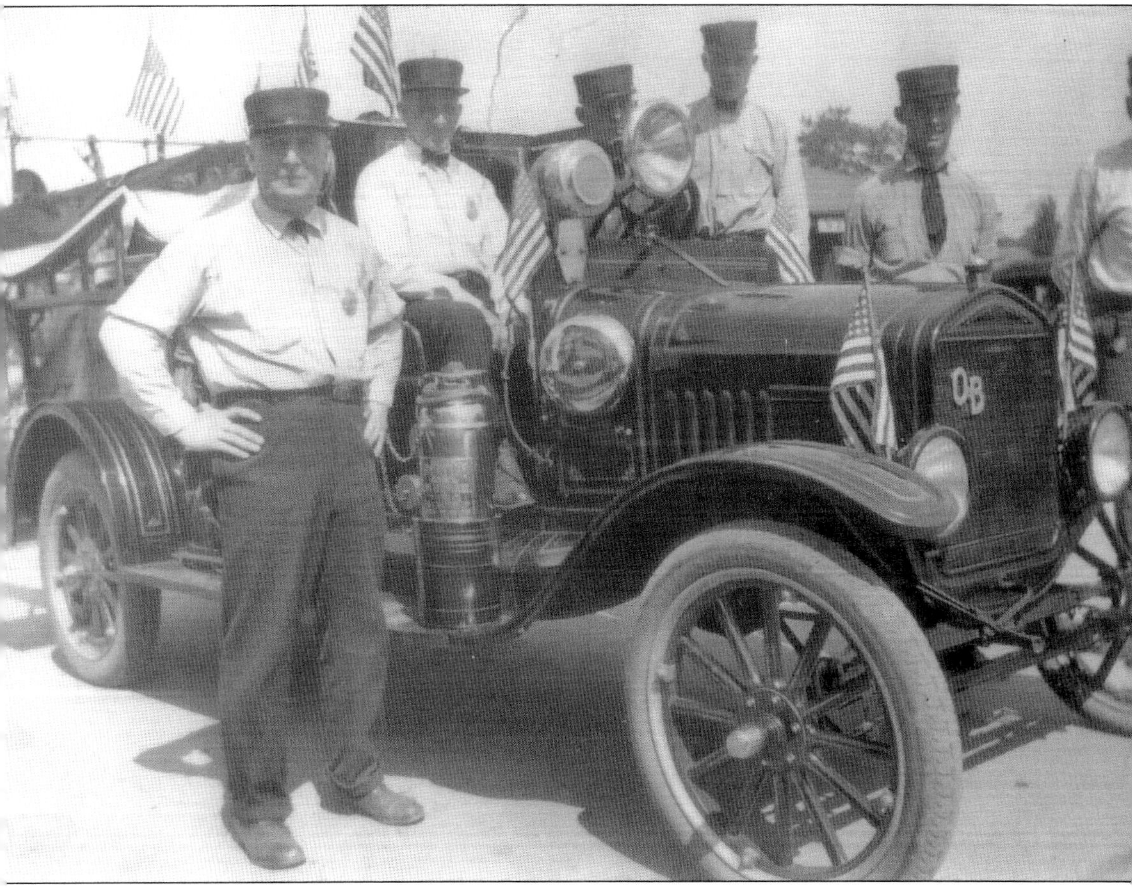

Westmont's fire department was founded on October 13, 1923. By 1924, it had acquired its first engine, a converted Model T truck. It was housed at the village's municipal building. Harry Woods was the first fire chief. Fires in the early days usually occurred in chimneys, sheds, and chicken coops, or on the prairie. (Courtesy of the Westmont Area Historical Society.)

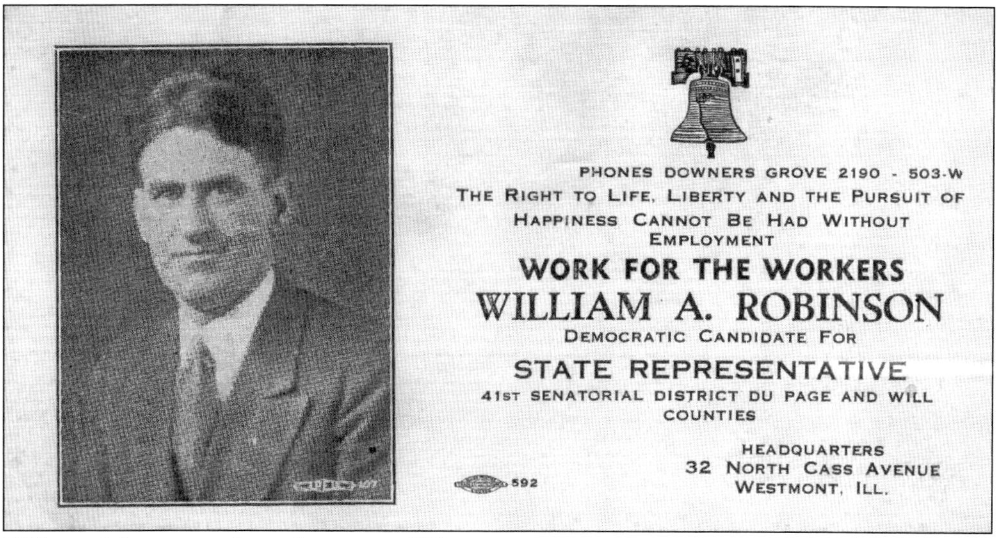

William Robinson is the only mayor of Westmont to serve two nonconsecutive terms. He was first in office from 1929 to 1935 and again from 1953 to 1961 following a failed bid for state representative. His campaign headquarters were at 32 North Cass Avenue. (Courtesy of the Westmont Area Historical Society.)

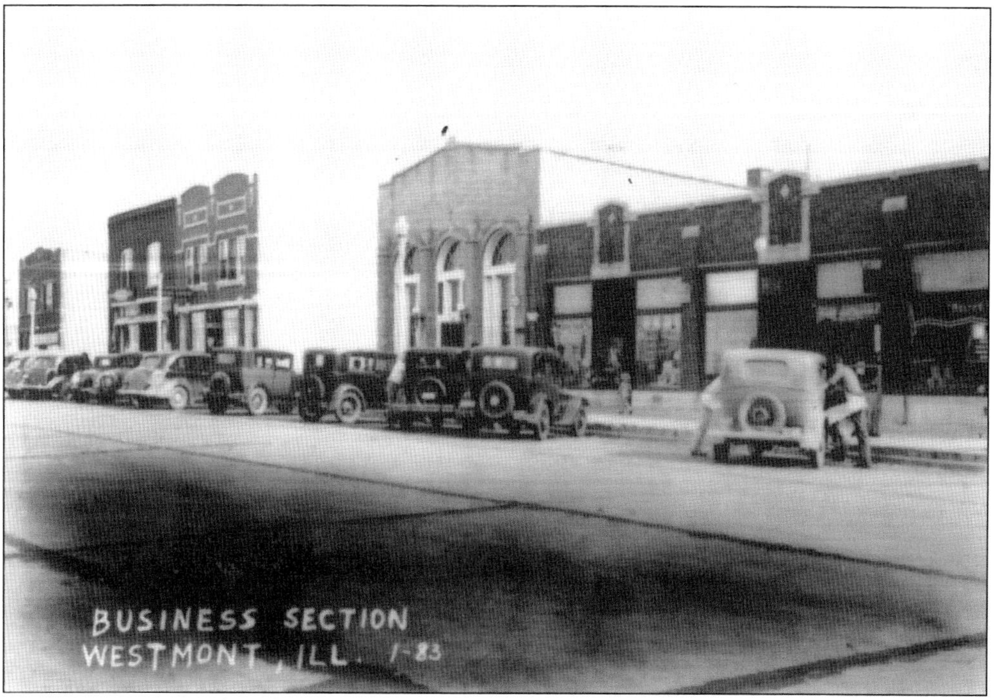

Quincy Street served as the home for many local businesses, including the First State Bank of Westmont and Webster's Pharmacy. Today, Quincy Street is the home of several dining establishments and village hall and is the future site of a luxury condominium development. (Courtesy of the Westmont Area Historical Society.)

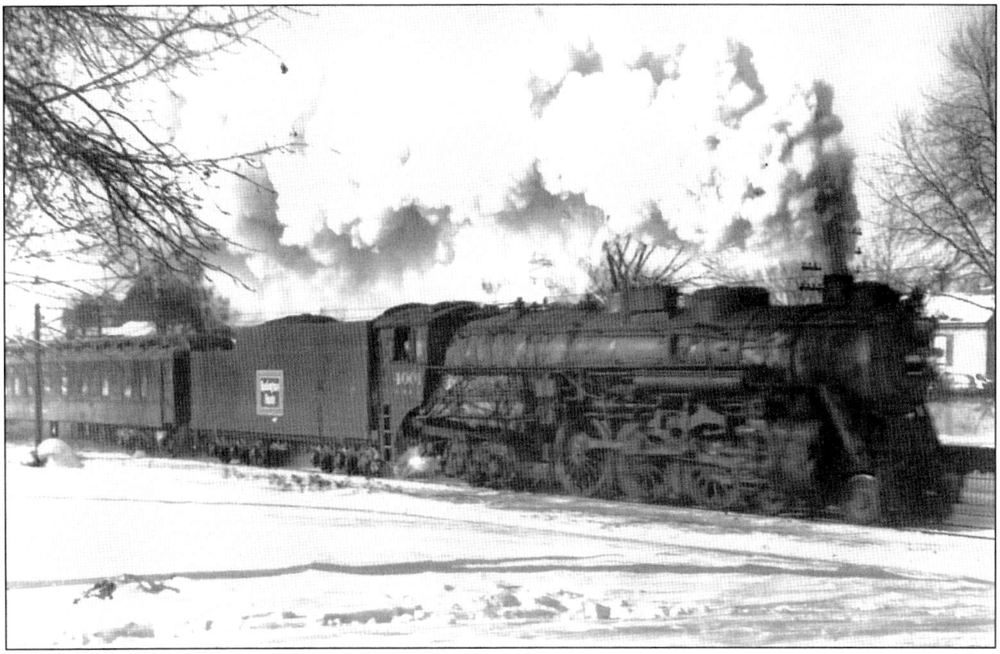

Nothing was more important to the development of the village of Westmont than the Chicago, Burlington & Quincy Railroad's establishment in 1864. The train line carried produce and milk from local farms into Chicago to be sold, and transported workers from Westmont to their jobs at places like Western Electric. The railroad also provided local farmers with a link to the city's stockyards. (Both, courtesy of the Westmont Area Historical Society.)

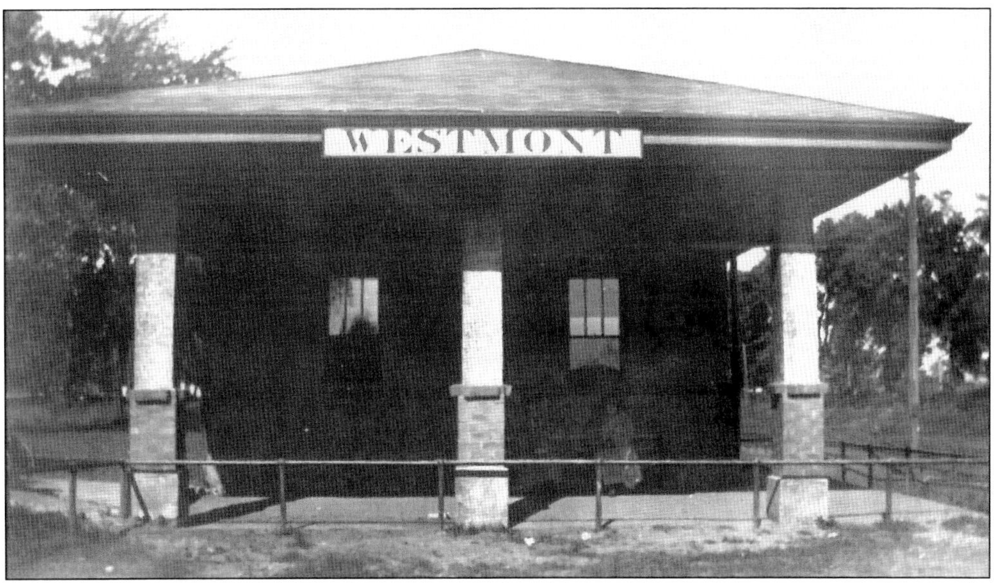

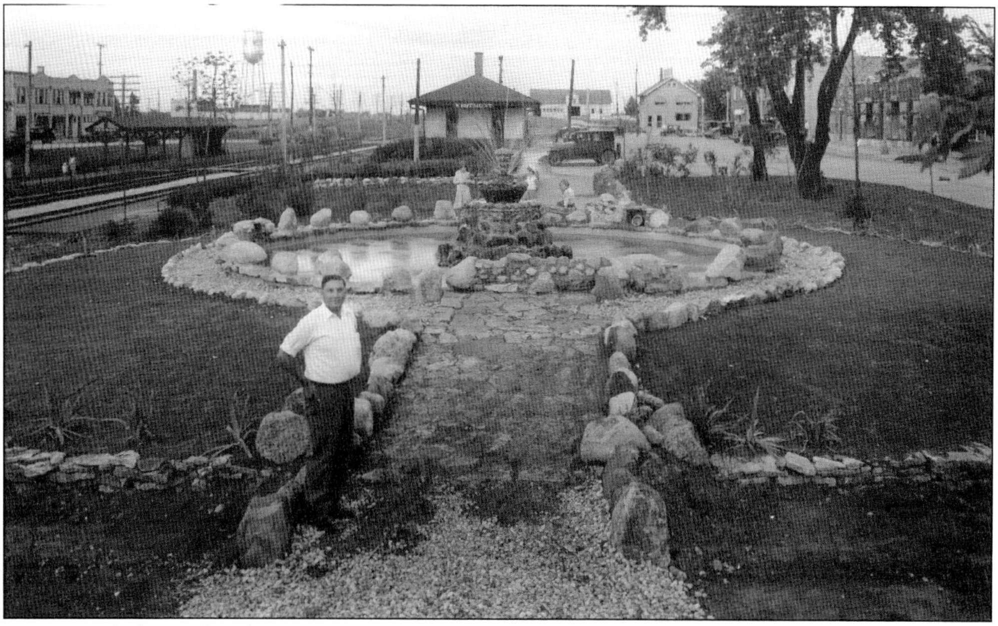

In 1932, to help combat the Great Depression, newly elected president Franklin D. Roosevelt formed the Works Progress Administration (WPA). One of the WPA's projects was the construction of a park and fountain on Quincy Street, near the train tracks. The construction of the fountain provided jobs to local people who had lost theirs. People used to swim in the fountain during the warm summer months. The project was completed between 1935 and 1943. Today, it is the site of a commuter parking lot. (Courtesy of the Westmont Area Historical Society.)

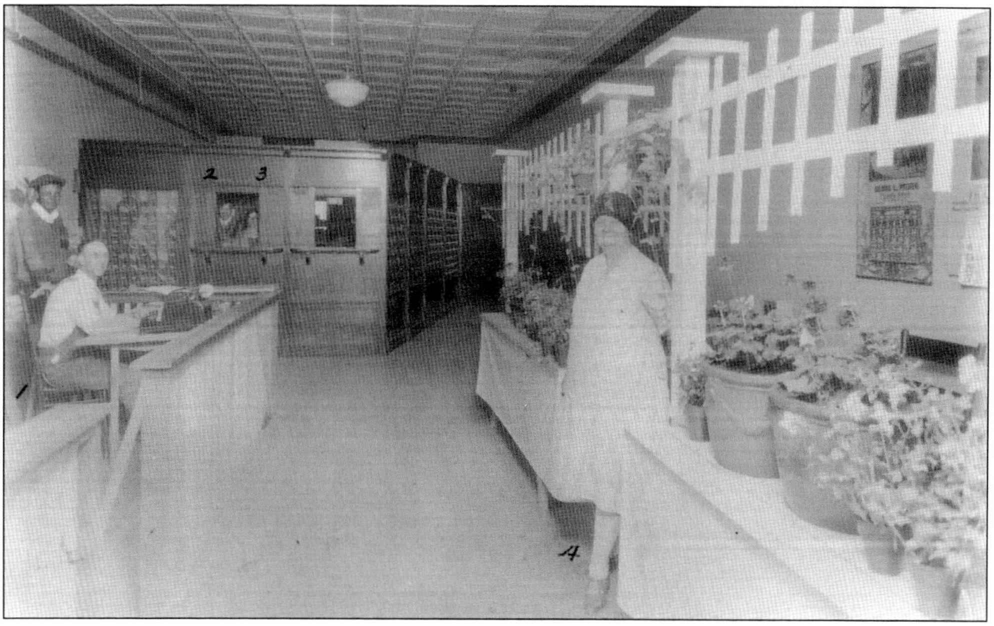

Westmont's first post office was at 7 West Quincy Street. Seated at left is Irvin Green. He served as the postmaster and was mayor from 1926 until 1927. The post office has occupied many locations over the years and is now on Cass Avenue, near Maercker School. (Courtesy of the Westmont Area Historical Society.)

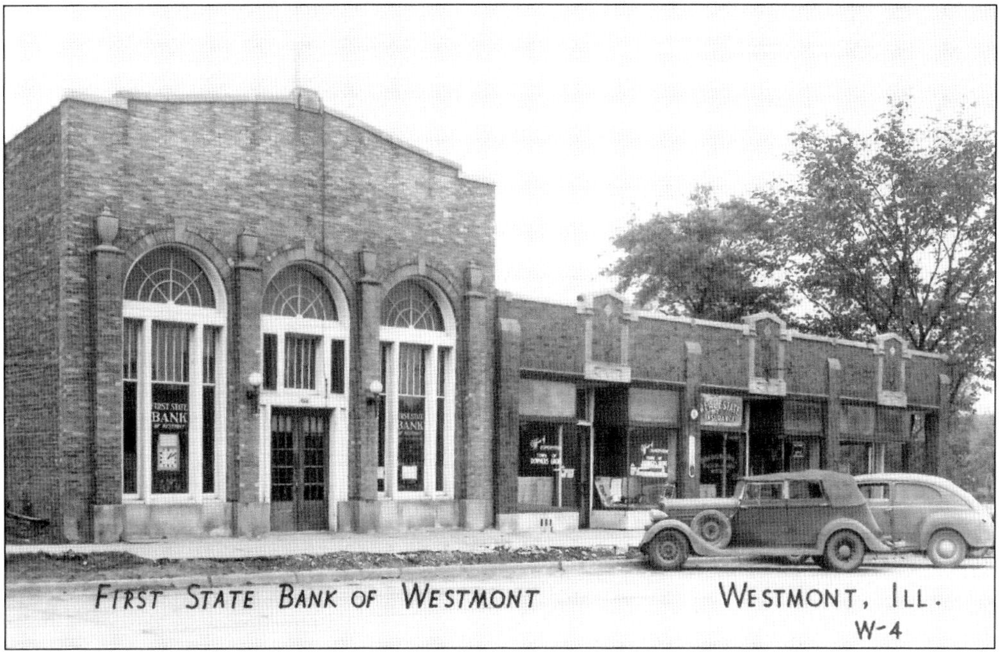

The First State Bank of Westmont was at 17 West Quincy Street. Although the bank did not go under during the Great Depression, customers still lined up around the block to withdraw their money for safekeeping. In 1931, the bank was robbed by four bandits who made off with $8,000. They were later apprehended in a neighboring town. (Both, courtesy of the Westmont Area Historical Society.)

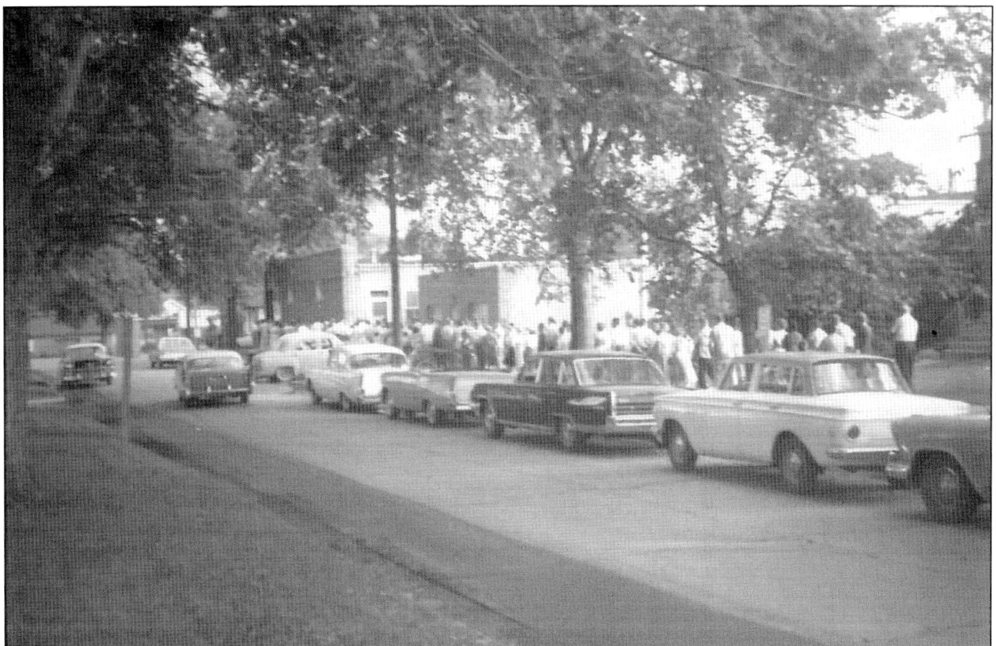

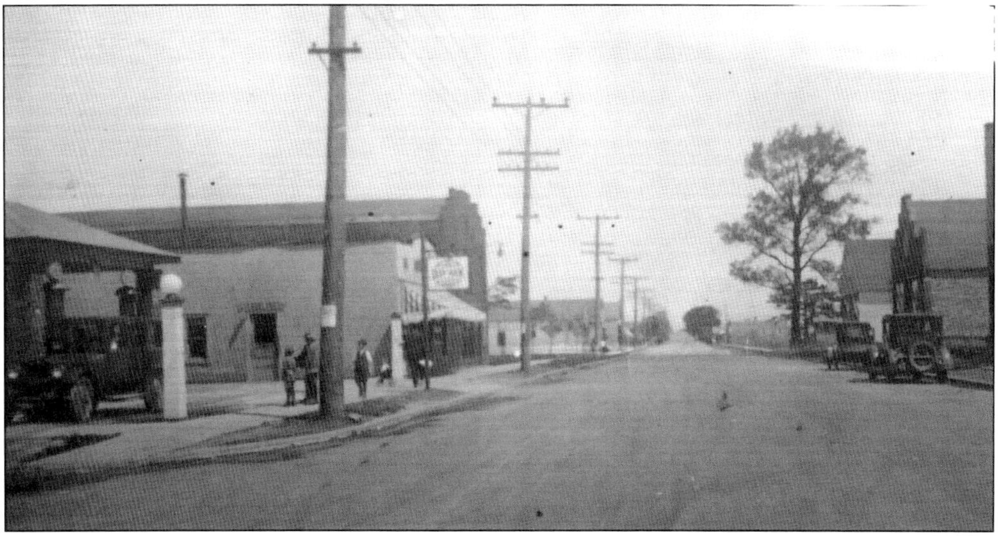

Archie Logan opened Logan's Theater on Cass Avenue. When it opened, the seats had not been installed, and theatergoers had to sit on planks resting on boxes or stand to watch the movie. Later, the theater became a boxing club. (Courtesy of the Westmont Area Historical Society.)

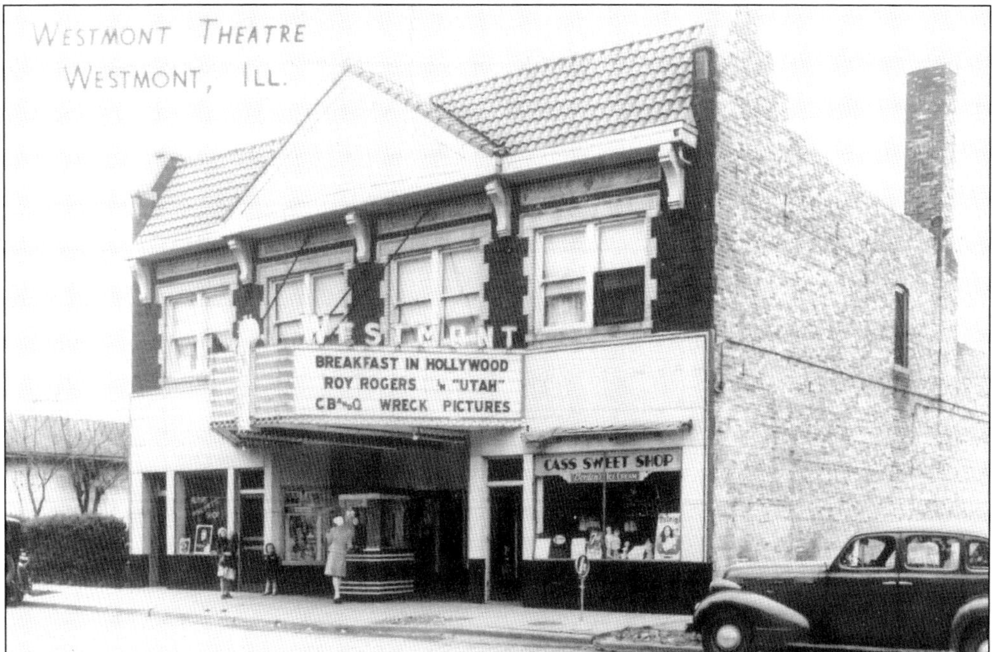

The Cass Theatre opened in 1928. Four years later, it changed its name to the Westmont Theatre. Owned and operated by the Zulas and Avegeris families, the theater became a gathering place for residents. Tickets were 20¢, and there were up to three different movies per week. A car outfitted with a loudspeaker would cruise through town to advertise that week's features. During World War II, theatergoers took a special interest in the war newsreels that aired with the main feature. Another popular newsreel topic was the local train crashes of the late 1940s. Central School held its graduation ceremony at the theater in 1947. The Westmont Theatre closed in 1957. Also pictured is the Cass Sweet Shop, another popular hangout. (Courtesy of the Westmont Area Historical Society.)

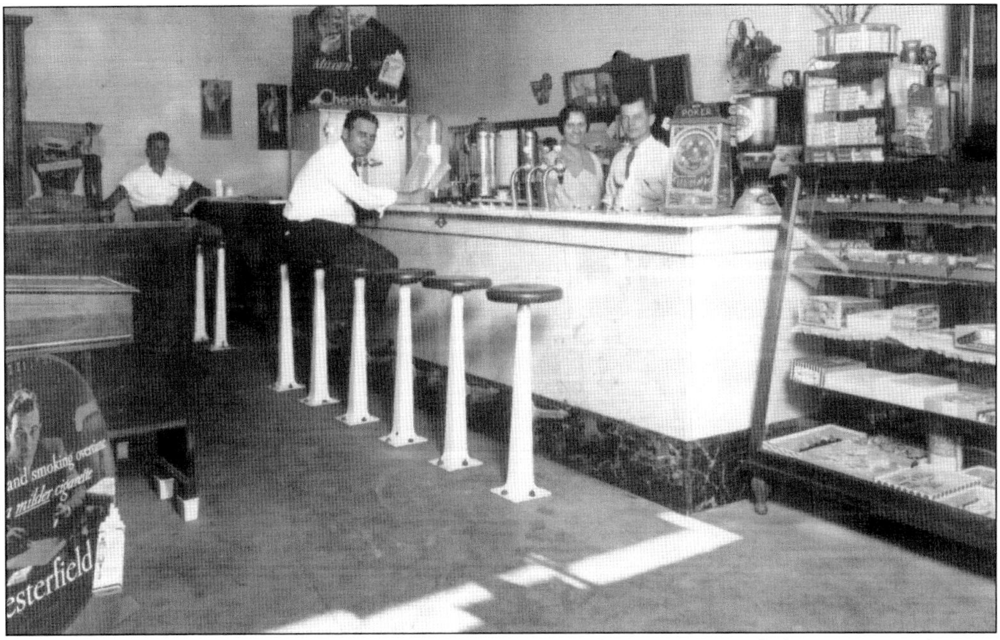

The Misek family owned and operated the Cass Sweet Shop. It occupied the prime retail space next to the Westmont Theatre and became a popular gathering place after shows. The Misek family got its start selling lots in Westmont for Arthur McIntosh in the early 1920s. (Courtesy of the Westmont Area Historical Society.)

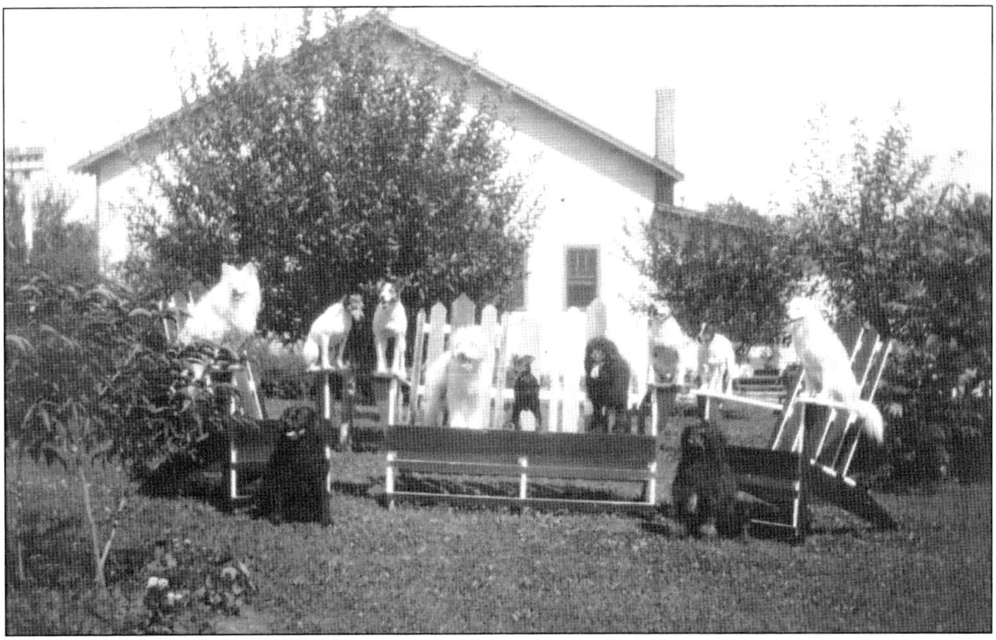

In 1934, Westmont was home to the Curtis-Gregg Circus. Dennie Curtis and Clifford Gregg (no relation to William Lampas of brick manufacturing fame) operated an act that featured acrobats, clowns, trained animals such as these dogs, and even the world's largest living elephant. However, the circus was only in business for five very entertaining weeks. (Courtesy of the Westmont Area Historical Society.)

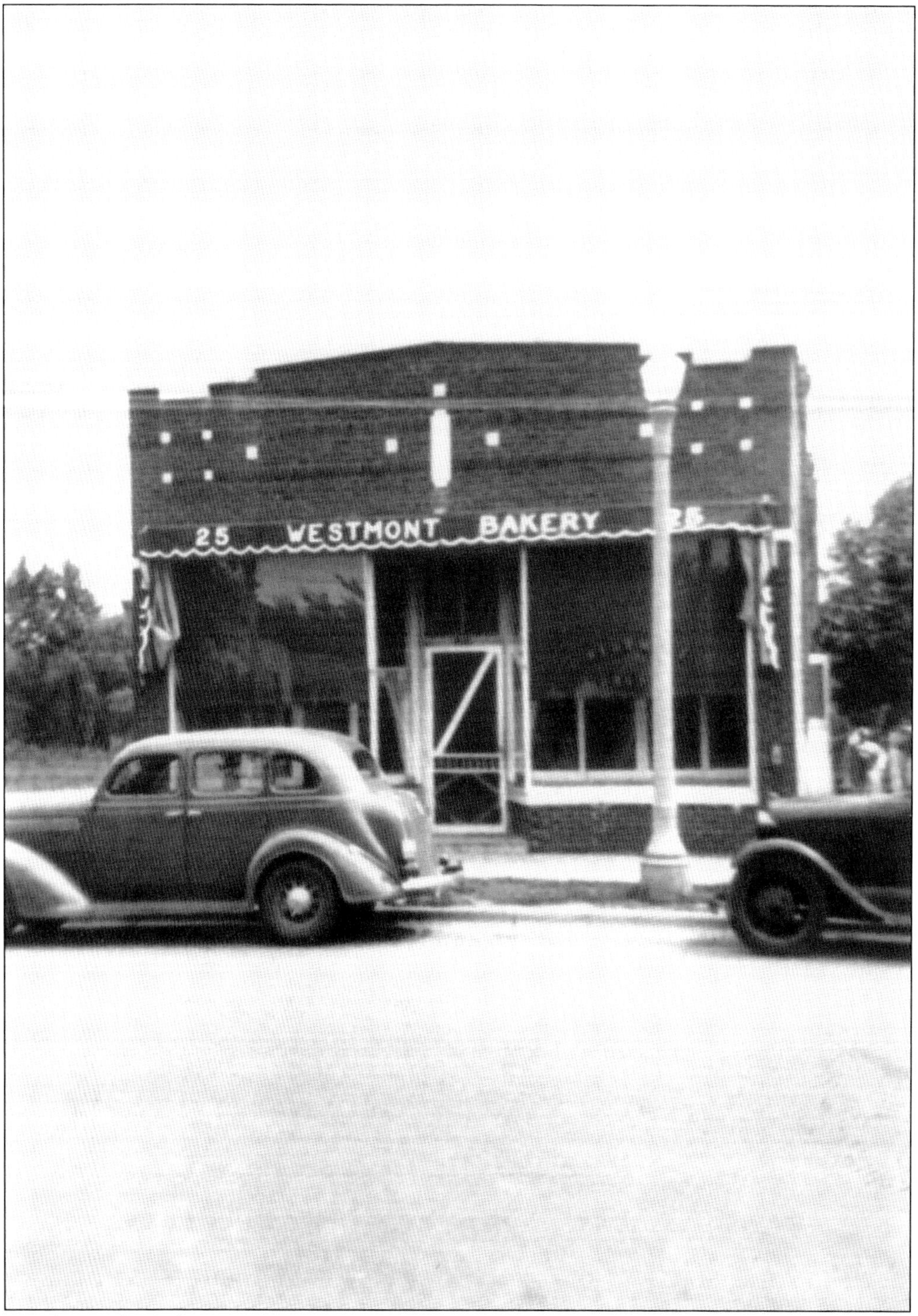

Joseph Marek's bakery was the first bakery in Westmont. Its construction was unusual because it had been built to house the bakery's ovens, making it long and narrow. Today, it houses the Knights of Columbus. (Courtesy of the Westmont Area Historical Society.)

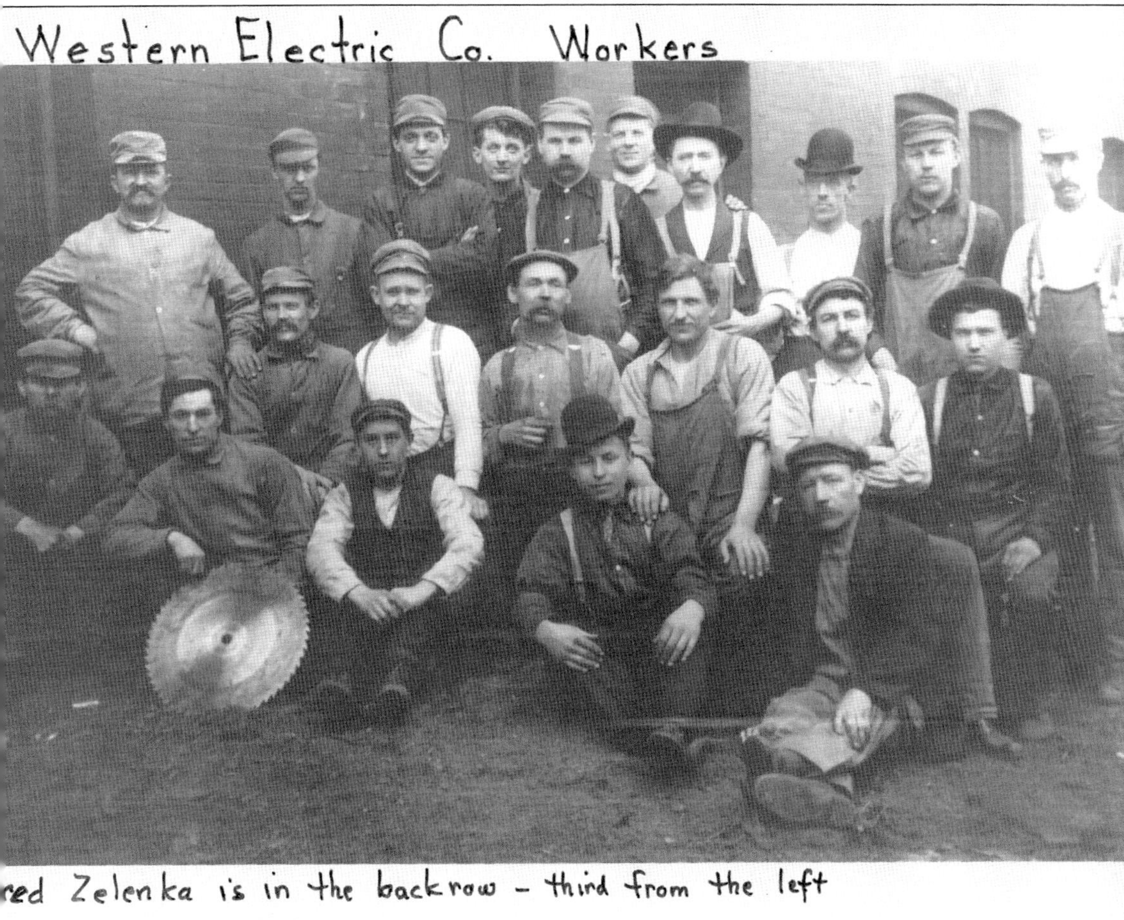

Many of Westmont's earliest residents were farmers. Others, like the men pictured here, worked for Western Electric in Chicago, making Westmont more blue collar than the surrounding suburbs. By 1917, Western Electric was one of the largest manufacturing companies in the world. It employed up to 25,000 people, many of whom were Czech and Polish immigrants. (Courtesy of the Westmont Area Historical Society.)

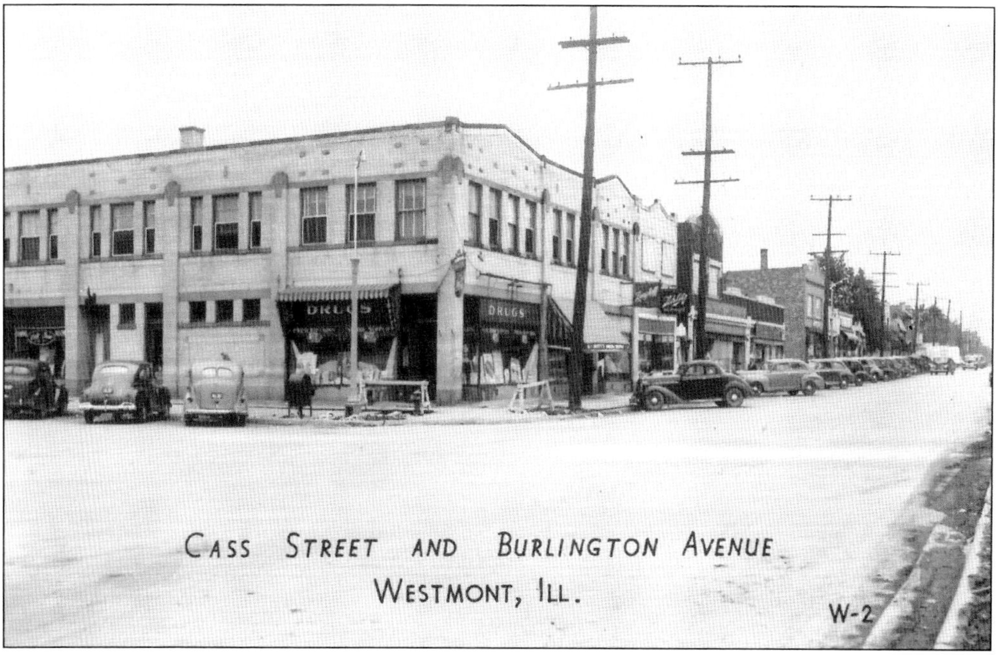

Pleshar's Pharmacy was one of the original businesses in Westmont. The building, which still stands on the western corner of Cass and Burlington Avenues, was built from Milwaukee cream brick. The upper level housed the Carillon Dance Hall, a popular dance hall for young people. Today, the building houses Westmont Pharmacy, while the dance hall space has been converted into apartments. (Courtesy of the Westmont Area Historical Society.)

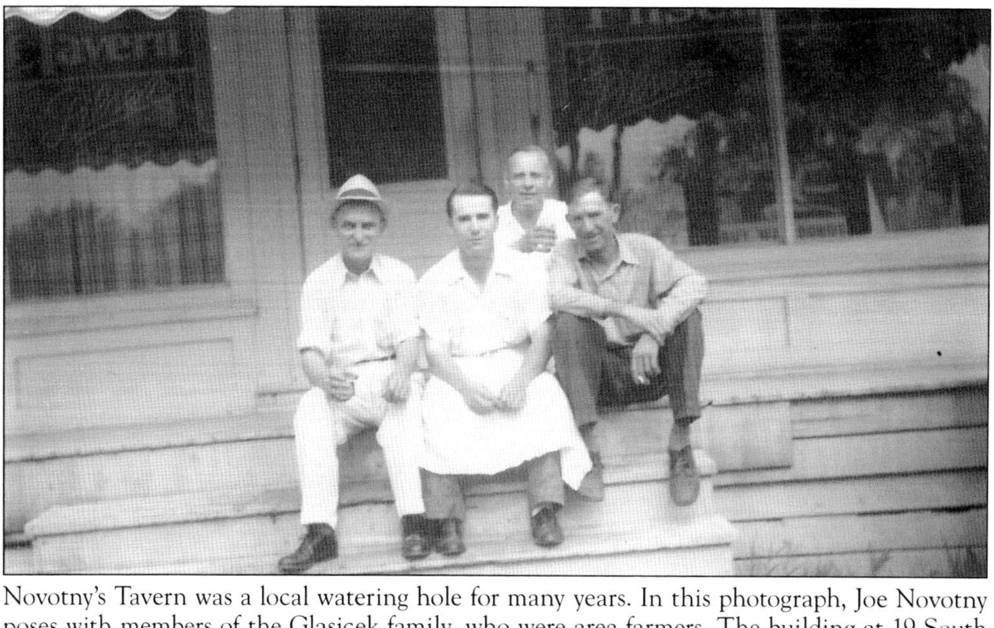

Novotny's Tavern was a local watering hole for many years. In this photograph, Joe Novotny poses with members of the Glasjcek family, who were area farmers. The building at 19 South Cass Avenue is now the home of Tasty Treat and Everything Southwestern. (Courtesy of the Westmont Area Historical Society.)

LIONS CLUB – 25 YEARS AGO

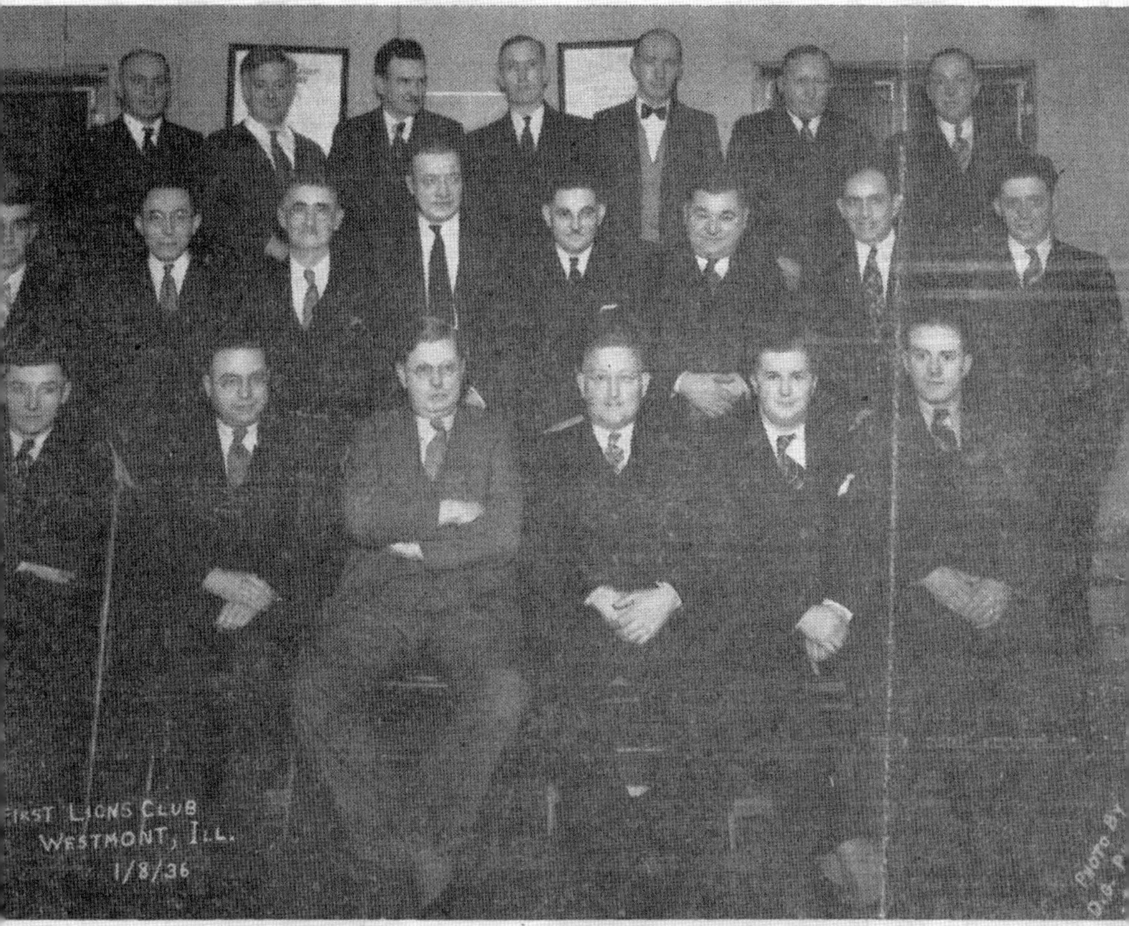

W — Dr. R. Manning, James Furlong, Edward Balch, Kuysin, Wm. Clark, Wm. Wehrmeister, Glen Moun... ROW — Seymour Waterfall, H. Berkowitz, Adam Feller, Kaler, H. Hartman, Eiken, Natkin.
THIRD ROW — Wm. Lossie, C. E. Miller, M. R. Bates, Ant... Dudek, Geo. Pleshar, Clyde Gleason.

The Westmont Lions Club has been one of the most fundamental groups in Westmont's history. Founded January 8, 1936, with 22 members, the all-male group consisted of mayors, school board presidents, and school superintendents. In July 1995, the Lions Club began admitting women as members. (Courtesy of the Westmont Area Historical Society.)

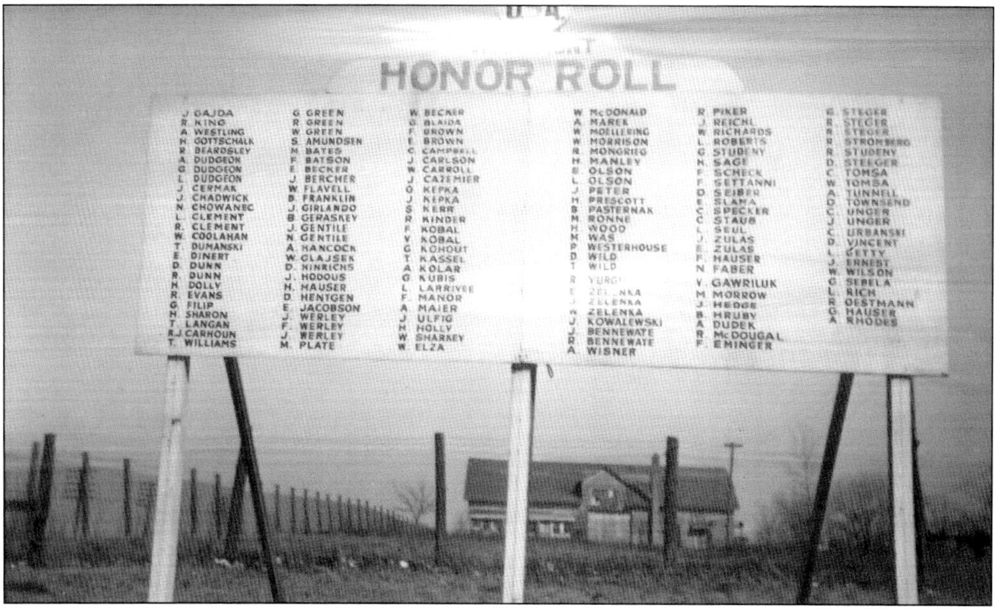

The Westmont Honor Roll billboard was erected on a hill near the railroad tracks. It listed the names of all of Westmont's servicemen and women during World War II. A name with no star meant that the soldier was still in training. Stars near the soldiers' names symbolized several things: a red star indicated a servicewoman, a blue star showed that the soldier was in active combat, and a gold star noted a soldier who had been killed in combat. (Both, courtesy of the Westmont Area Historical Society.)

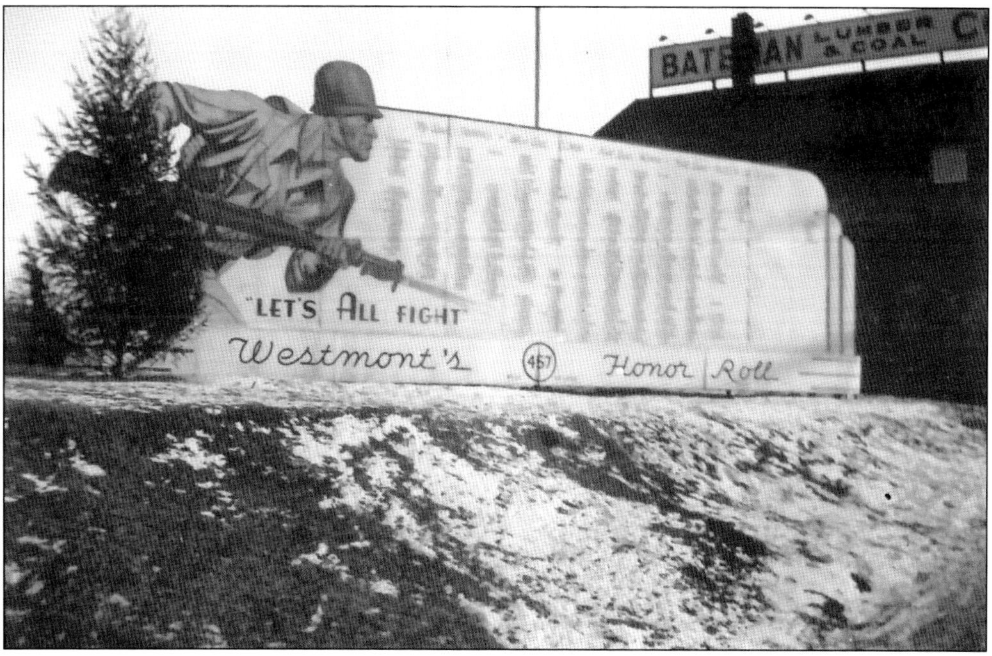

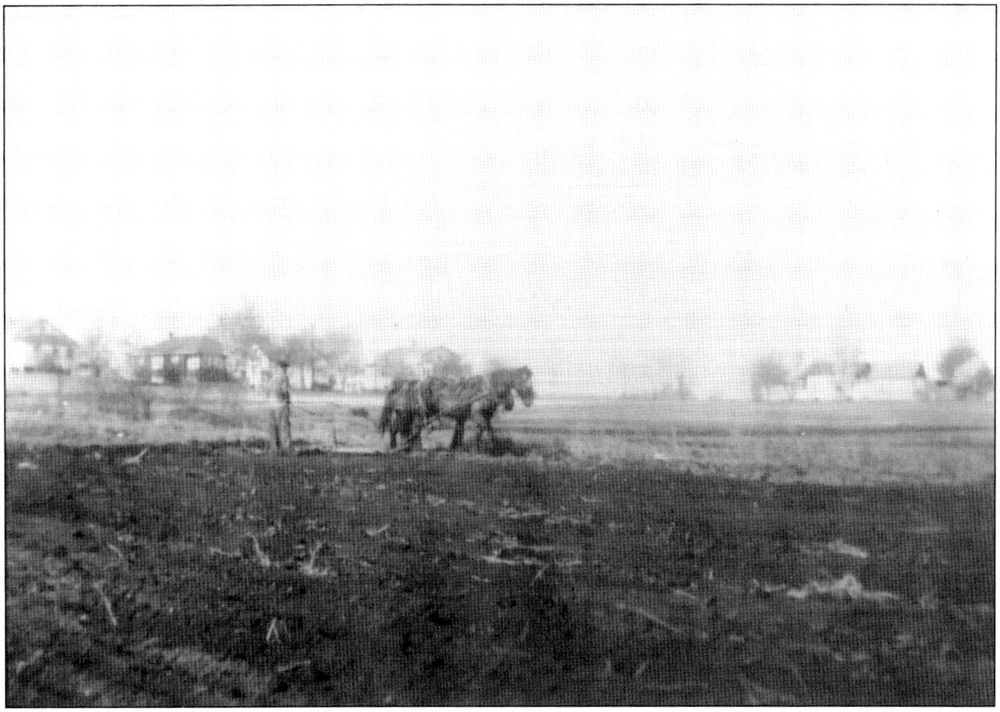

This field was at the present-day location of Veterans Memorial Park. Even through the Great Depression, many of the village's residents were farmers and maintained large acreages of land. (Courtesy of the Westmont Area Historical Society.)

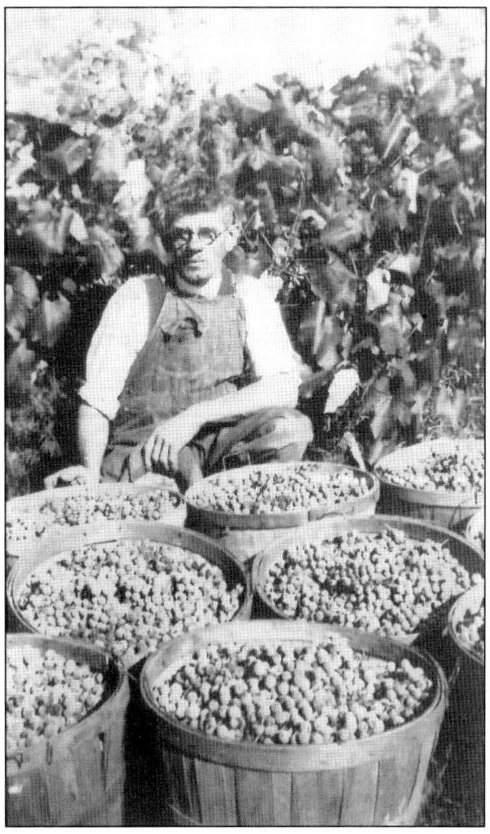

The Glasjcek family maintained a vineyard and farm near the North Acres School on Traube Street on the north side of Westmont. The back of this photograph boasts that the vineyard was "the largest in Westmont." (Courtesy of the Westmont Area Historical Society.)

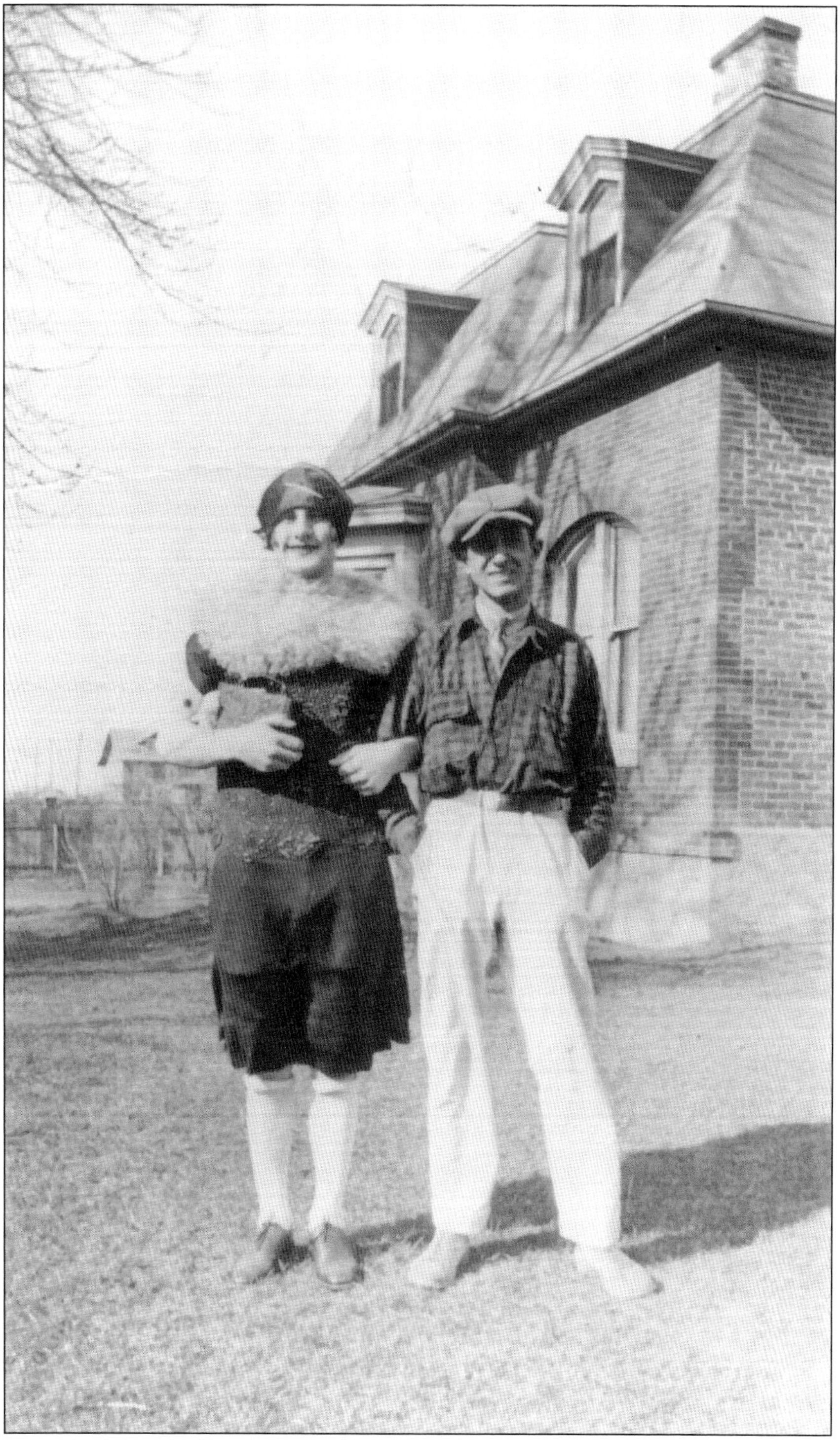

Al Politowicz (right) and a friend pose in front of William L. Gregg's former house. Politowicz lived in the house from 1924 to 1929. He bottled beer in the basement during Prohibition. (Courtesy of the Westmont Area Historical Society.)

Before becoming a museum, William Gregg's house served many different purposes. In 1937, it was being used as a recreation center for the community. These residents posed outside the house during that time. (Courtesy of the Westmont Area Historical Society.)

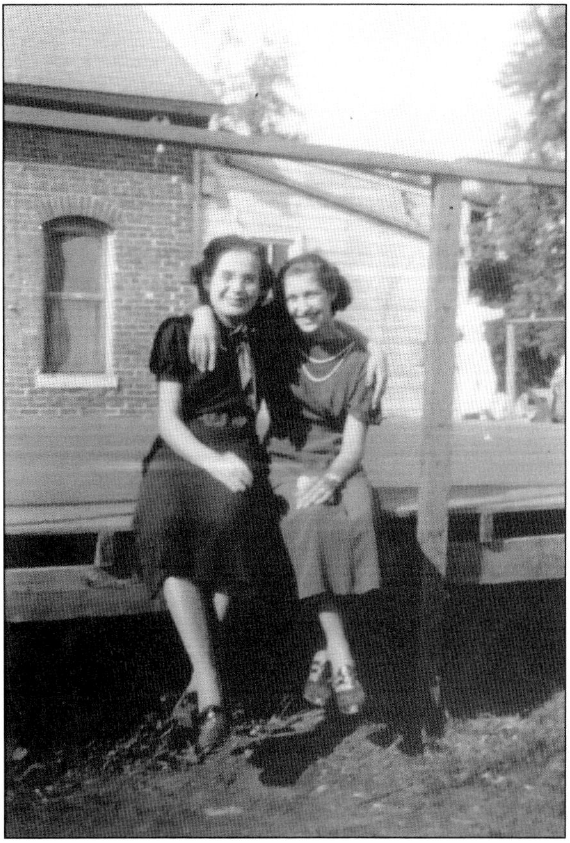

This plane carried the first airmail to leave Westmont on May 19, 1938, during National Airmail Week. Postmaster General James Farley organized National Airmail Week to celebrate the 20-year anniversary of the US airmail system. At this time, stamps cost 6¢ per ounce—much less than today! (Courtesy of the Westmont Area Historical Society.)

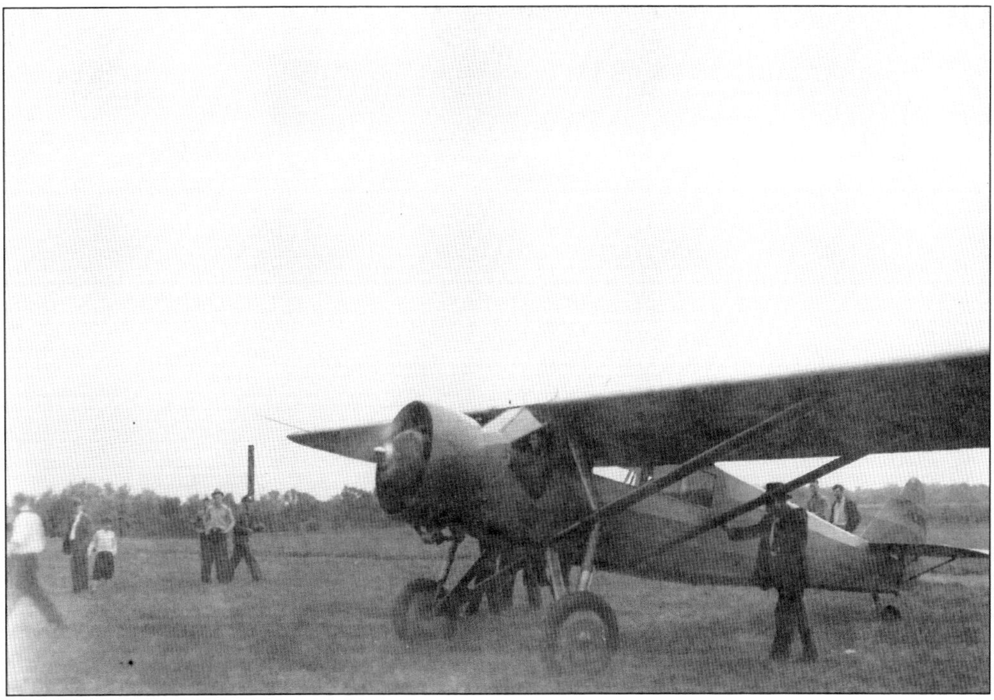

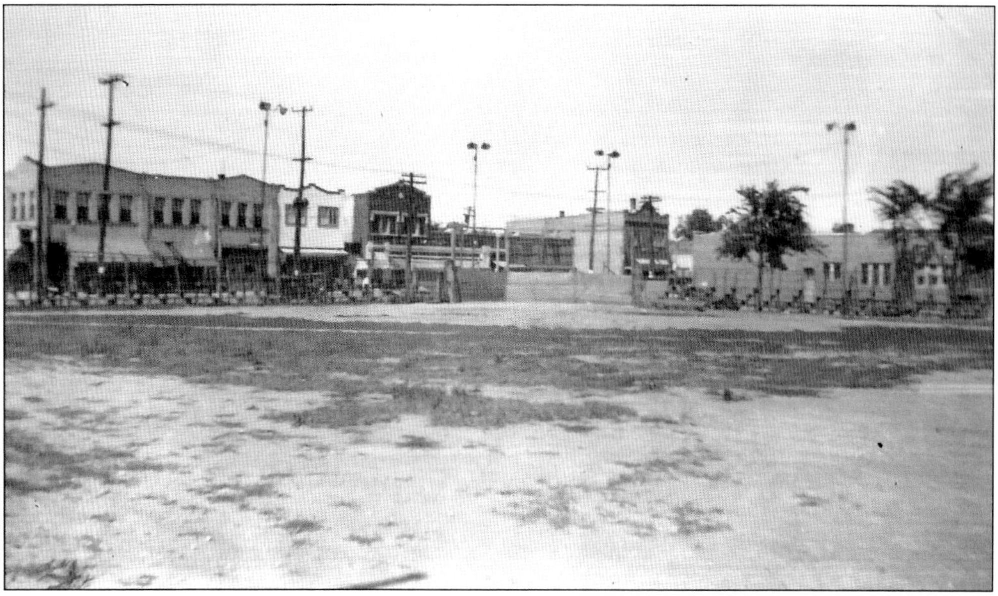

Recreation has always been vital to Westmont's residents. The first lighted baseball field was built near the CB&Q tracks and was used for baseball and other events, including soapbox derbies. (Both, courtesy of the Westmont Area Historical Society.)

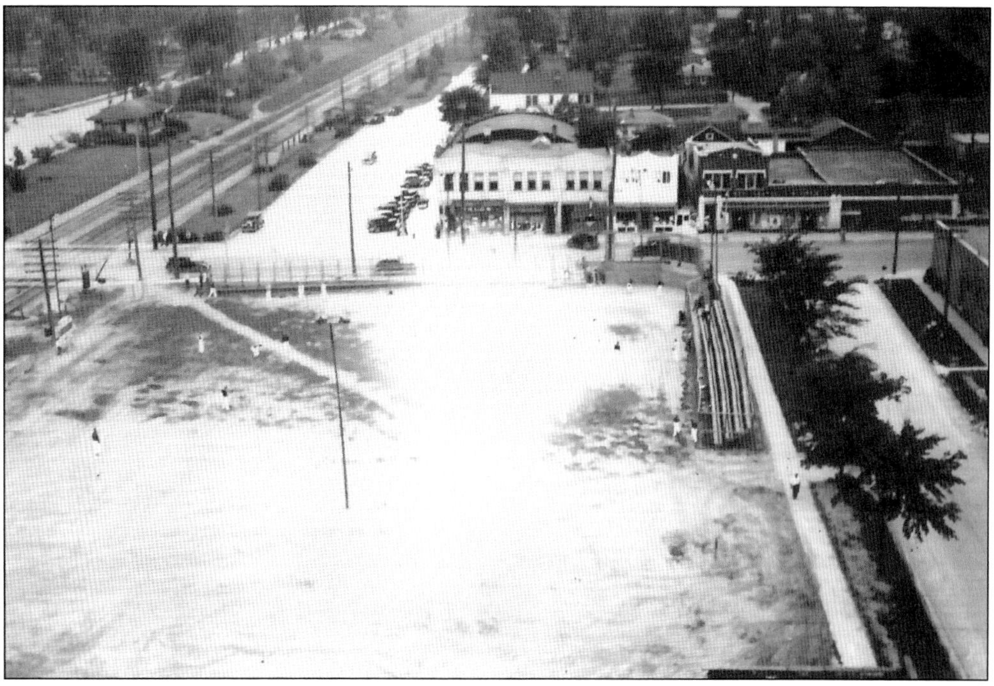

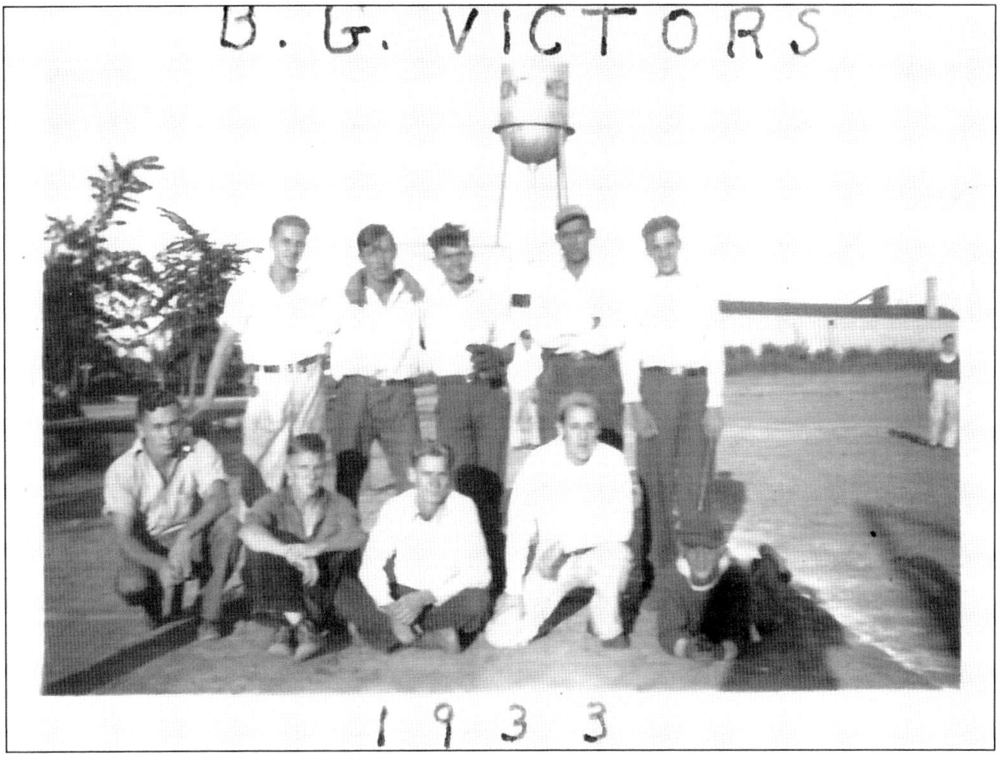

Playing on the lighted field was a popular pastime. Both men's and women's teams took advantage of the playing space. Above are the "BG Victors" in 1933, and below are the Westmont Red Hots. (Both, courtesy of the Westmont Area Historical Society.)

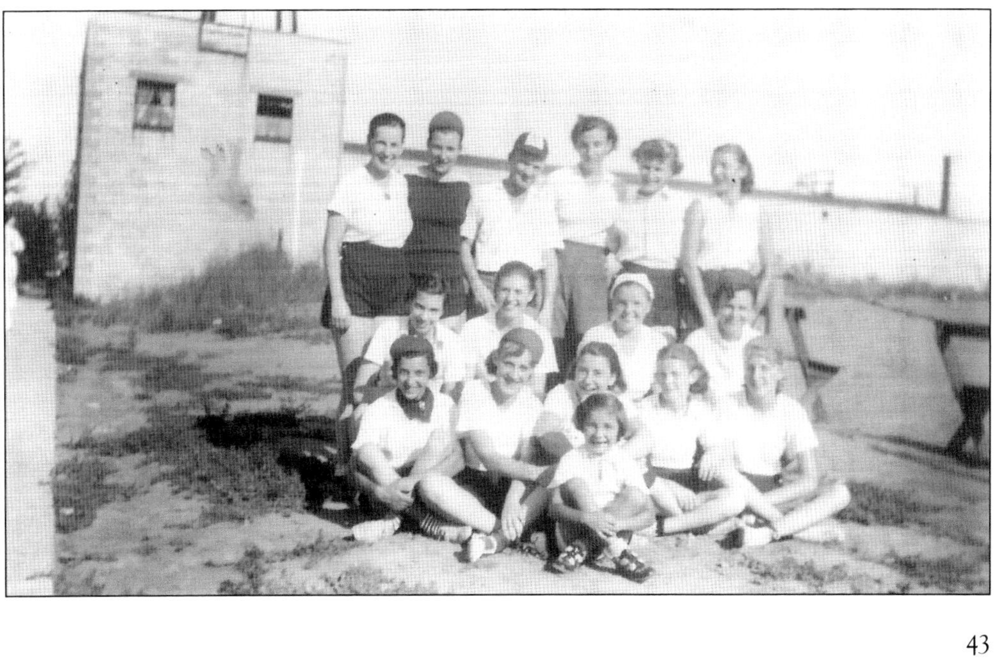

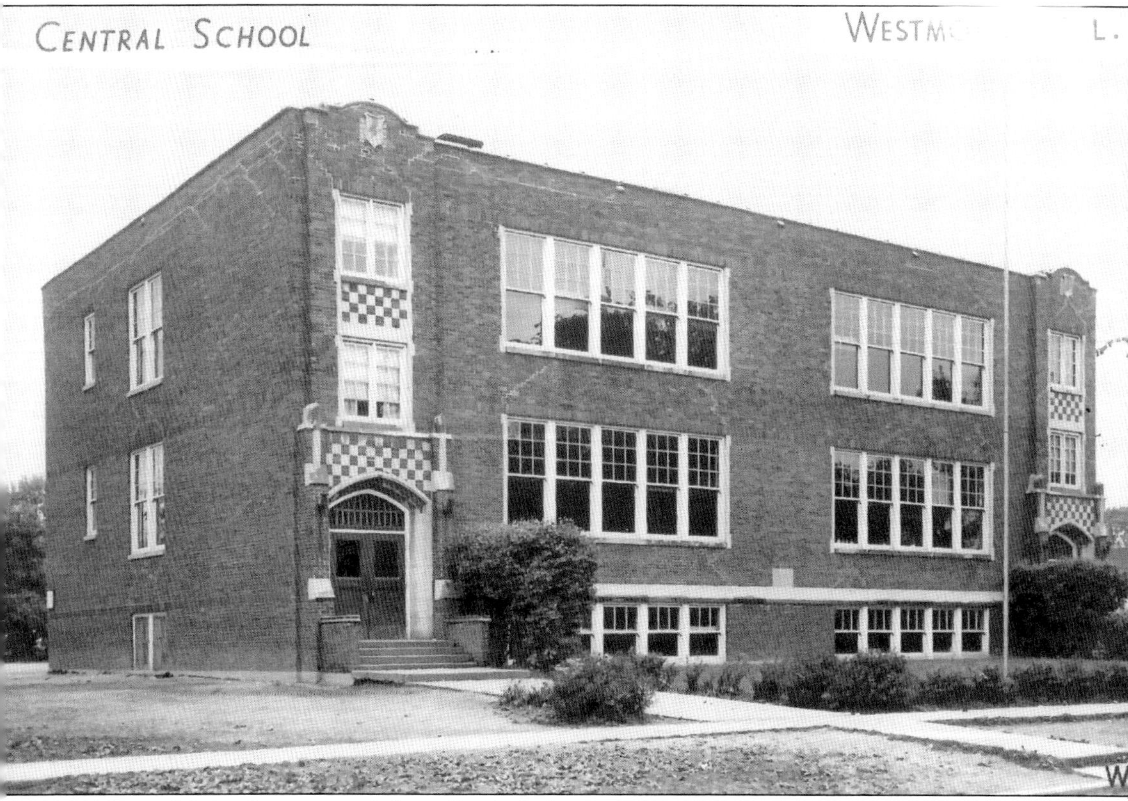

Central School was one of the village's earliest schools. After it outgrew its original one-room building, mobile classrooms were added, and then an updated, brick school was constructed to accommodate the growing number of students. Central School was renamed Manning School in honor of superintendent James T. Manning's many accomplishments. (Courtesy of the Westmont Area Historical Society.)

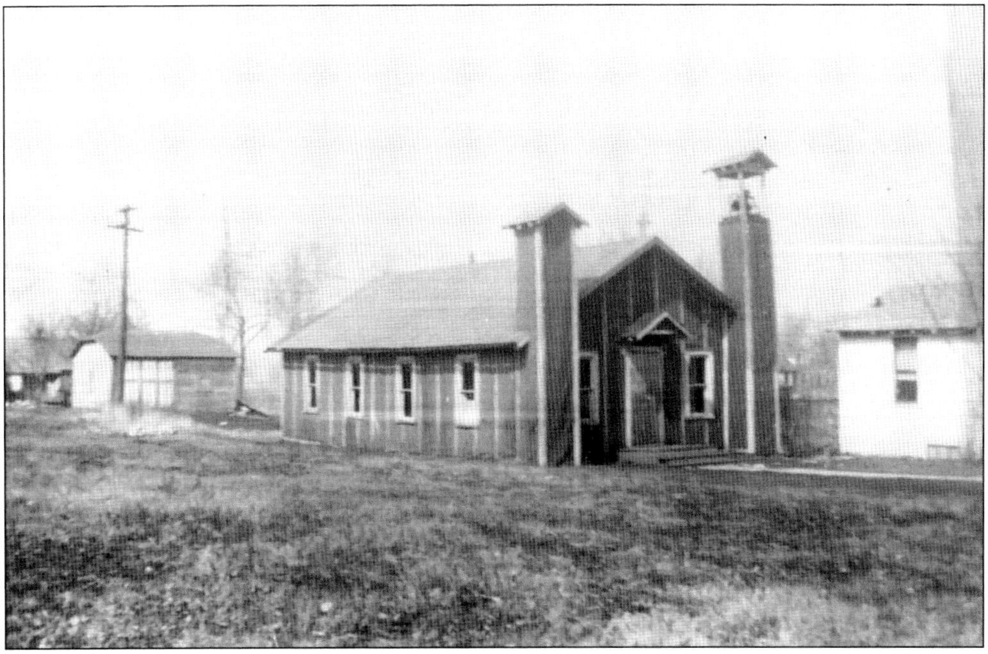

In 1923, Fr. Eneas B. Goodwin wrote Archbishop George W. Mundelein of Chicago petitioning him to establish a Catholic parish in the new development, citing a need to minister to the blue-collar Bohemian farmers. This led to the creation of Holy Trinity Parish. (Courtesy of the Westmont Area Historical Society.)

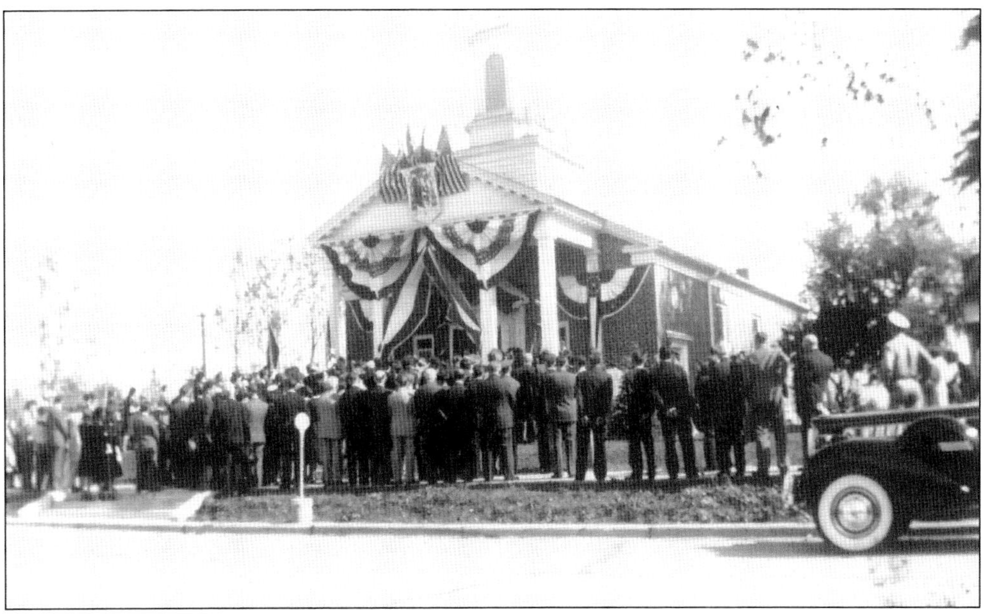

By the 1950s, Holy Trinity had outgrown its early structure and was rebuilt. In this photograph, parishioners celebrate the construction of the new church building. (Courtesy of the Westmont Area Historical Society.)

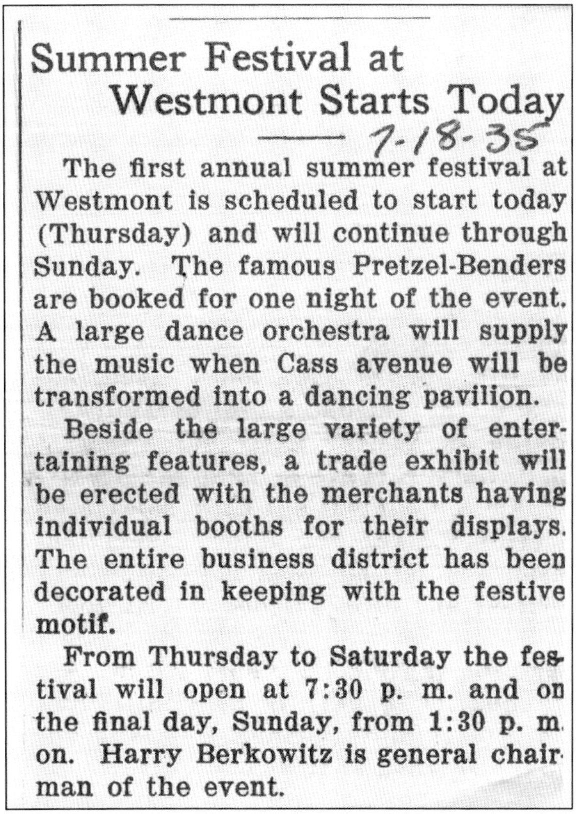

Summer Festival at Westmont Starts Today

7-18-35

The first annual summer festival at Westmont is scheduled to start today (Thursday) and will continue through Sunday. The famous Pretzel-Benders are booked for one night of the event. A large dance orchestra will supply the music when Cass avenue will be transformed into a dancing pavilion.

Beside the large variety of entertaining features, a trade exhibit will be erected with the merchants having individual booths for their displays. The entire business district has been decorated in keeping with the festive motif.

From Thursday to Saturday the festival will open at 7:30 p. m. and on the final day, Sunday, from 1:30 p. m. on. Harry Berkowitz is general chairman of the event.

In 1935, the village hosted its first summer festival. Activities included music, dancing, and merchants on Cass Avenue. This served as the precursor to Summer Fest, and later, the Taste of Westmont. (Courtesy of the Westmont Area Historical Society.)

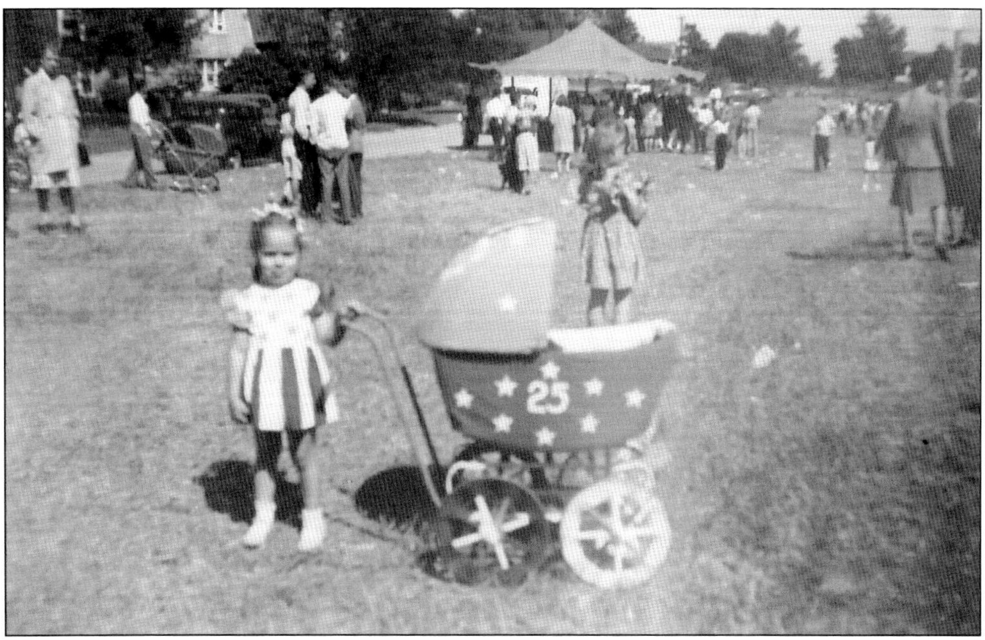

In 1946, Westmont celebrated the 25th anniversary of its incorporation. Here, a young girl poses with a decorated baby buggy to celebrate the occasion. (Courtesy of the Westmont Area Historical Society.)

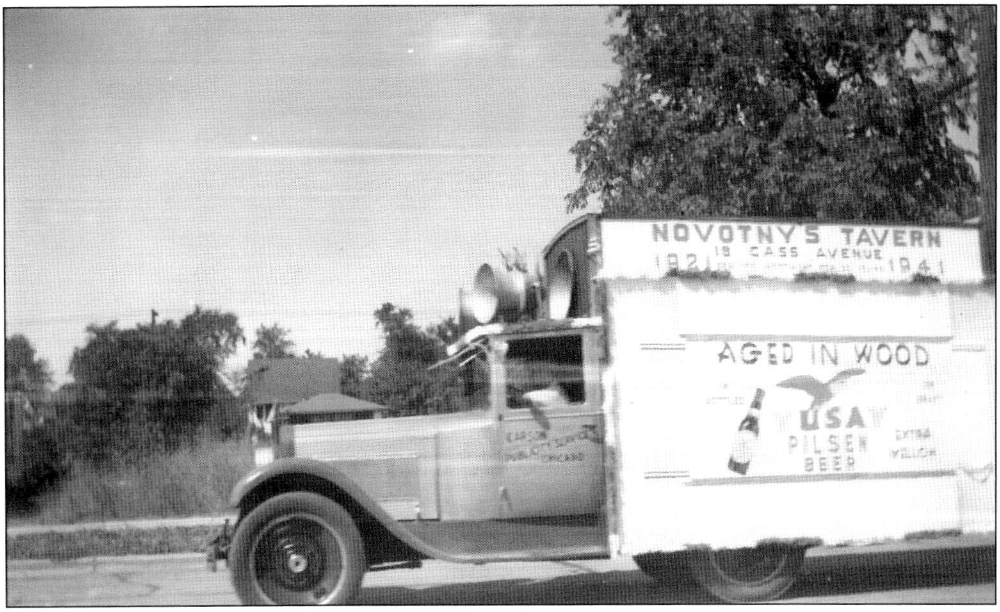

As a form of celebration and entertainment, parades have always been an important part of Westmont. Even today, parades serve as community touchstones. In this 20th anniversary parade, businesses like Novotny's Tavern and Westmont Restaurant decorated vehicles to participate. (Both, courtesy of the Westmont Area Historical Society.)

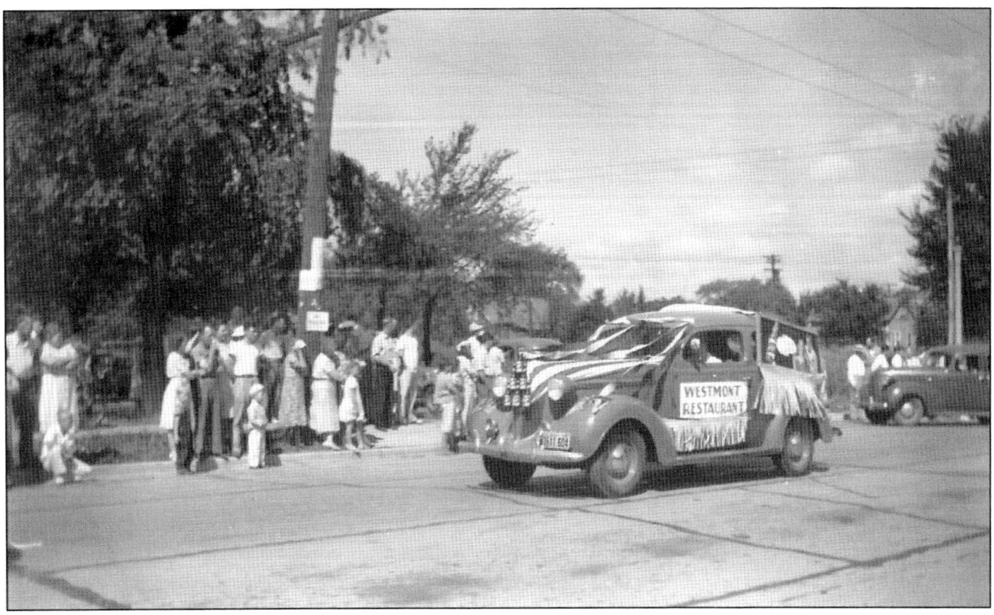

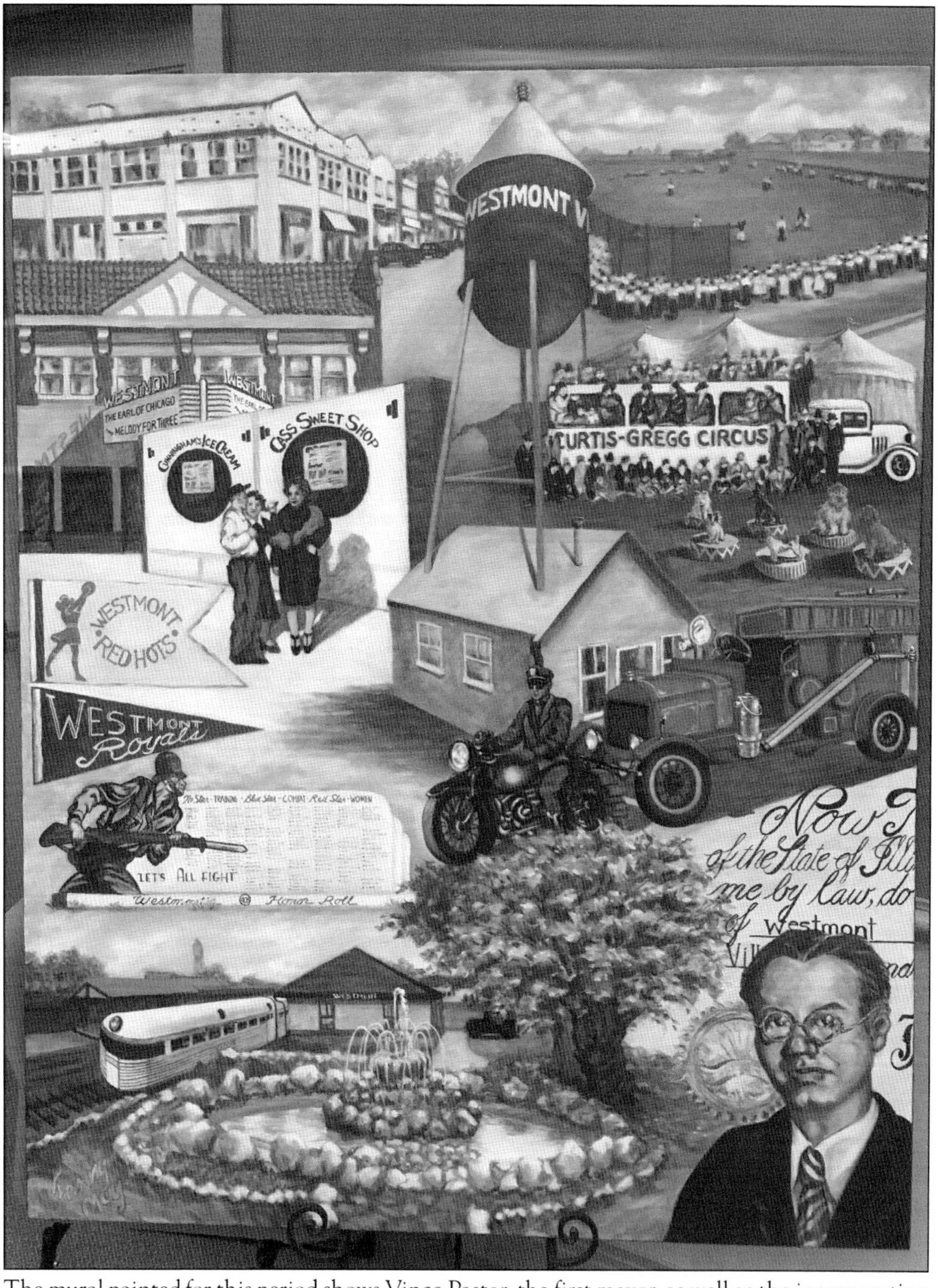

The mural painted for this period shows Vince Pastor, the first mayor, as well as the incorporation certificate for the village. Fanny Moy has painted in local businesses, such as the Westmont Theater and Cass Sweet Shop, as well as sports teams like the Red Hots. (Courtesy of the Village of Westmont.)

Three

The Golden Years 1950s to 1970s

After World War II, building in Westmont boomed. More housing was built for middle- and upper-class families, and by the 1960s, there were very few lots left to build on in town. In 1959, the Westmont Park District was established by referendum and acquired its first two parks, Kiwanis Park and LeBeck Park. It also purchased Veterans Memorial Park from the American Legion. Veterans Memorial Park became the home of the park district's community center in 1975. After the Westmont Area Historical Society was formed in 1976, it also became the site of William Gregg's home, now the Gregg House Museum. Other notable service clubs formed during this time include the Kiwanis Club and Rotary Club.

Despite the establishment of Central School and Maercker School in the earliest days, no secondary school system existed in the village until the 1970s. In 1976, Westmont Public High School opened its doors. Before this, students attended either Hinsdale Central High School or Downers Grove North High School.

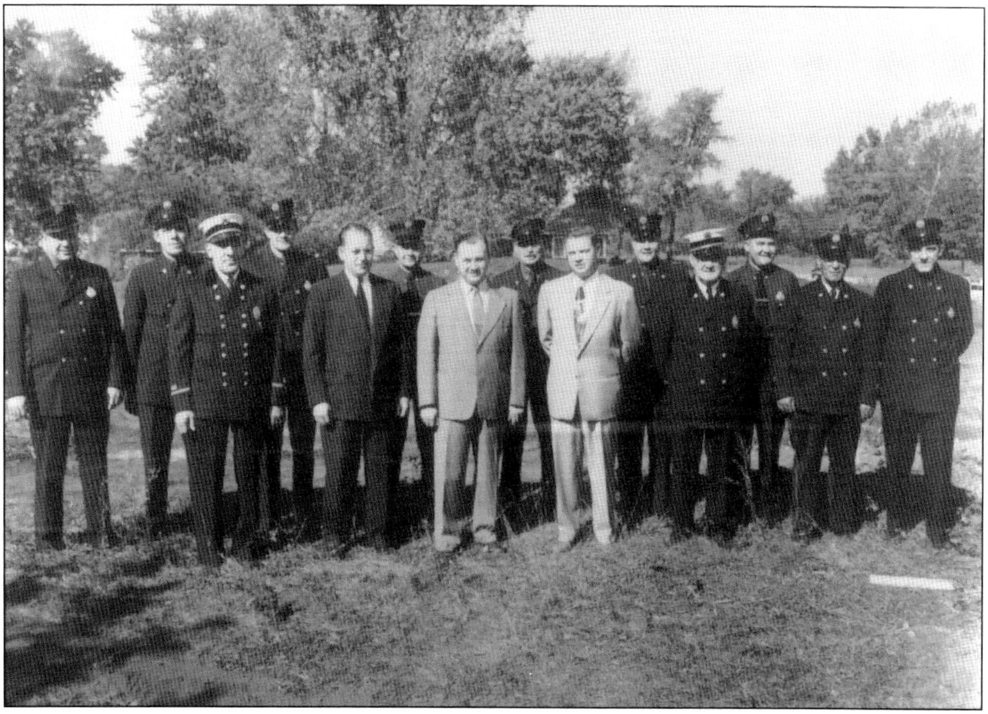

Mayor George Pukis (left center, in light suit) poses with other village officials at a ground-breaking ceremony. Pukis lost his reelection race against William Robinson, who then served his second term as mayor. (Courtesy of the Westmont Area Historical Society.)

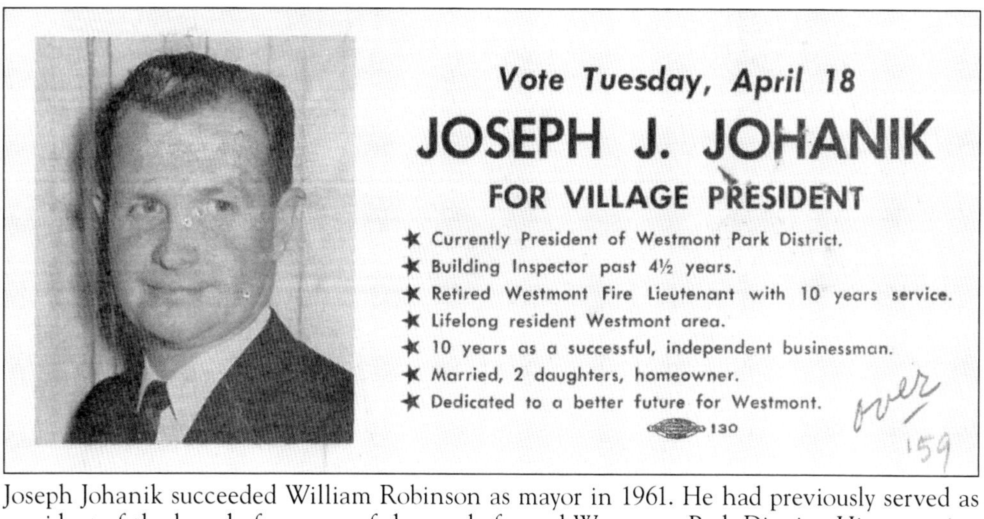

Joseph Johanik succeeded William Robinson as mayor in 1961. He had previously served as president of the board of trustees of the newly formed Westmont Park District. His campaign card lists his qualifications as retired fire lieutenant, building inspector, and lifelong resident of Westmont. (Courtesy of the Westmont Area Historical Society.)

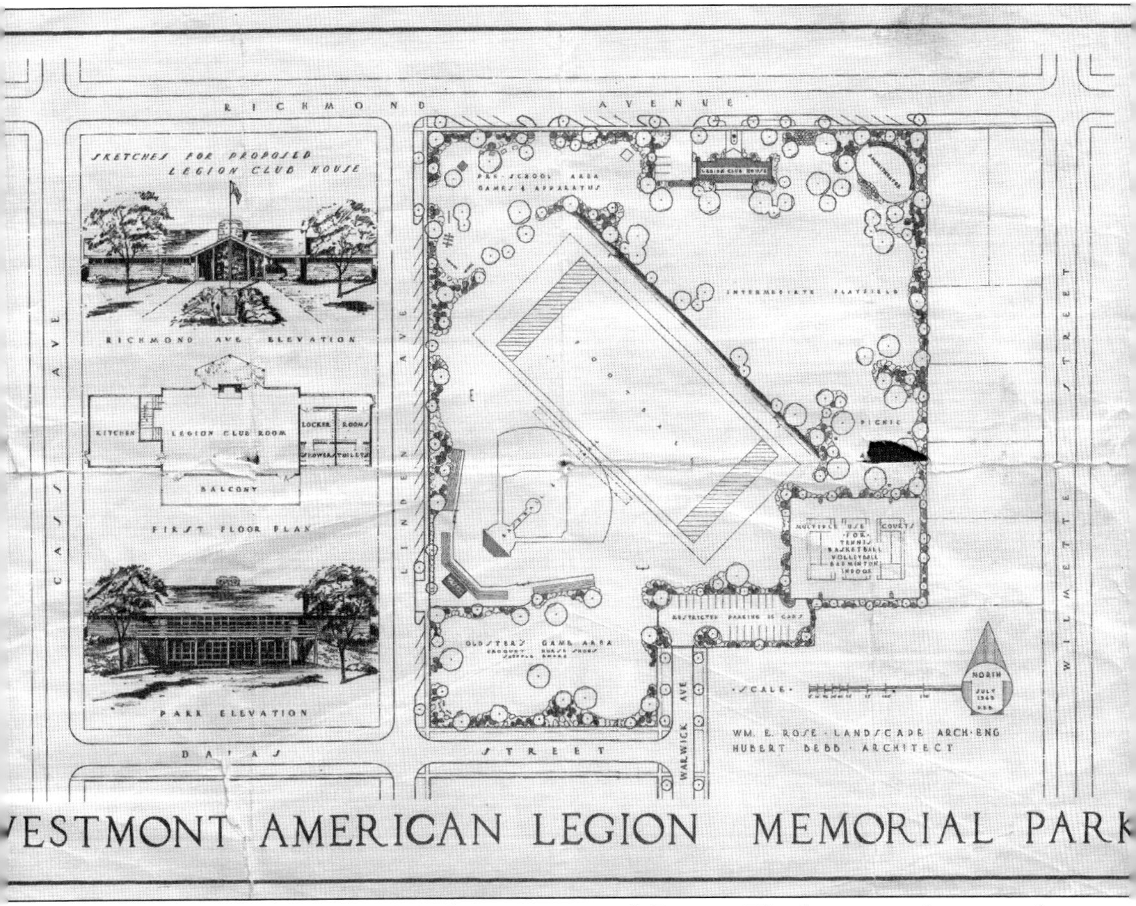

In 1959, residents voted to establish the Westmont Park District. The first two parks acquired by the district were Kiwanis Park and LeBeck Park, which amounted to one and a half acres combined. The park district also purchased Veterans Memorial Park from the American Legion. Before the park district purchased the park, plans were drawn up by the legion. These included a clubhouse for the American Legion; baseball and football fields; basketball, volleyball, and tennis courts; and game areas for different age groups. Today, it is the home of a playground; basketball, tennis, and volleyball courts; baseball fields; and a picnic shelter. (Courtesy of the Westmont Area Historical Society.)

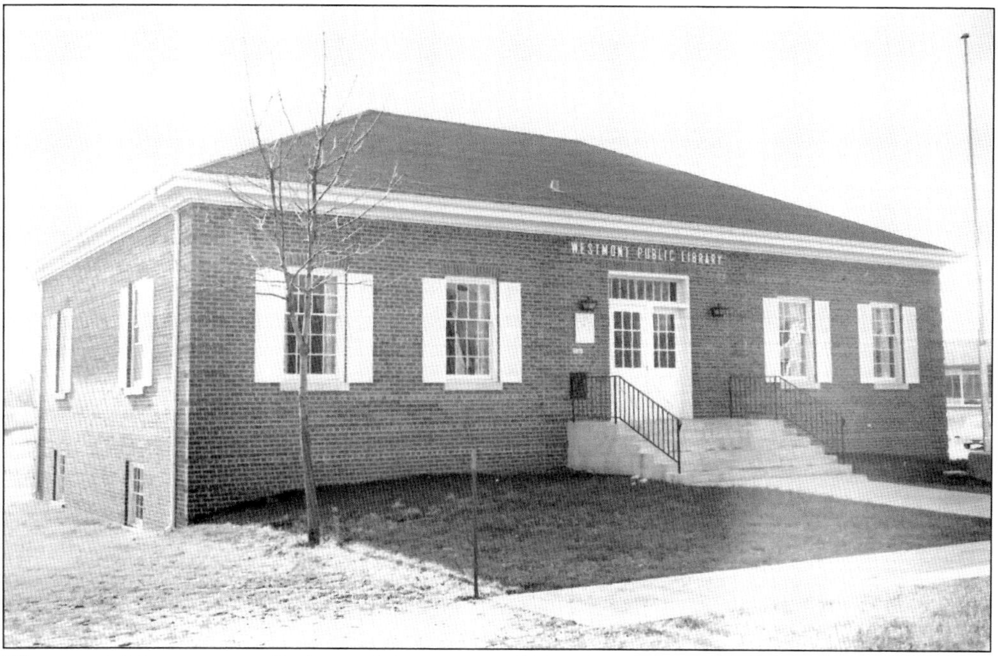

Westmont's library was on Richmond Street, east of Cass Avenue in a building constructed by the American Legion in 1960, until its new facility was completed north of the tracks. Prior to this, the library was run by Everett Meservey from his office on the corner of Burlington Avenue and Lincoln Street. Meservey also printed the first local newspaper, the *Community Press*, beginning in 1924. Today, the former library building is the home of the Westmont Park District's administrative staff and senior center. (Courtesy of the Westmont Area Historical Society.)

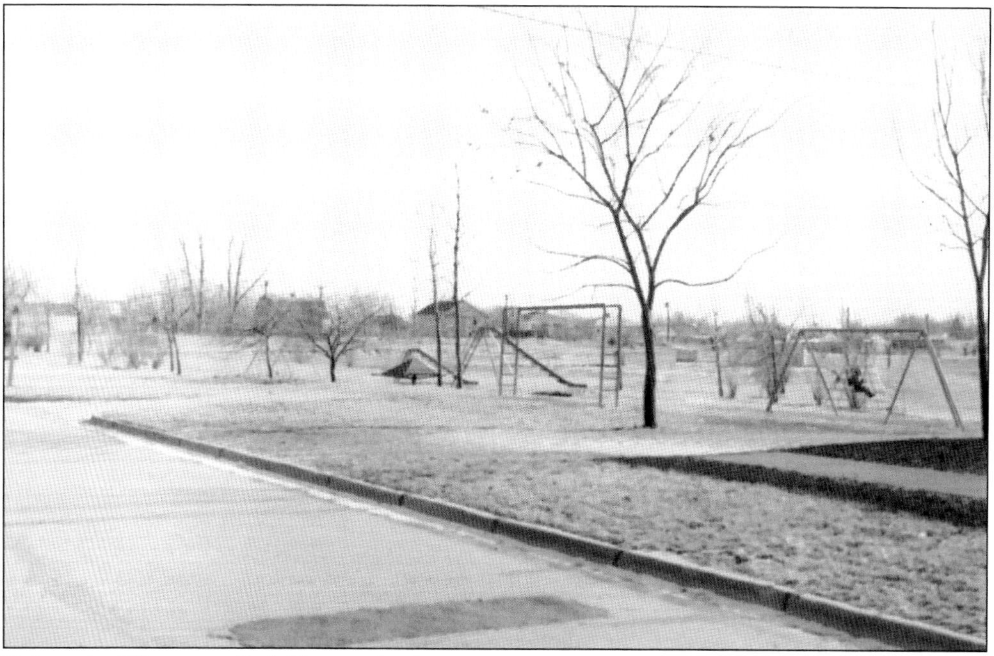

Before the Westmont Park District built its community center, the land was used for a small playground next to the library. (Courtesy of the Westmont Area Historical Society.)

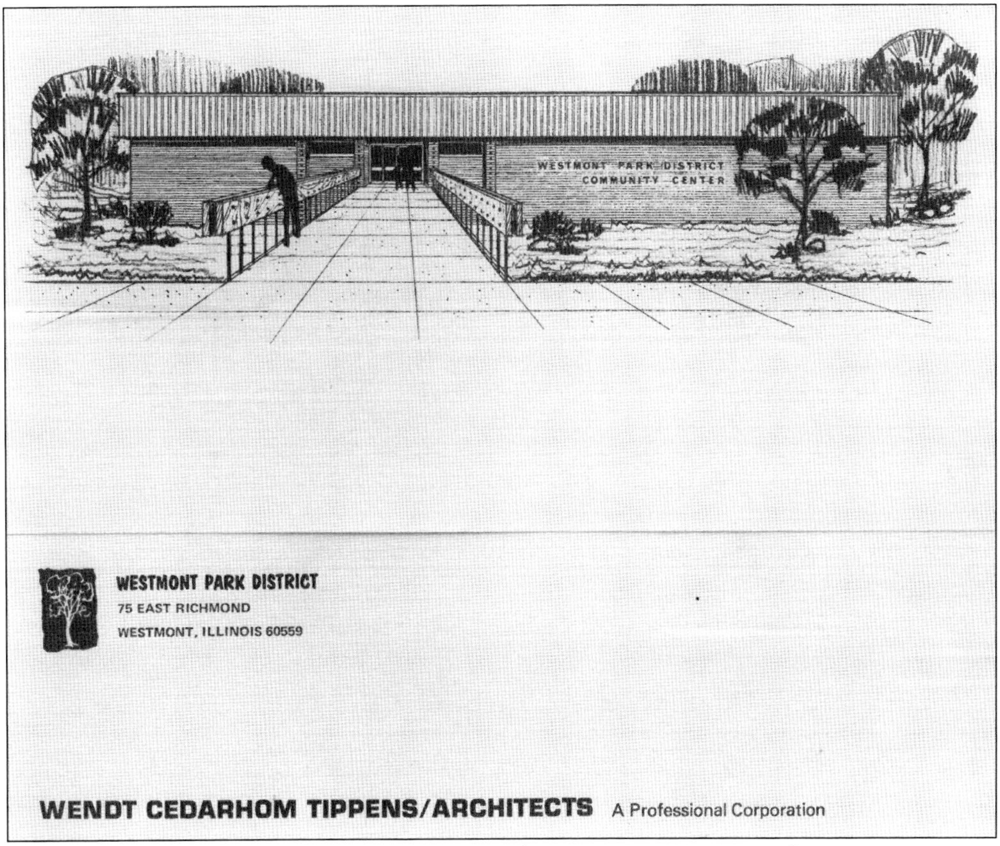

In 1975, the Westmont Park District constructed a community center to house its recreation activities. The facility includes a basketball court, rooms for recreation programming, and offices for the park district's recreation staff. (Both, courtesy of the Westmont Area Historical Society.)

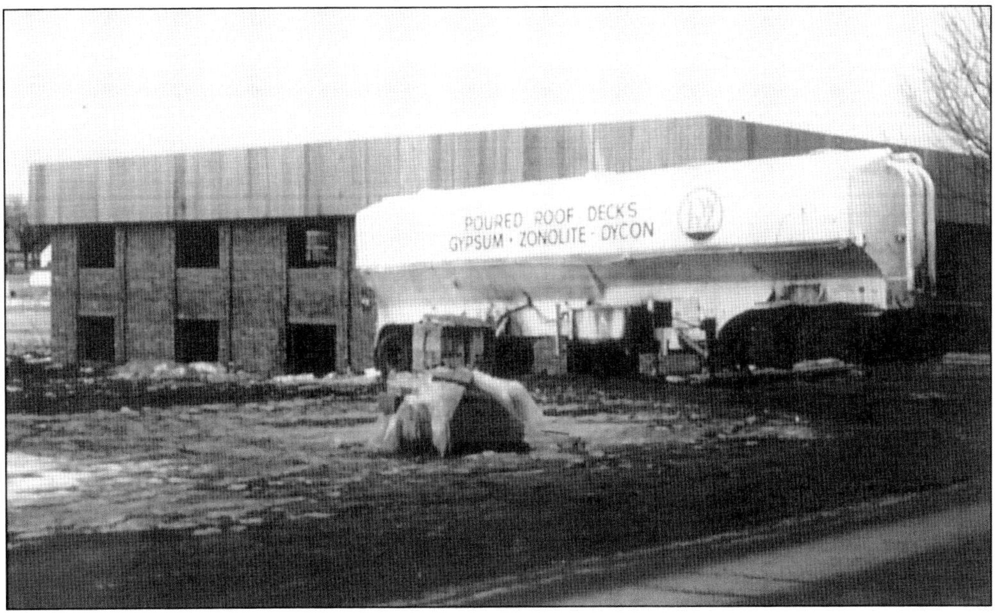

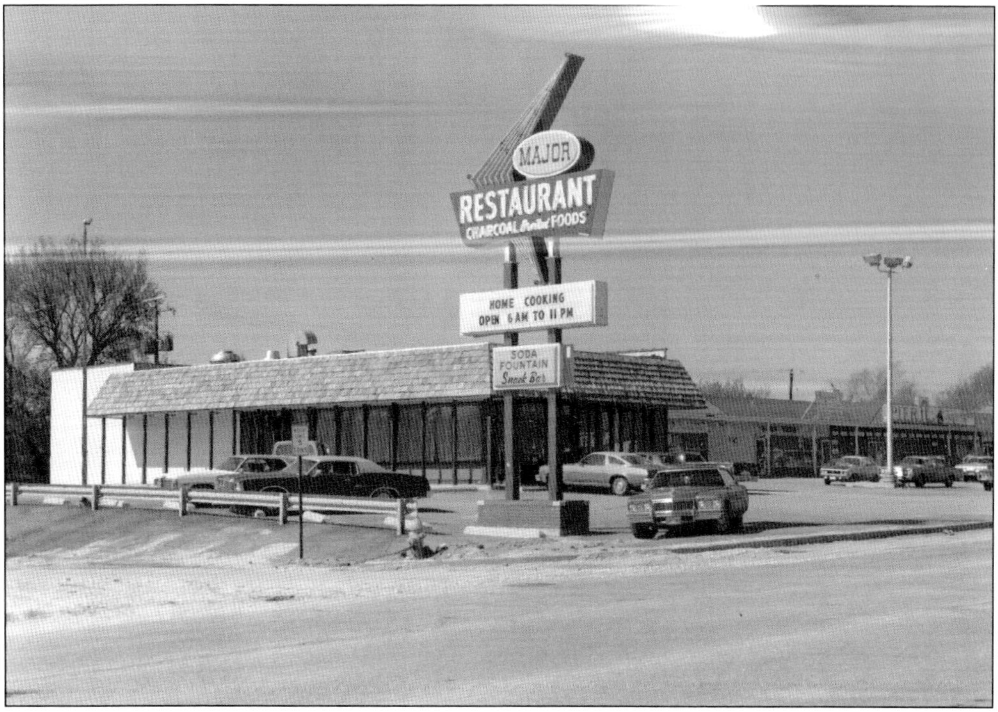

During the 1950s and 1960s, businesses on the north side of town flourished. Restaurants, like Major Restaurant, and recreation centers, like Suburbanite Bowl, thrived. The north side of Westmont was also home to a golf driving range and a roller rink. While Major Restaurant has since been demolished, Suburbanite Bowl remains a popular place to pass the time. (Both, courtesy of the Westmont Area Historical Society.)

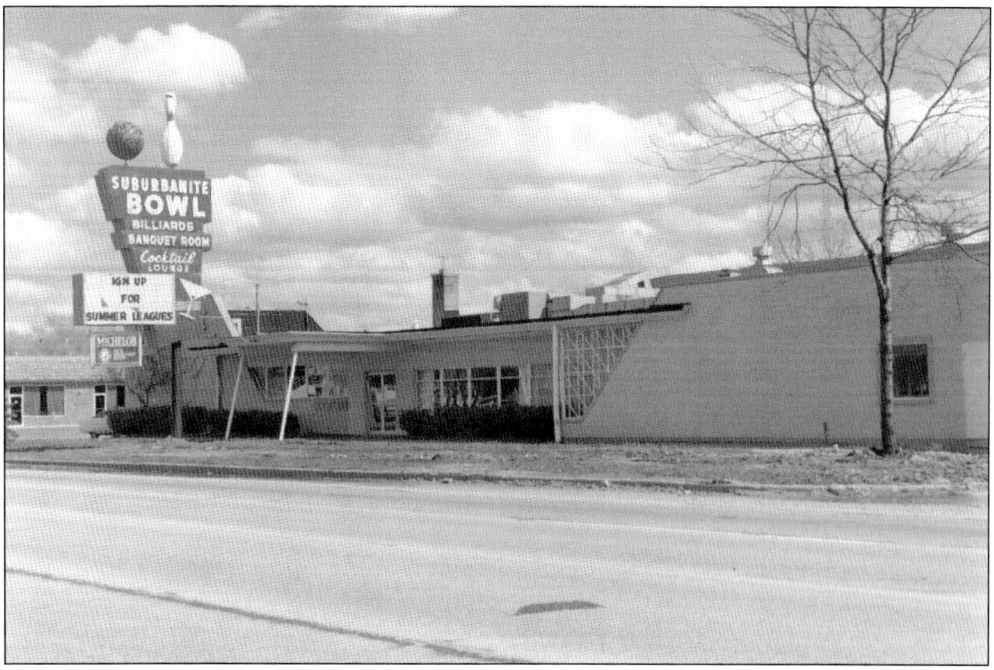

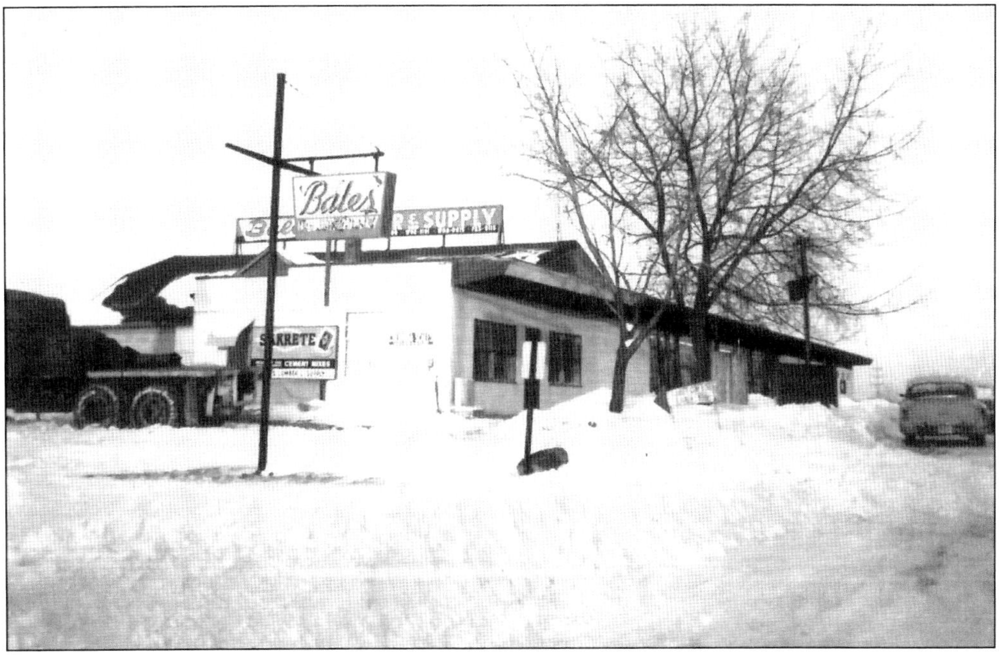

Bales Ace Hardware opened during this period. Despite a massive fire, it has remained an important business for locals with home improvement in mind. (Courtesy of the Westmont Area Historical Society.)

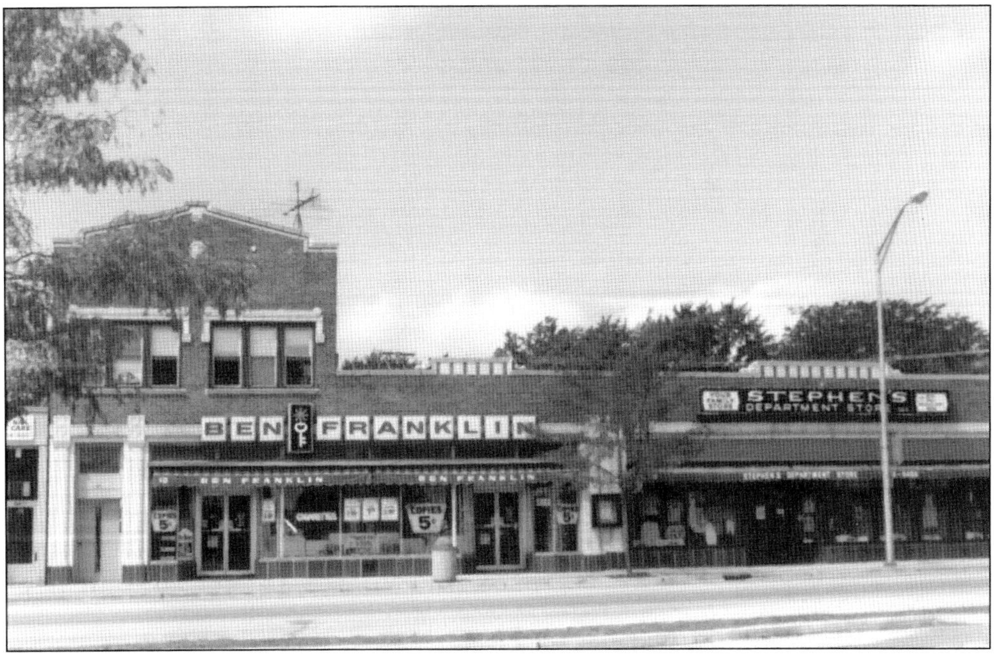

Ben Franklin was a national chain of five-and-dime stores. It is usually recognized as the first national chain store in the United States. This Ben Franklin stood on Cass Avenue until the 1990s, when the company became insolvent and had to close several stores across the country. Today, this building houses the Vincitori Italian restaurant. (Courtesy of the Westmont Area Historical Society.)

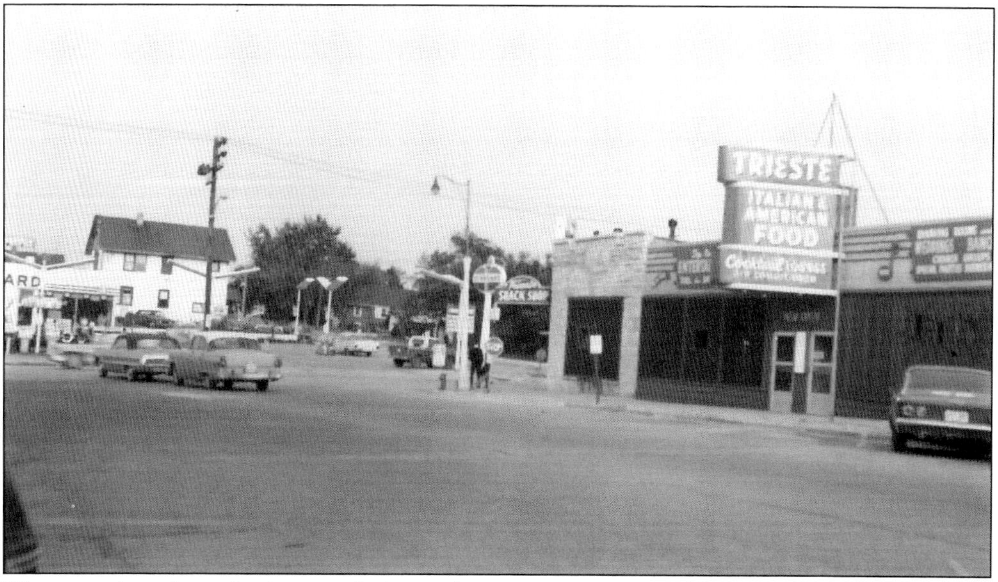

Westmont has always had strong links to the music community. Trieste was a popular lounge where blues players would perform, some of whom were drawn to the area by Muddy Waters. The building, also home to Villa Roma restaurant, was destroyed by a fire. (Courtesy of the Westmont Area Historical Society.)

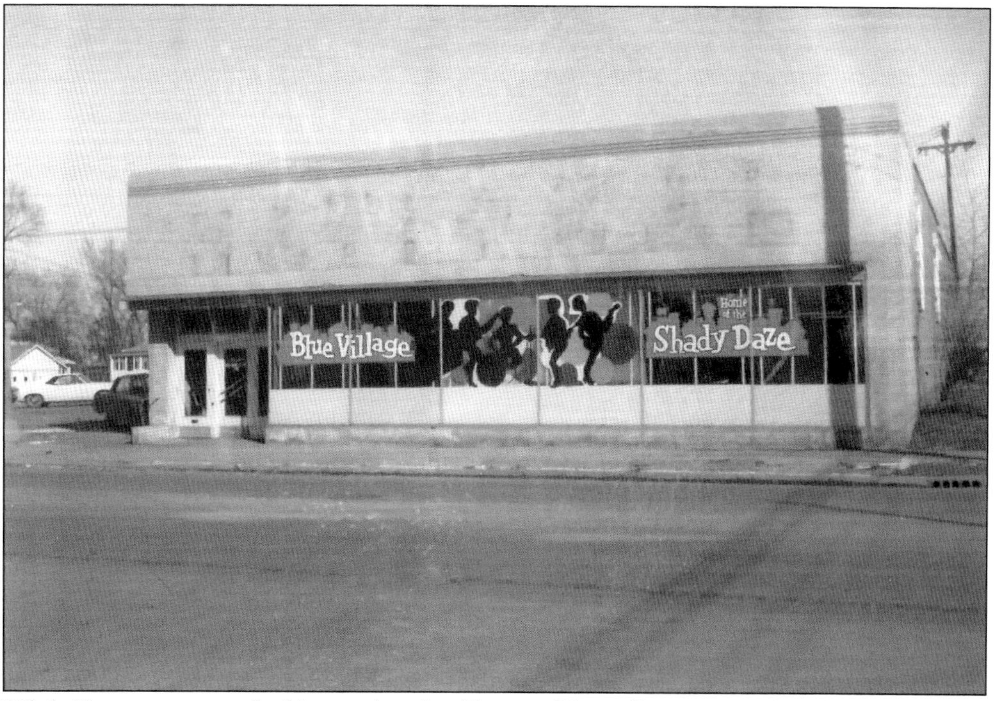

While Trieste was a popular blues and cocktail lounge, Blue Village was a rock and roll club. Local suburban bands got their start there by playing to crowds of Westmont's young people. The club was originally in the VFW hall when it opened in 1966, before moving to 1 North Cass Avenue in 1967, site of the former National grocery store. Admission was $2. Blue Village closed in 1970. (Courtesy of the Westmont Area Historical Society.)

Over the years, some well-known groups have played at Blue Village, including Deep Purple, New Colony 6, the Buckinghams, the Ides of March, Shadows of Knight, and the Yardbirds. These bands in particular went on to receive national acclaim and are still widely played today. The Cryan' Shames were the house band. (Both, courtesy of the Westmont Area Historical Society.)

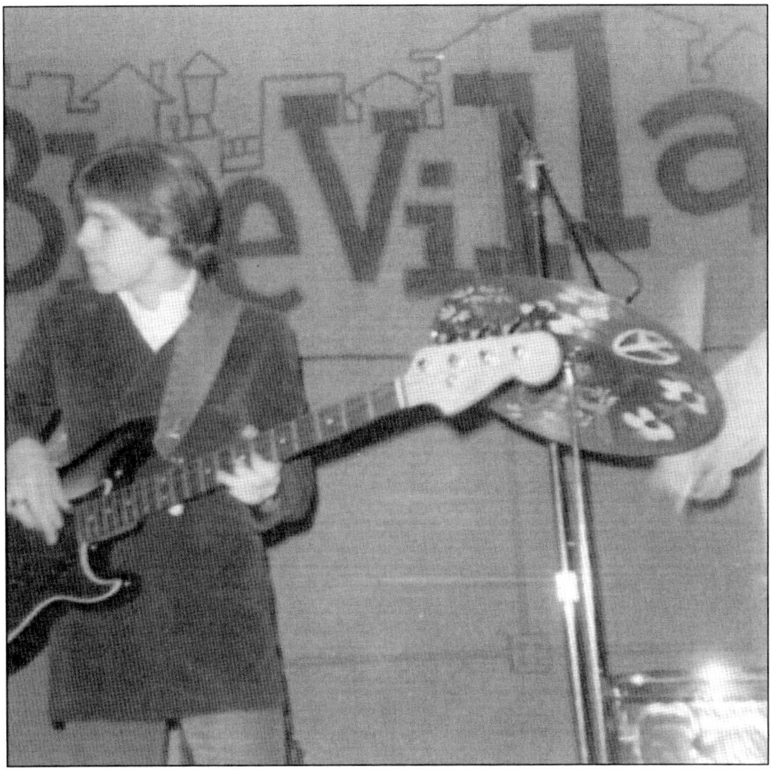

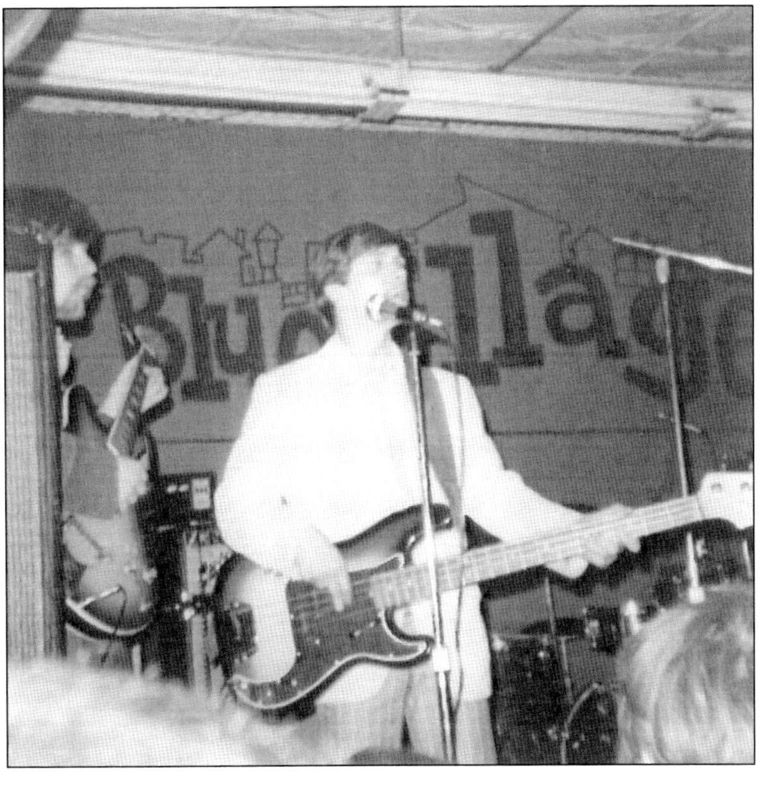

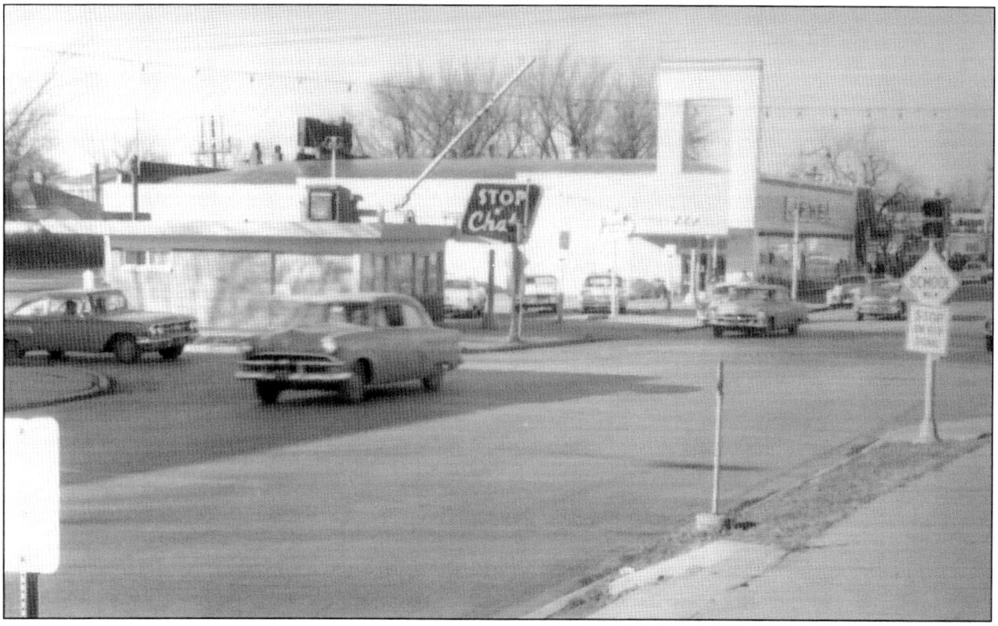

One of Westmont's most legendary businesses, the Stop N Chat (1967–1999) on Cass Avenue is fondly remembered by residents. Today, the site of Stop N Chat and the Jewel grocery store on the south side of town are the home of the Richmond Station condominiums and several retail businesses. (Courtesy of the Westmont Area Historical Society.)

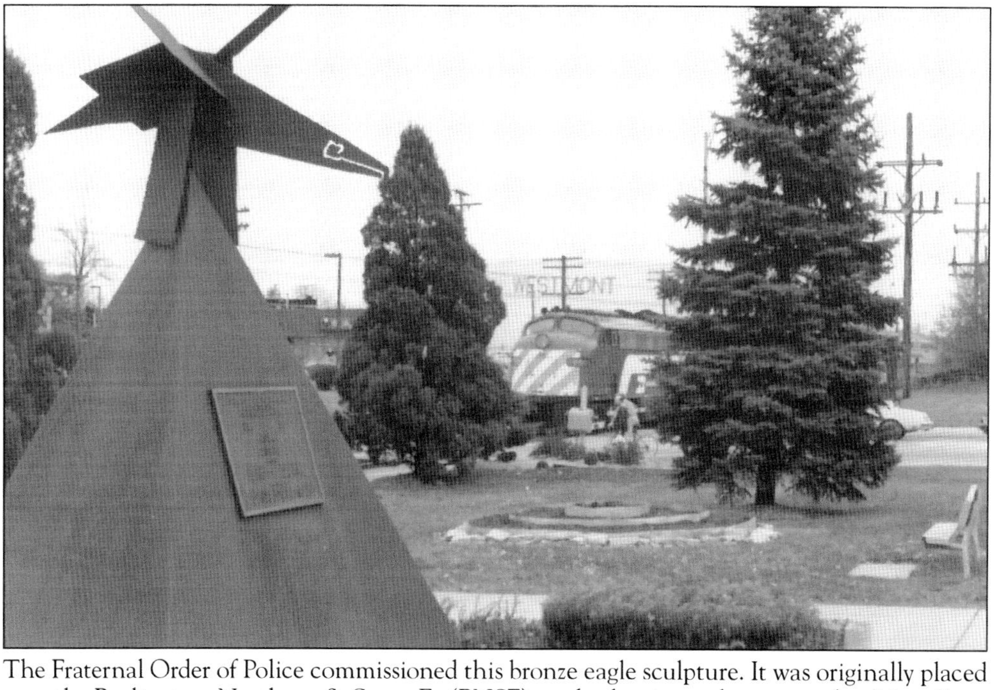

The Fraternal Order of Police commissioned this bronze eagle sculpture. It was originally placed near the Burlington, Northern & Santa Fe (BNSF) tracks, but it was later moved to Mary Egan Plaza, where a time capsule was buried in its base. In 2019, the eagle was relocated again to facilitate the Quincy Street condominium development. It can now be found at Wilderness Park. (Courtesy of the Westmont Area Historical Society.)

Suburban Trib

South Du Page County
Friday, April 6, 1979

ɅIayor hutters ;ame room

Anne Little

DOWNERS Grove game room, which ce contend was the operation center of a g ring, was closed Wednesday by the yor.

t a public hearing, during which police businessmen testified to several other ged state and municipal law violations at Electric Game World, 6400 S. Woodward , Mayor Frank Houck suspended the ne room's license. The suspension could up to 30 days. Houck, who held the ring, said during that time he will issue formal order relating to more permanent position" of the establishment.

And I must warn you that I am not npathetic to this business' continuation," ck told the game room owner, Donald ore of Hoffman Estates. Moore didn't pond.

CCORDING TO village ordinance, which es game room licenses in a category ilar to liquor licenses, the mayor has the hority to revoke or to suspend for more n seven days a game room license after a lic hearing. He may suspend a license for aximum seven-day period without a

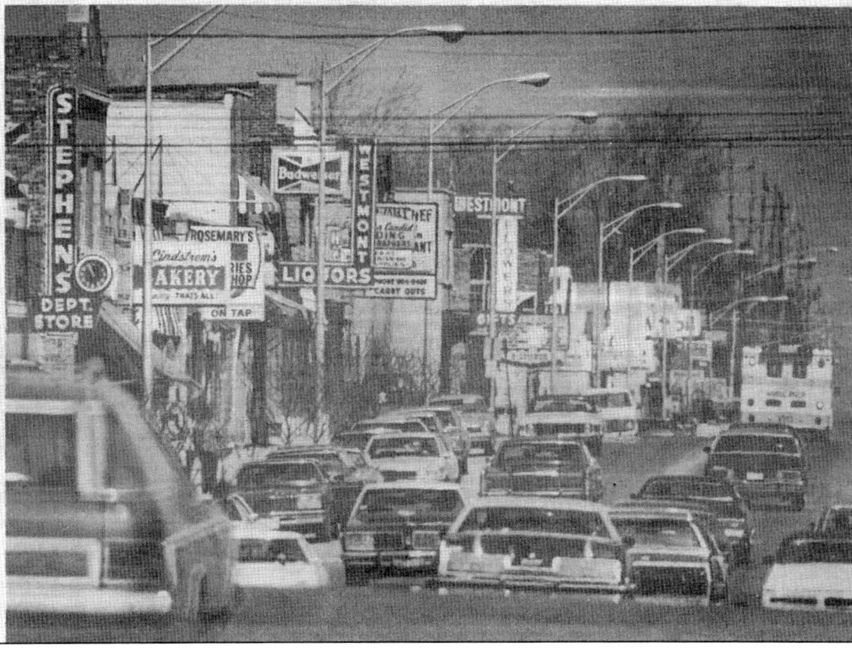

This 1979 issue of the *Suburban Trib* shows downtown Westmont facing north from the train tracks in the 1970s. The type of signs seen here, which hung over the sidewalk, are now prohibited. Some of Westmont's most well-known businesses, such as Stephen's Department Store, Lindstrom's Bakery, and Westmont Floral, are seen here. (Courtesy of the Westmont Area Historical Society.)

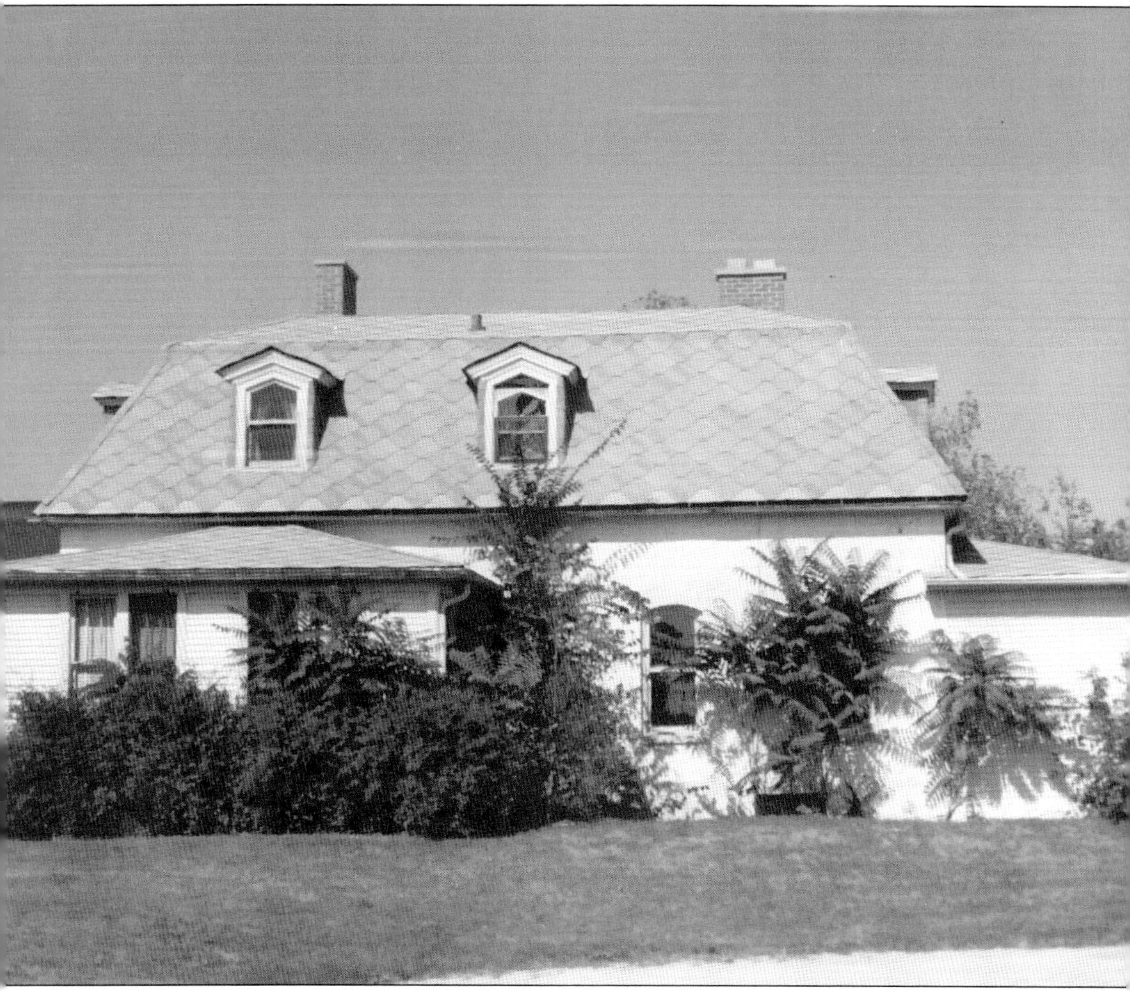

By the 1970s, William Gregg's former home at 107 South Cass Avenue was showing its age. Holy Trinity Church, which was using the house as a caretaker's cottage, made the decision to demolish the building. However, in 1976, a group of citizens formed the Westmont Area Historical Society to save the house and were ultimately successful. (Courtesy of the Westmont Area Historical Society.)

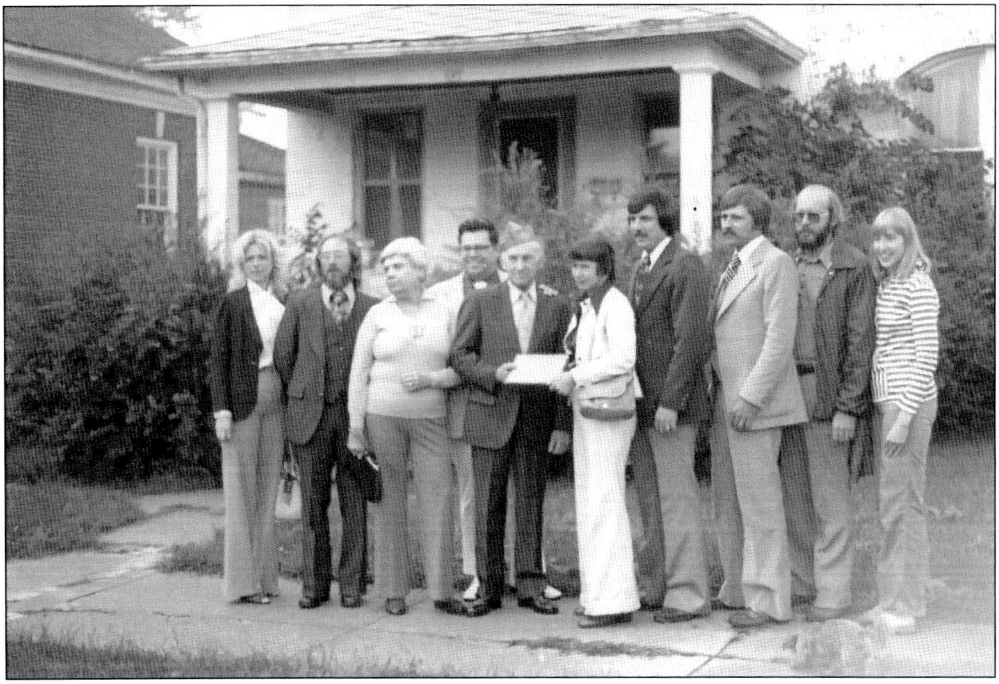

Members of the newly formed Westmont Area Historical Society and village representatives pose outside of the Gregg House before it was moved to its new site in 1977. Fifth from right is Marge Smejkal, who was instrumental in founding the society and raising $10,000 to move the house. (Courtesy of the Westmont Area Historical Society.)

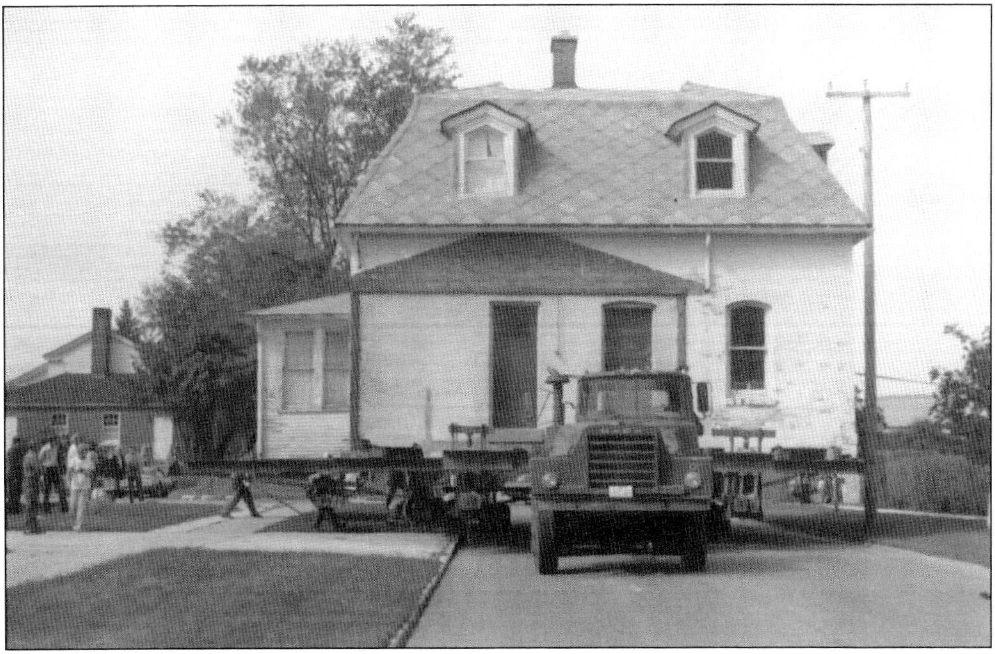

The Gregg House was hoisted onto a trailer and moved to its present location. The trip around the block from Cass Avenue to Linden Avenue was observed by members of the community and the new historical society. (Courtesy of the Village of Westmont.)

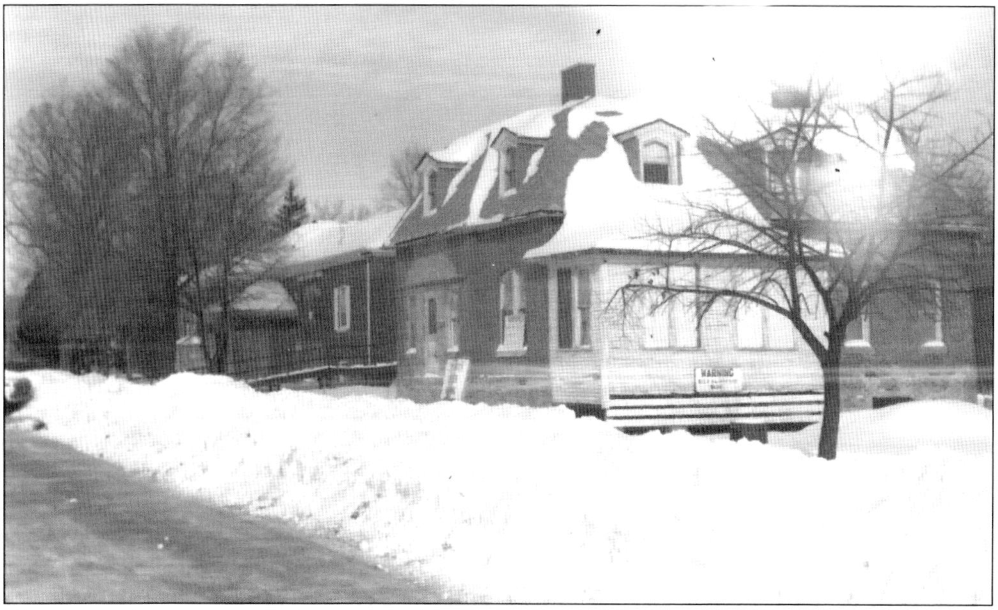

The Gregg House was moved to its new location on Linden Avenue to become the home of the Westmont Area Historical Society and Gregg House Museum. It is adjacent to the Westmont Park District's administrative staff and senior center, as well as Veterans Memorial Park. (Courtesy of the Westmont Area Historical Society.)

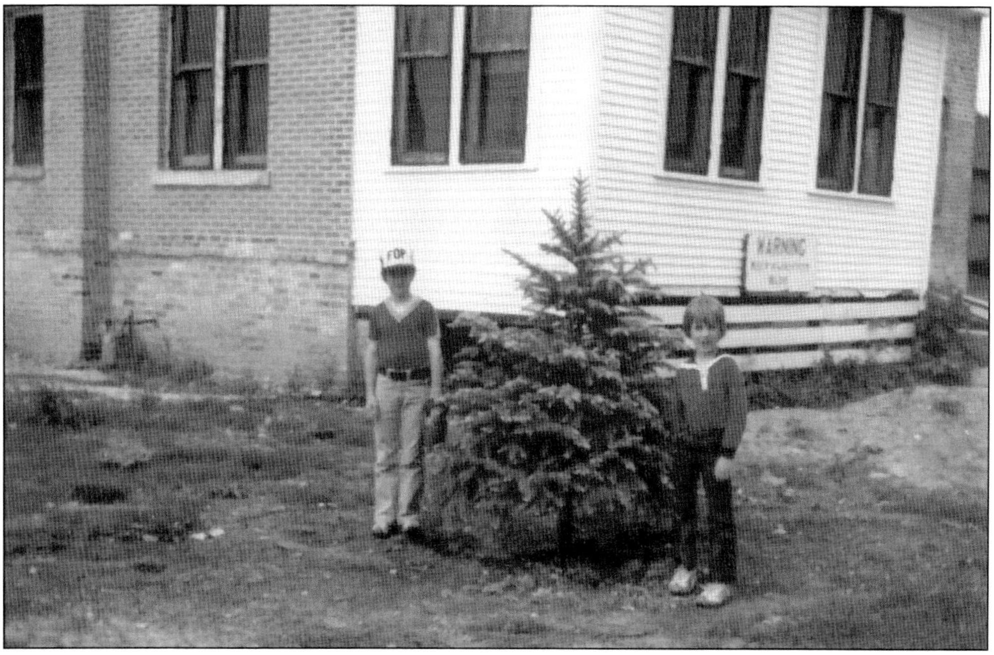

Members of the Fleck family pose outside of the Gregg House in June 1980. In over 100 years, the house has served as a residence, a restaurant, a speakeasy, a community recreation center, a funeral home, a convent, and a rectory. Today, the building serves as a reminder of Westmont's humble beginnings. The historical society serves to teach Westmont and the surrounding area about the early days in DuPage County. (Courtesy of the Westmont Area Historical Society.)

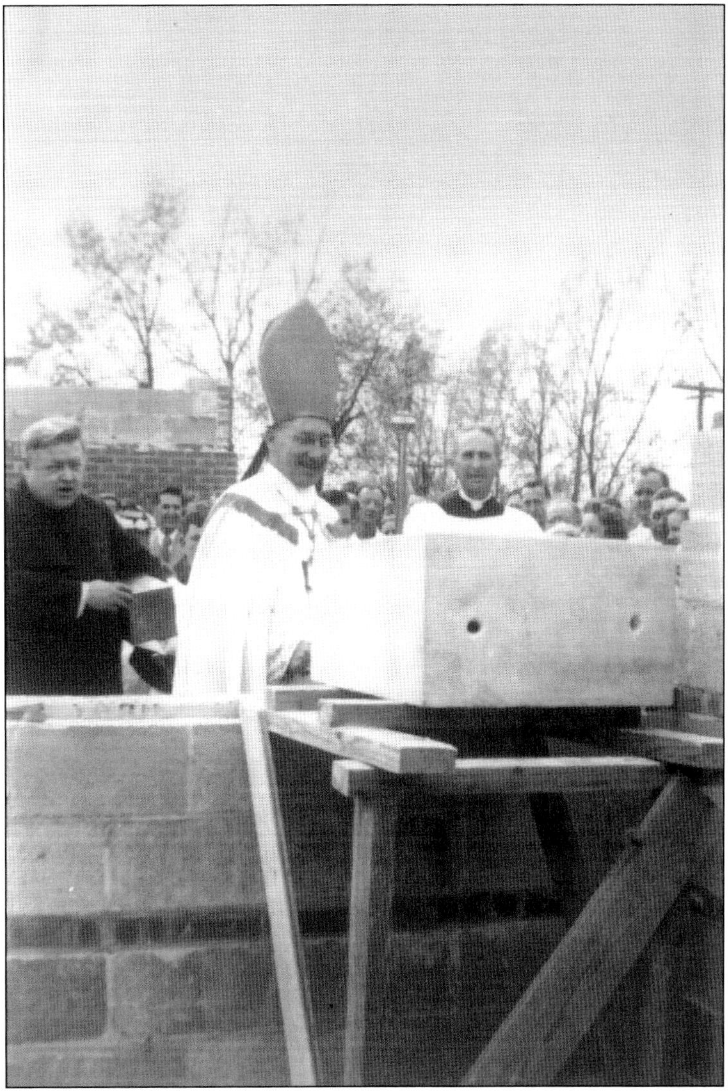

In 1952, Holy Trinity School opened its doors under the auspices of Holy Trinity Parish. At right, the archbishop makes a speech during construction. Its earliest teachers, nine nuns, lived in the Gregg House. Today, the school serves students in preschool through eighth grade. (Right, courtesy of the Westmont Area Historical Society; below, courtesy of the Village of Westmont.)

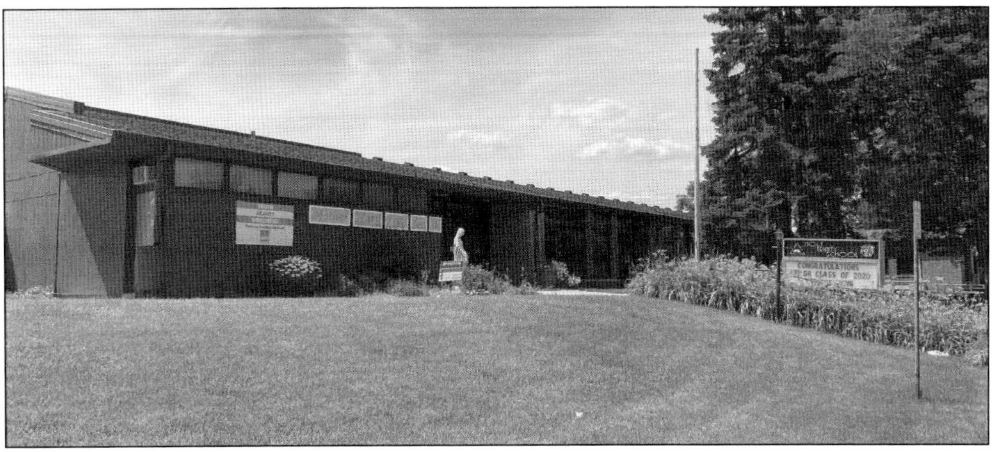

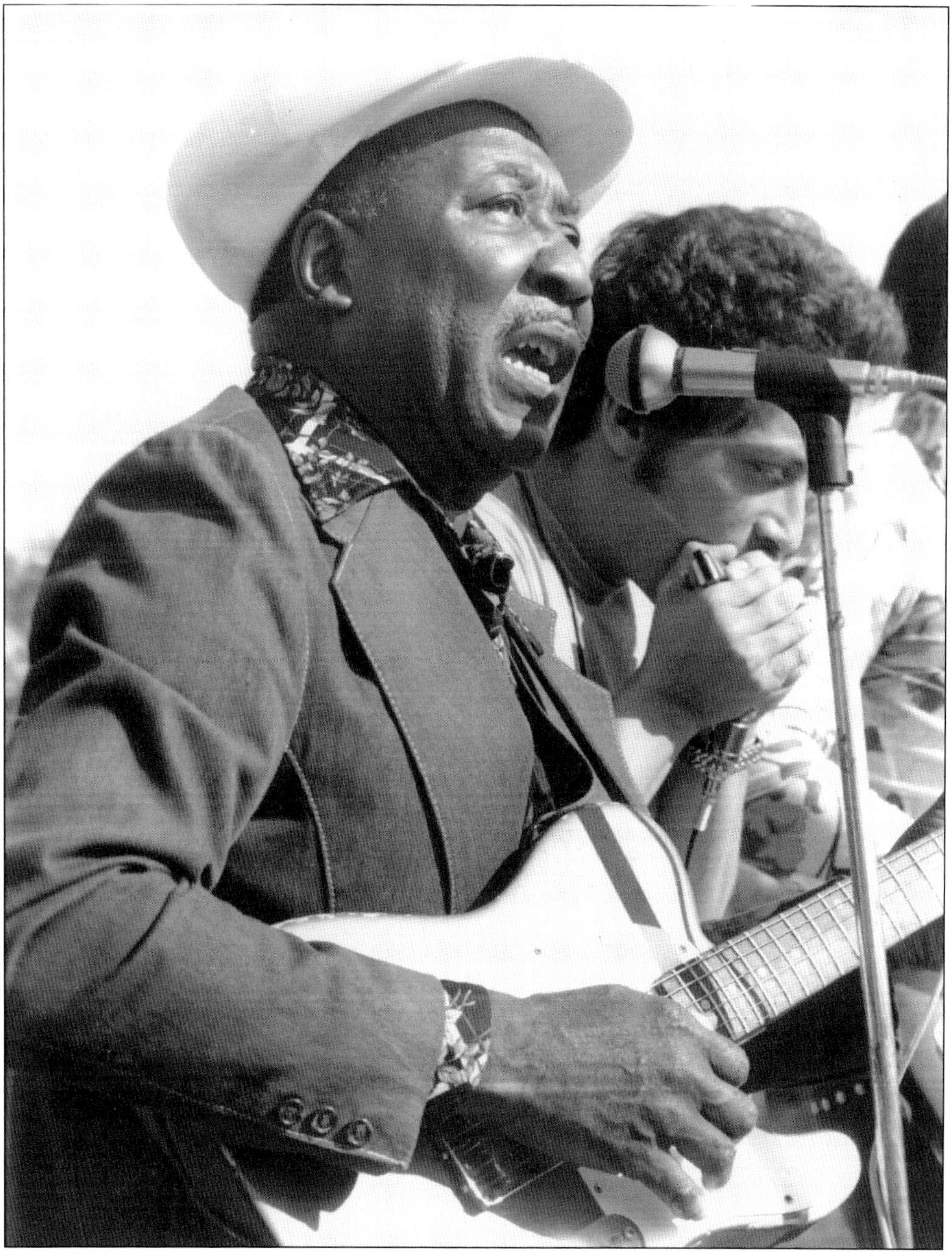

McKinley Morganfield, better known as Muddy Waters, made Westmont his home during the last decade of his life. When he married his second wife, Marva Jean Brooks, in 1979, Eric Clapton served as his best man. Known as "the father of modern Chicago blues," his music influenced groups like the Beatles and the Rolling Stones and continues to be influential today. (Courtesy of the Westmont Area Historical Society.)

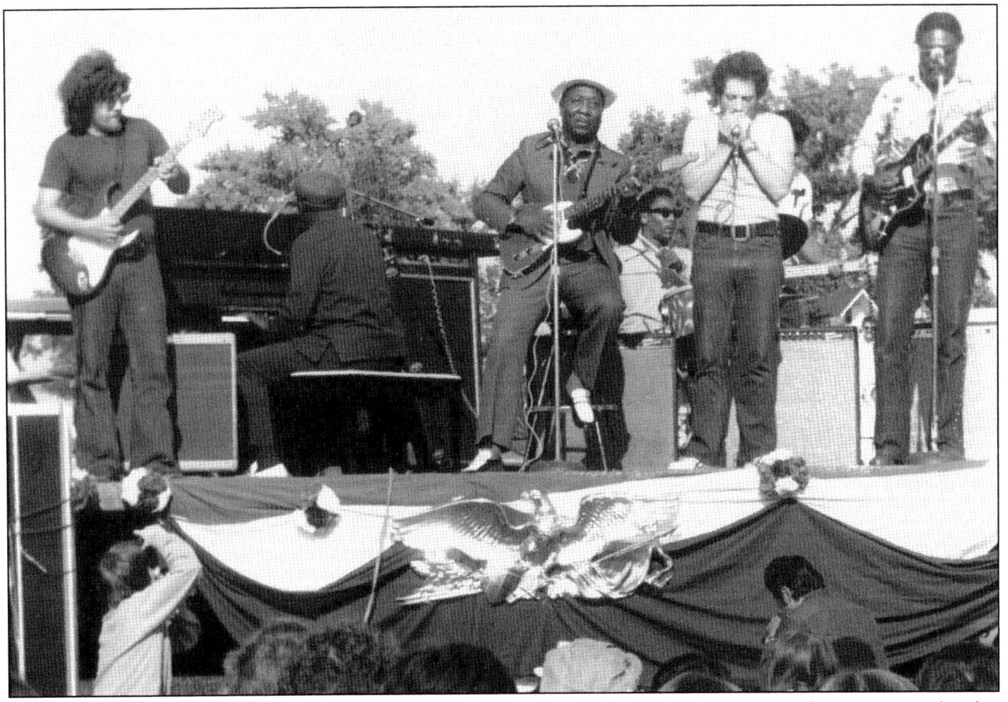

Waters left his fingerprints on Westmont. Here, he performs at an event in the 1970s and rides in a parade. Following his death in 1982, the village named a section of Cass Avenue "Honorary Muddy Waters Way." A museum in his honor, featuring artifacts including one of his six Grammy Awards, was opened in Westmont Centre at 1 South Cass Avenue. (Both, courtesy of the Westmont Area Historical Society.)

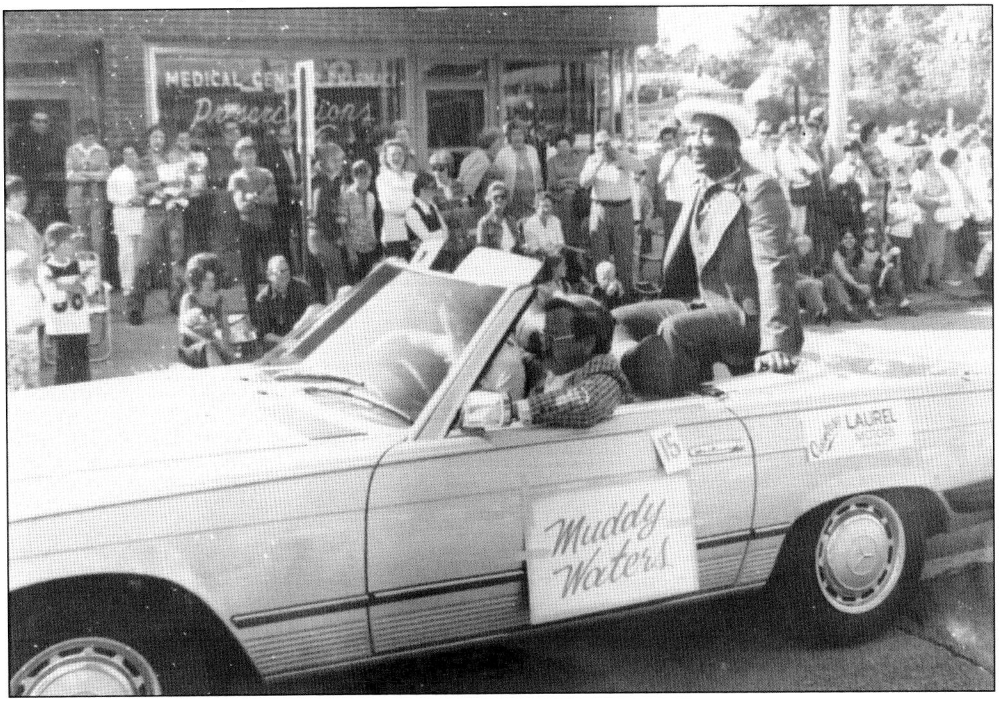

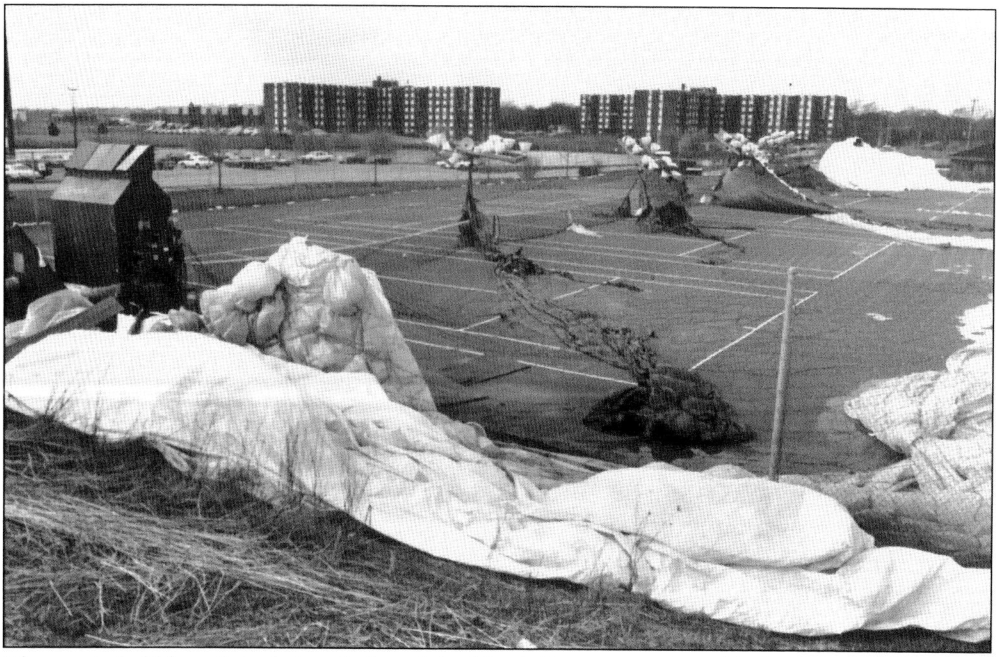

The tennis bubble at Twin Lakes Park on Fifty-Ninth Street caused trouble for several years. While the bubble made it possible to play tennis in inclement weather, it also blew over or "popped" in high winds. This photograph shows the aftermath of one such event and was captioned "when the bubble burst." (Courtesy of the Westmont Area Historical Society.)

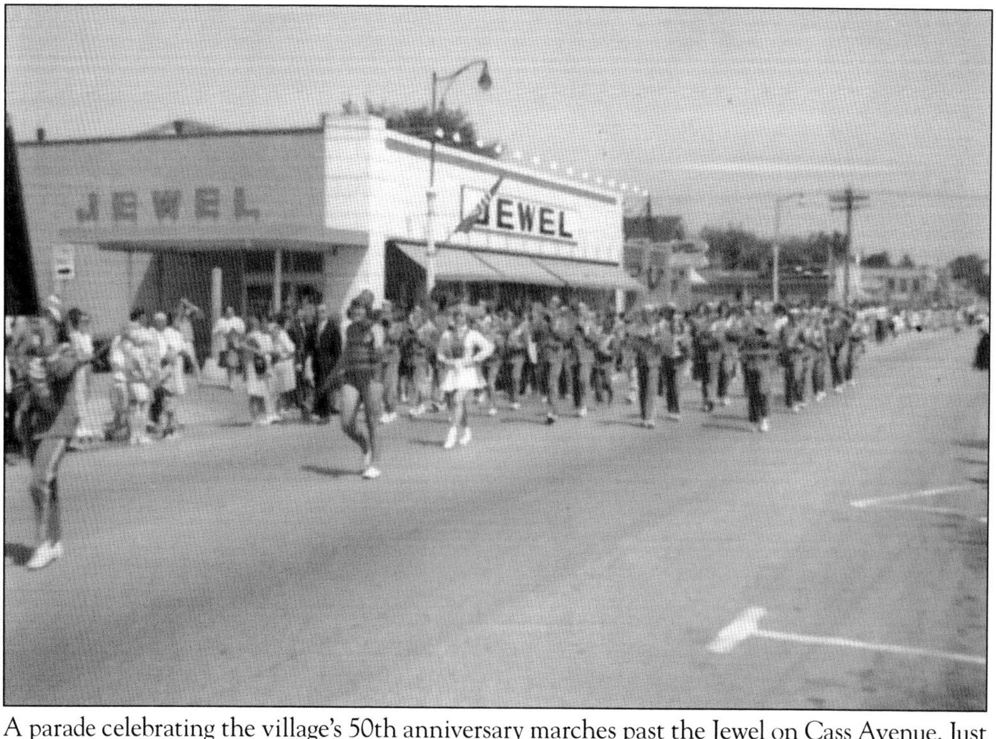

A parade celebrating the village's 50th anniversary marches past the Jewel on Cass Avenue. Just out of frame is the Stop N Chat. (Courtesy of the Westmont Area Historical Society.)

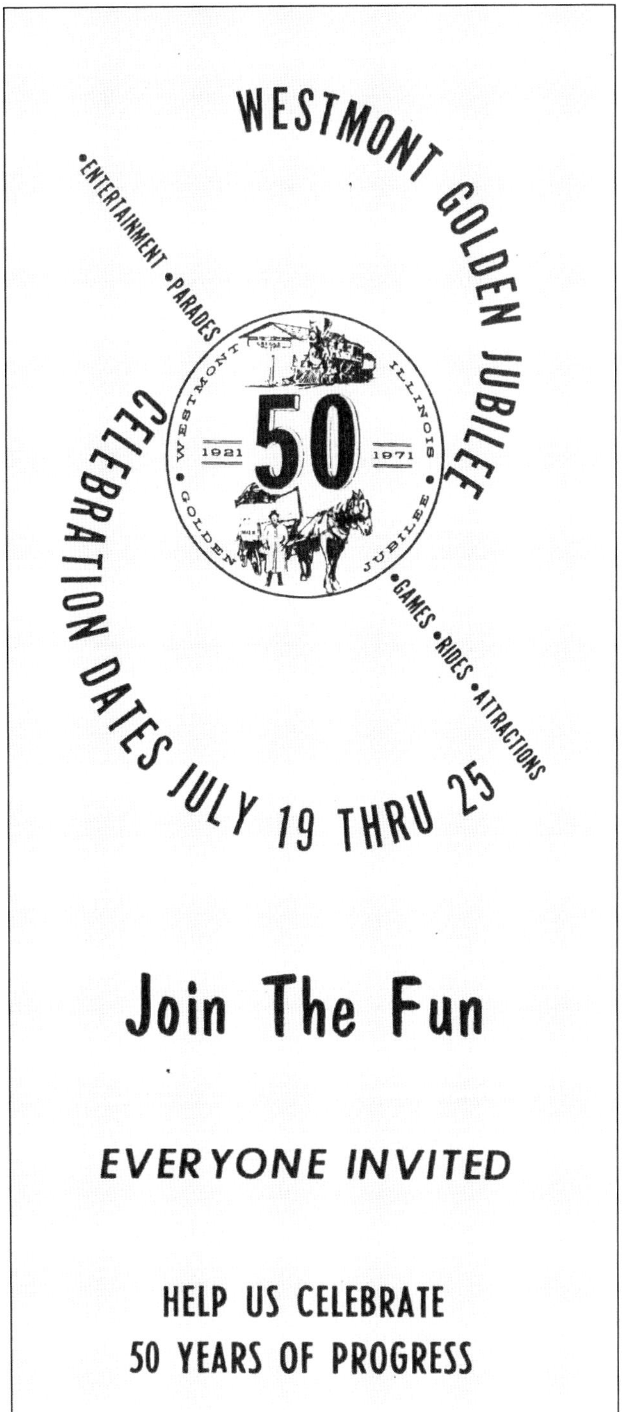

In 1971, the village celebrated its 50th anniversary with a weeklong celebration in July. The occasion included parades, pageants, picnics, dress-up days, and live music. In just 50 years, the village had blossomed from a small farming community to a prosperous modern suburb. (Courtesy of the Westmont Area Historical Society.)

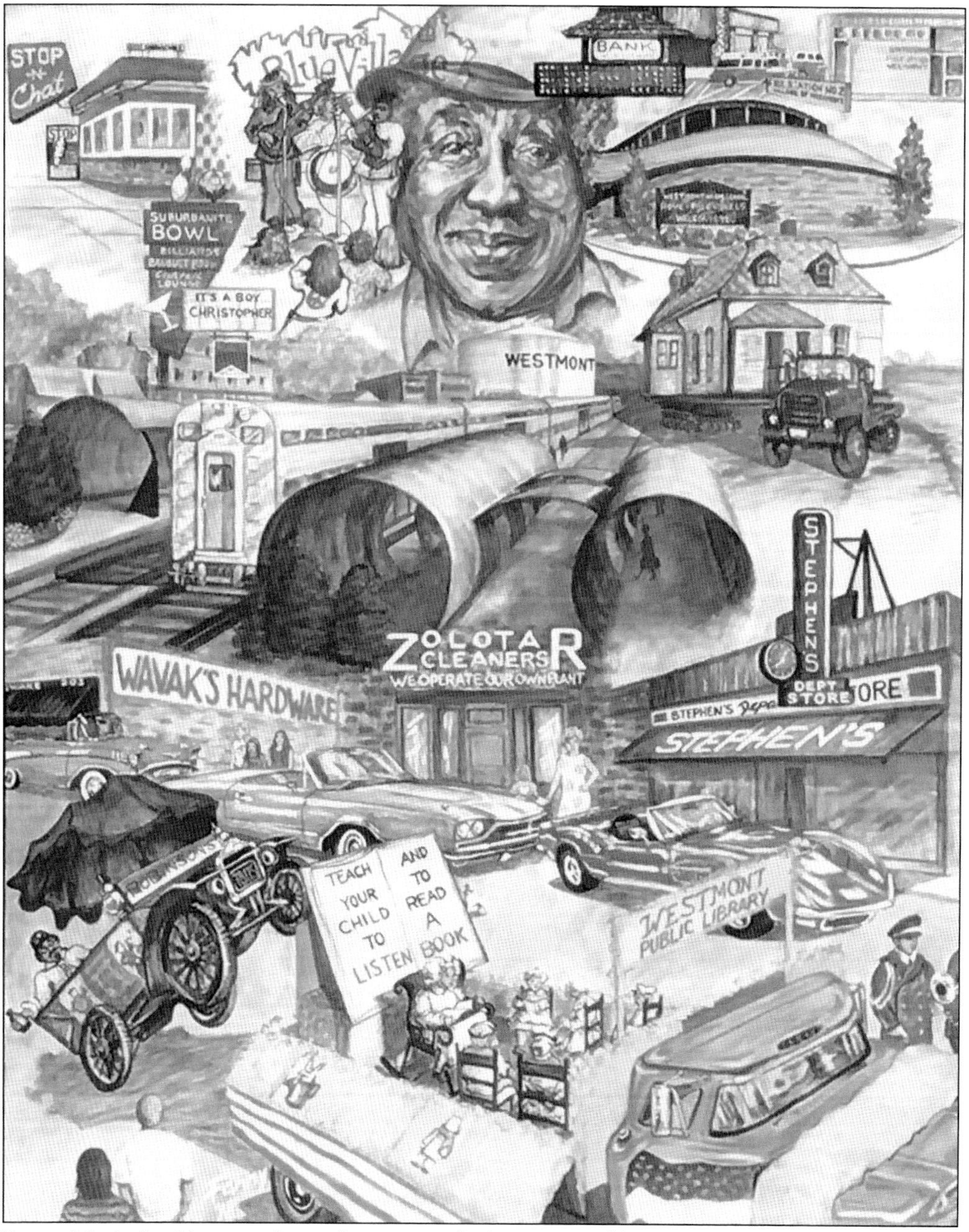

Fanny Moy's third historical mural prominently features Muddy Waters at top. The Blue Village and Stop N Chat also feature, along with other local businesses like Zolotar cleaners and Stephen's Department Store. (Courtesy of the Village of Westmont.)

Four

International Advancement 1980s to 1990s

In the 1980s, Westmont was booming. One of the last remaining farms, the Healy farm, had been sold off piecemeal for years to make way for schools, residential development, and commercial construction. In 1985, what remained of the farm became the Hilton Chicago/Oak Brook Hills Resort and Conference Center. The hotel and conference center has brought about 600,000 people to the area per year since its opening. Newer, upscale housing developments began to sprout up on the edge of town. In the 1980s, the park district acquired Twin Lakes Golf Course and eight new parks, meaning that this boom town also had a large amount of green space for recreation.

By 1990, Westmont was home to 21,228 residents, many of whom were renters. The car dealerships that dotted Ogden Avenue brought in about 40 percent of the village's sales tax revenue. Development continued along Pasquinelli Drive, including a hotel, office parks, two shopping centers, and the DiHo Market. Businesses chose Westmont as a home base because of its proximity to Chicago's Midway and O'Hare airports, the BNSF line into Chicago, and its amenities, including hotels and a wide variety of restaurants.

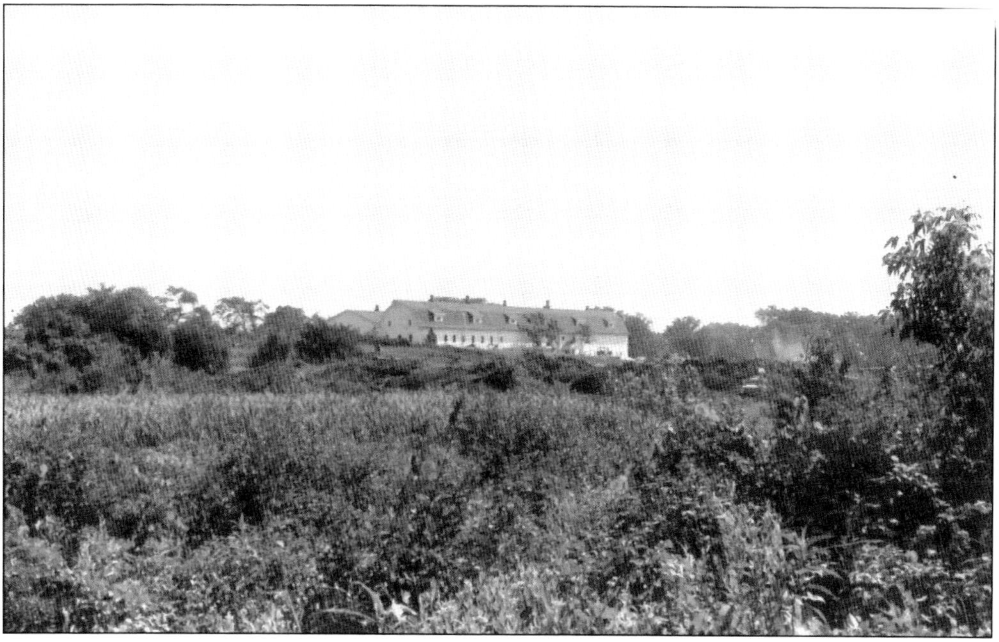

In 1936, the Healy family purchased 900 acres at the northernmost point of Westmont. The family boarded polo ponies and horses for the US Army. Over the years, the farm sold off acreage piecemeal to make way for new developments and businesses. The final few acres were sold in 1985 and became the site of the Hilton Chicago/Oak Brook Hills Resort and Conference Center. (Both, courtesy of the Westmont Area Historical Society.)

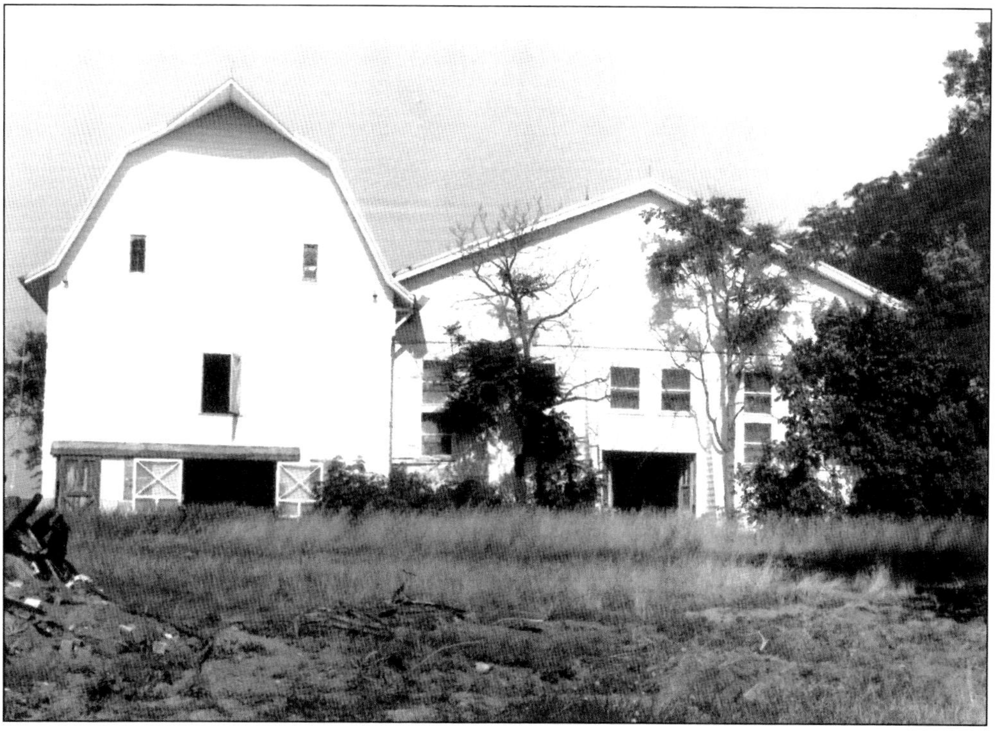

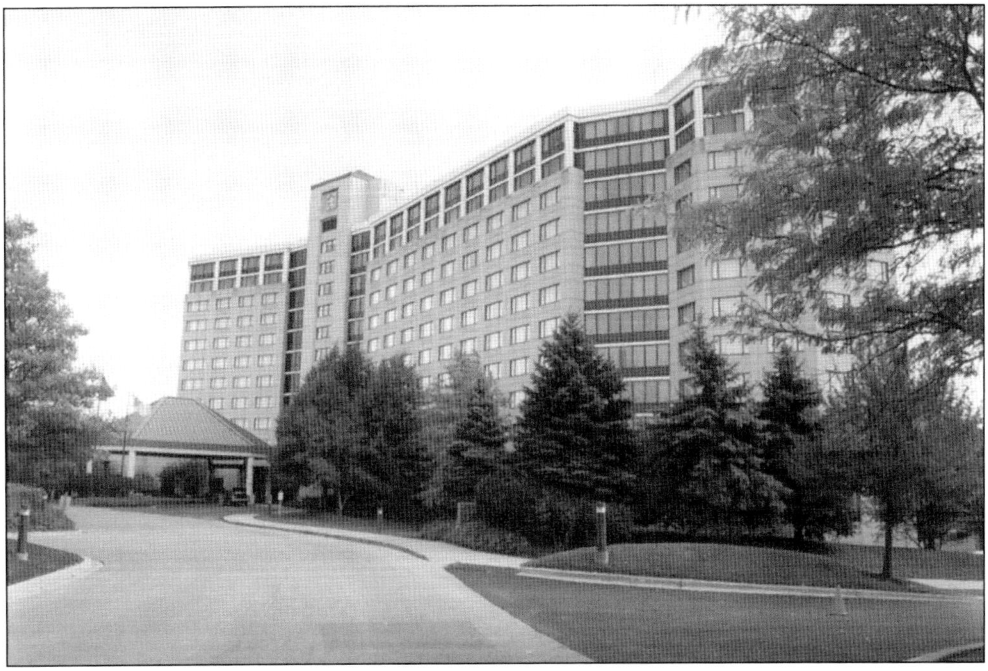

The Hilton Chicago/Oak Brook Hills Resort and Conference Center was built in 1985 on the site of the Healy farm. The hotel and its adjoining golf course bring approximately 600,000 visitors to the town each year. The German national soccer team stayed in the hotel during a visit to the village in the 1990s. The golf course has hosted several celebrity golf outings. (Both, courtesy of the Village of Westmont.)

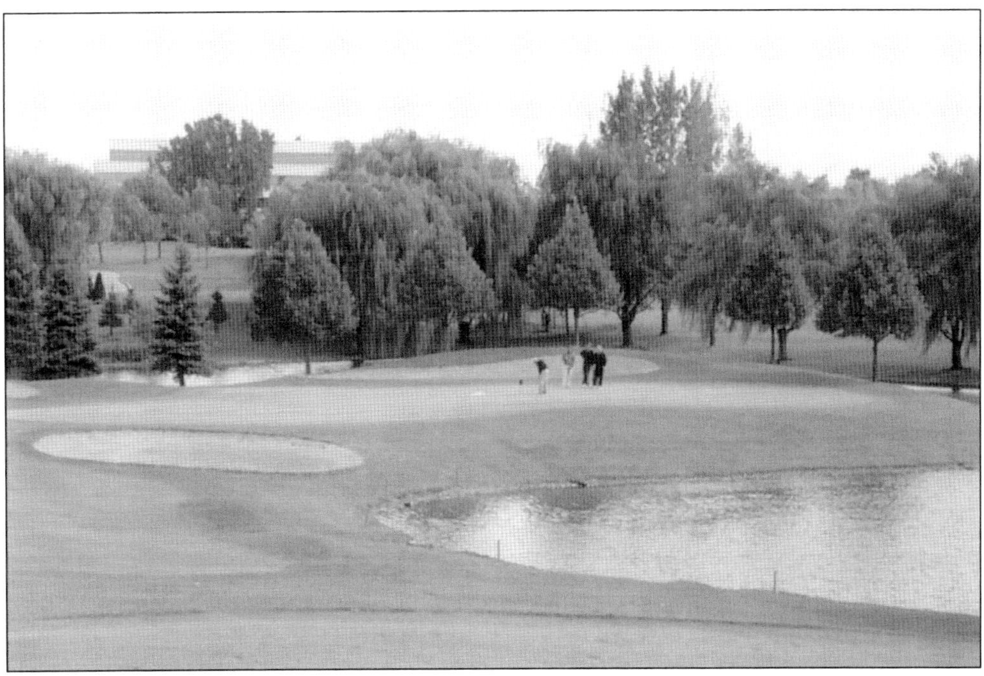

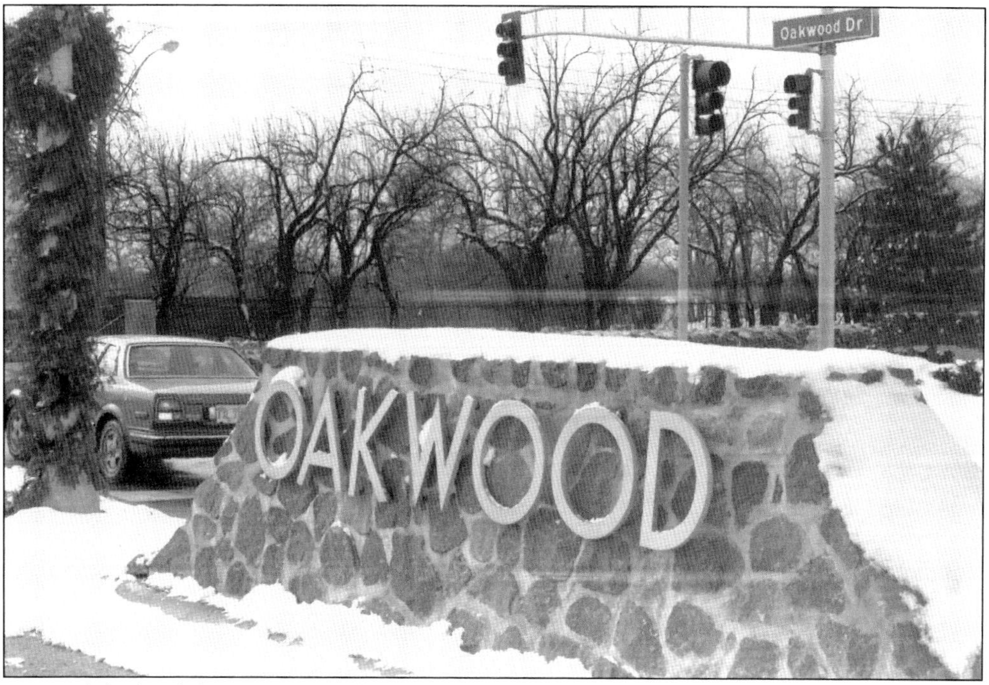

Some of the land that was originally part of the Healy farm became the Oakwood subdivision. This housing development consists of over 400 homes and is bordered by country clubs, golf courses, and a small lake. (Courtesy of the Westmont Area Historical Society.)

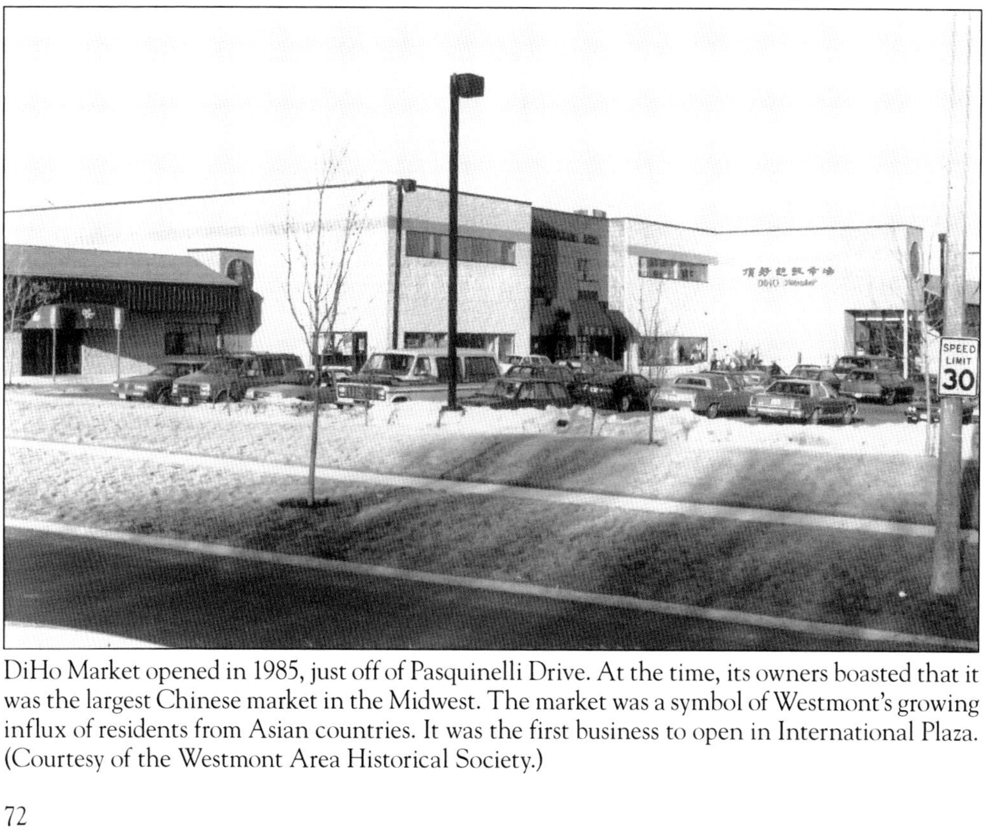

DiHo Market opened in 1985, just off of Pasquinelli Drive. At the time, its owners boasted that it was the largest Chinese market in the Midwest. The market was a symbol of Westmont's growing influx of residents from Asian countries. It was the first business to open in International Plaza. (Courtesy of the Westmont Area Historical Society.)

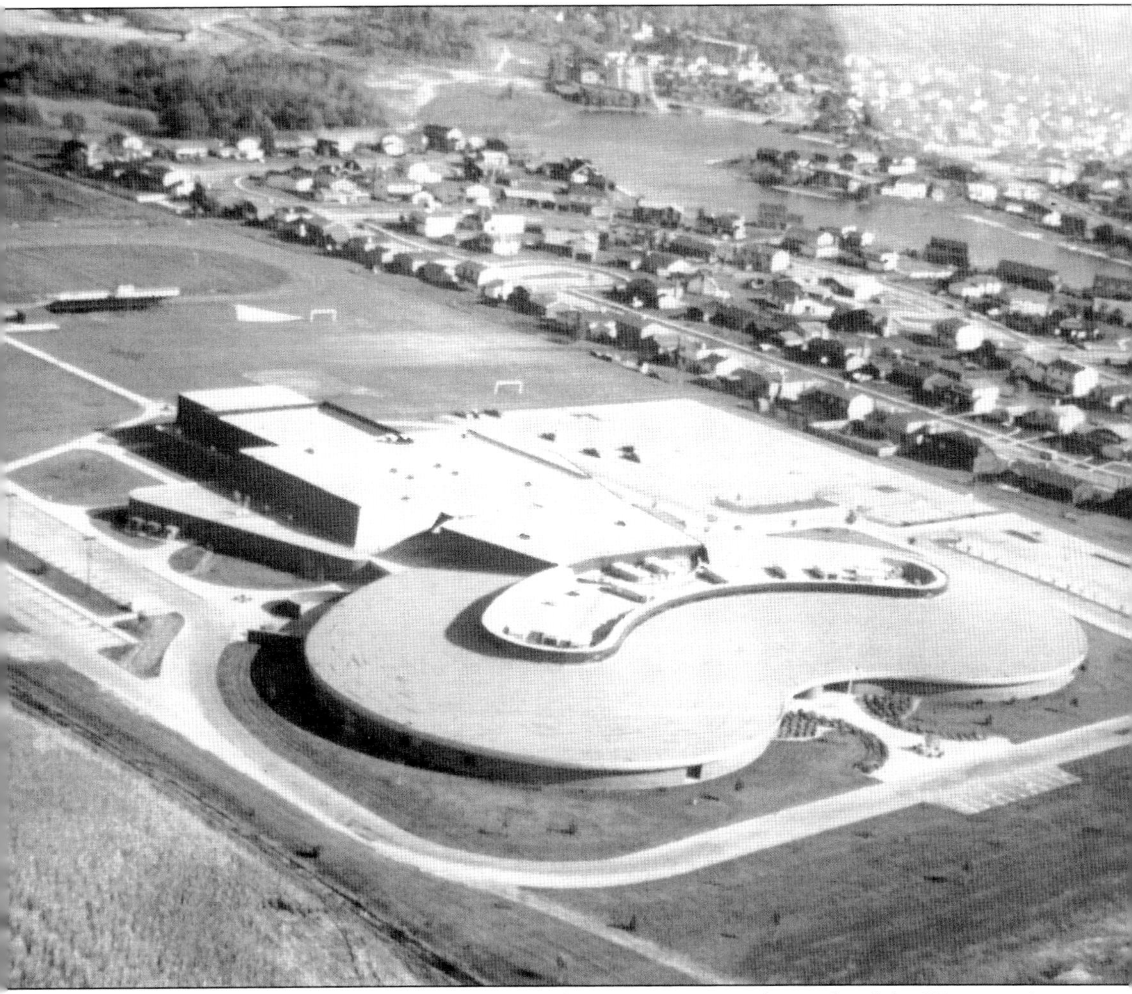

Until Westmont High School opened in 1976, there was no secondary school for Westmont's students. The high school is near Ty Warner Park and Sentinel Park, and the land on which it is built was once part of Healy farm. In this aerial photograph, the new Oakwood subdivision is seen at upper right. The school was built in a circular configuration; when it first opened, classrooms were blocked off with movable partitions. In recent years, permanent walls and doors were installed. (Courtesy of the South family.)

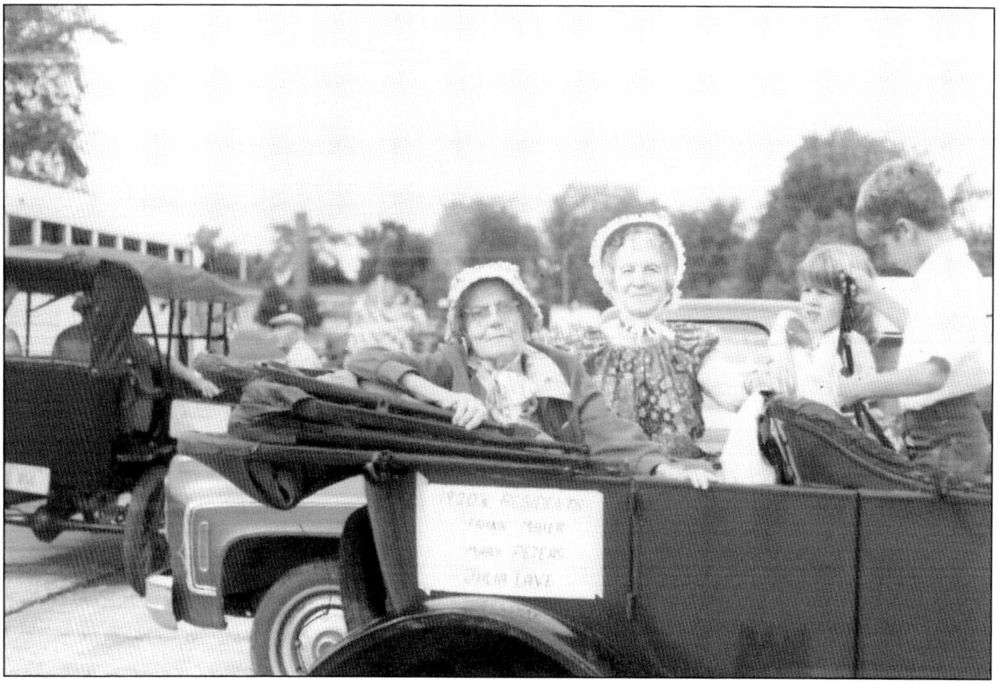

To commemorate its 75th anniversary, the village held celebrations throughout 1996. Here, some of Westmont's original residents ride in an antique car during a parade. (Courtesy of the Westmont Area Historical Society.)

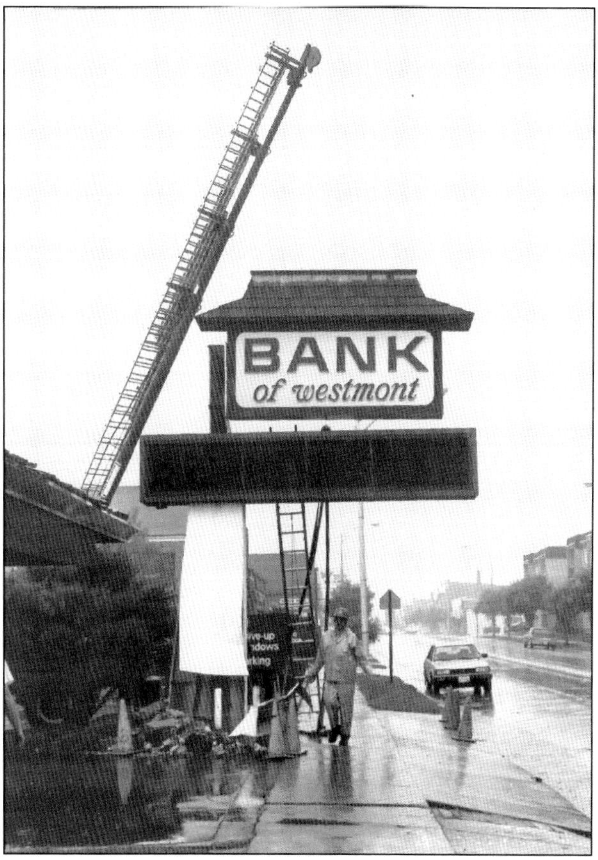

The Bank of Westmont replaced the First State Bank of Westmont. Located at 139 North Cass Avenue at Norfolk Avenue, the bank acquired a state-of-the-art electronic sign in the 1980s. Today, the building houses a Bank of America. (Courtesy of the Westmont Area Historical Society.)

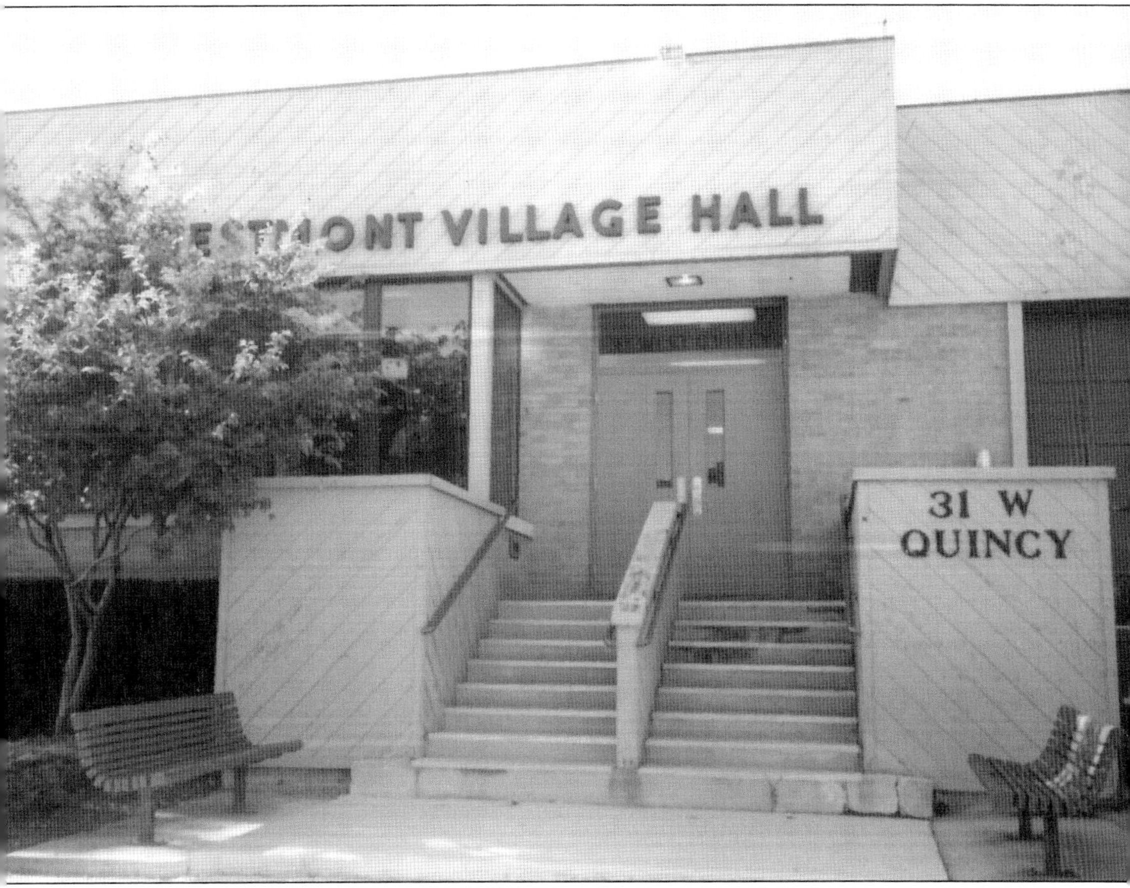

Village hall continued to share space with the police department until the late 1990s. This village hall was on Quincy Street, where the present village hall still stands. The "new" village hall was constructed as part of Project 2000, an ambitious effort to redesign Quincy Street and the BNSF corridor through Westmont. (Courtesy of the Village of Westmont.)

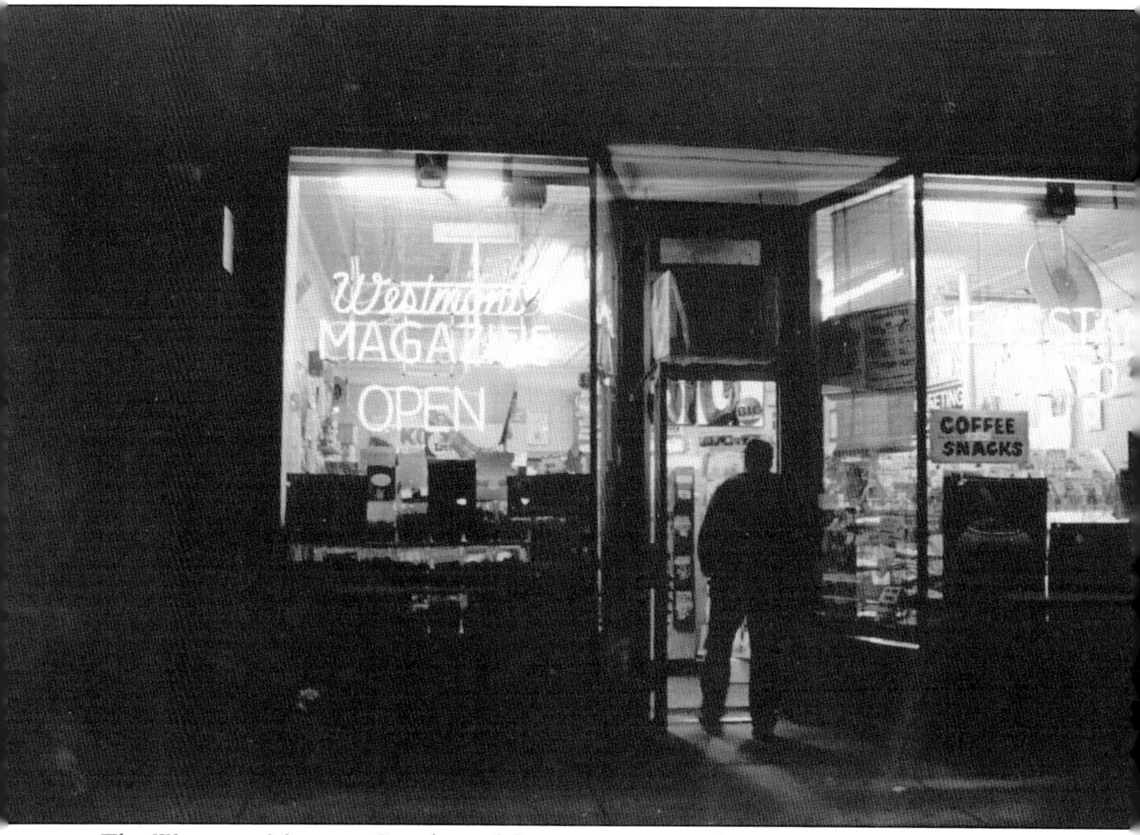

The Westmont Magazine Stand stood for many years on Quincy Street across from the train depot. It was a friendly place to pick up daily papers or magazines and lottery tickets. Sadly, this business closed and will be the future home of another famous Westmont business, Taco Express. (Courtesy of the Westmont Area Historical Society.)

In 1991, Westmont chose to honor local soldiers participating in Operation Desert Storm by erecting a billboard in their honor. It echoes the large World War II billboard. (Courtesy of the Westmont Area Historical Society.)

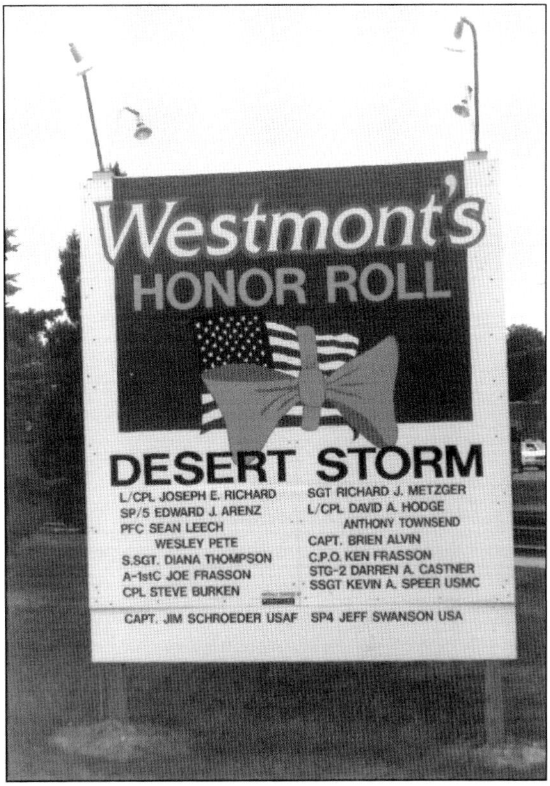

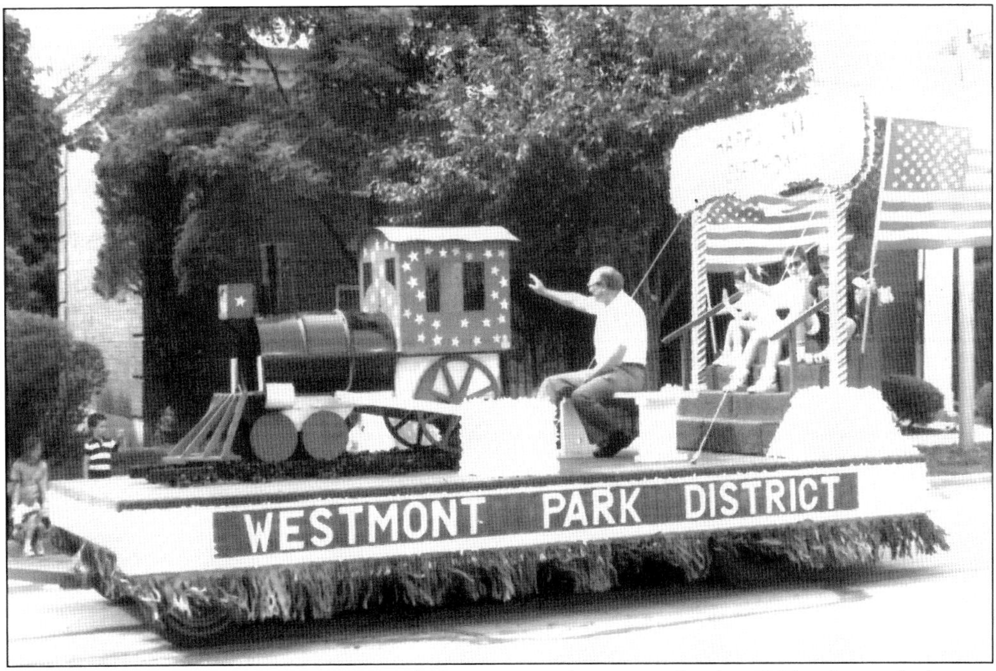

During this period, the Westmont Park District was booming. In the 1980s, the park district acquired eight new parks and a golf course, creating plenty of recreation opportunities for its residents. (Courtesy of the Westmont Area Historical Society.)

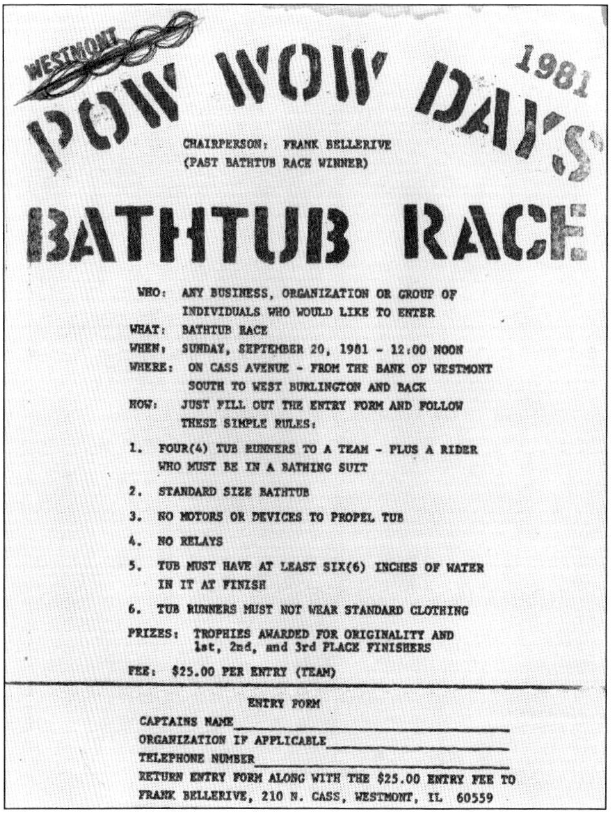

WESTMONT POW WOW DAYS 1981

CHAIRPERSON: FRANK BELLERIVE
(PAST BATHTUB RACE WINNER)

BATHTUB RACE

WHO: ANY BUSINESS, ORGANIZATION OR GROUP OF INDIVIDUALS WHO WOULD LIKE TO ENTER
WHAT: BATHTUB RACE
WHEN: SUNDAY, SEPTEMBER 20, 1981 - 12:00 NOON
WHERE: ON CASS AVENUE - FROM THE BANK OF WESTMONT SOUTH TO WEST BURLINGTON AND BACK
HOW: JUST FILL OUT THE ENTRY FORM AND FOLLOW THESE SIMPLE RULES:

1. FOUR(4) TUB RUNNERS TO A TEAM - PLUS A RIDER WHO MUST BE IN A BATHING SUIT
2. STANDARD SIZE BATHTUB
3. NO MOTORS OR DEVICES TO PROPEL TUB
4. NO RELAYS
5. TUB MUST HAVE AT LEAST SIX(6) INCHES OF WATER IN IT AT FINISH
6. TUB RUNNERS MUST NOT WEAR STANDARD CLOTHING

PRIZES: TROPHIES AWARDED FOR ORIGINALITY AND 1st, 2nd, and 3rd PLACE FINISHERS

FEE: $25.00 PER ENTRY (TEAM)

ENTRY FORM

CAPTAINS NAME____________________
ORGANIZATION IF APPLICABLE____________________
TELEPHONE NUMBER____________________
RETURN ENTRY FORM ALONG WITH THE $25.00 ENTRY FEE TO FRANK BELLERIVE, 210 N. CASS, WESTMONT, IL 60559

Pow Wow Days was a major social event in Westmont. The festival featured carnival games and rides, live music, food, and the very popular bathtub races. Teams would compete by running their bathtubs down Cass Avenue. (Both, courtesy of the Westmont Area Historical Society.)

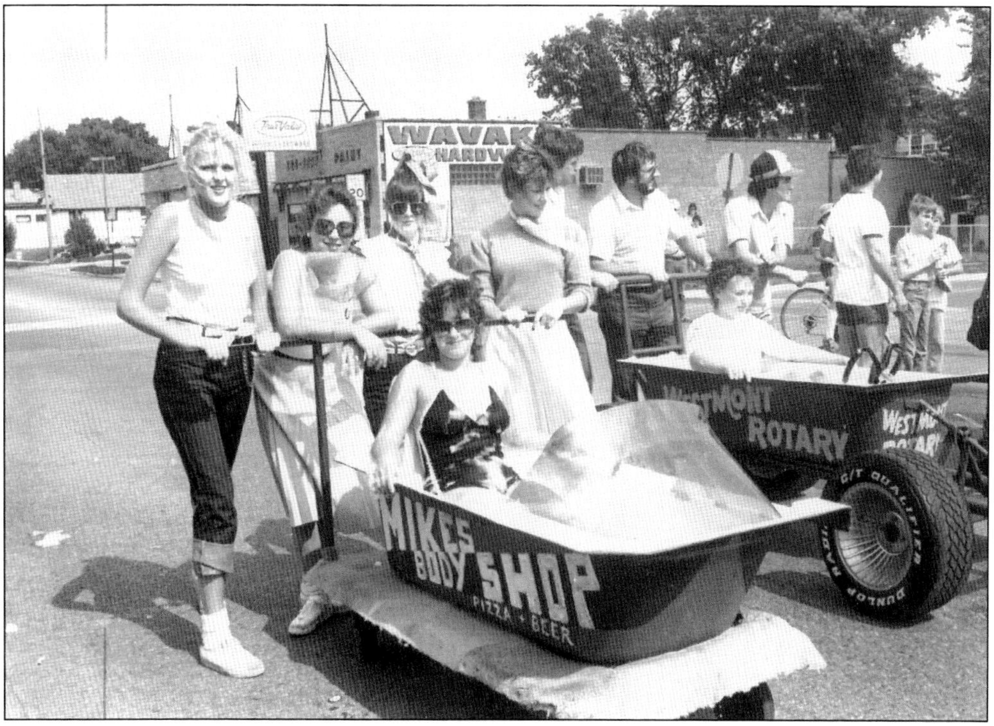

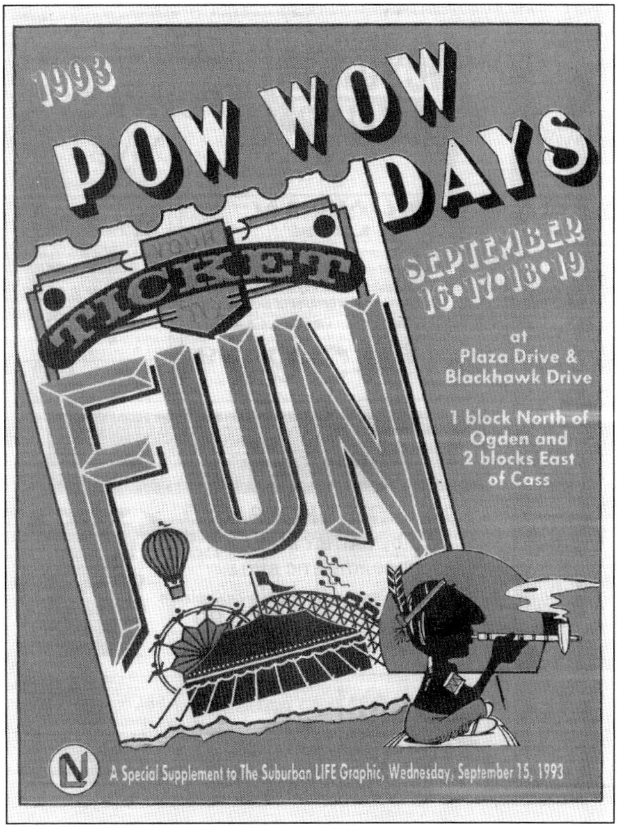

Pow Wow Days was held in the open space on Blackhawk Drive, which was previously a part of the Healy farm. The festival continued until the late 1990s, until the Taste of Westmont began in 1996 during the village's 75th anniversary. This section of open green space was developed into Ty Warner Park. (Both, courtesy of the Westmont Area Historical Society.)

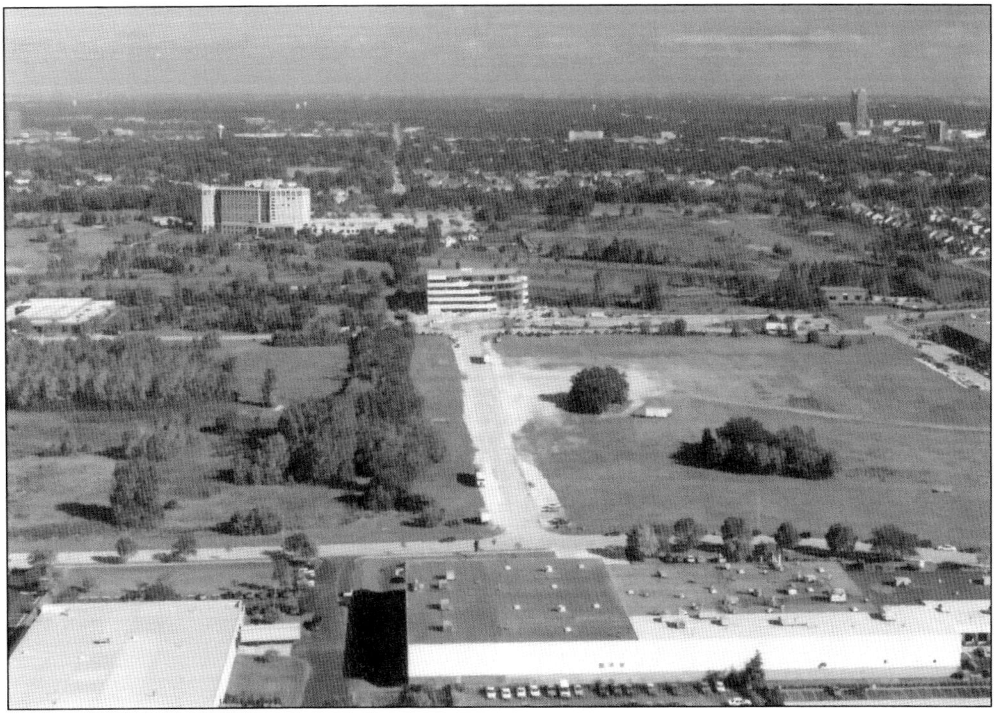

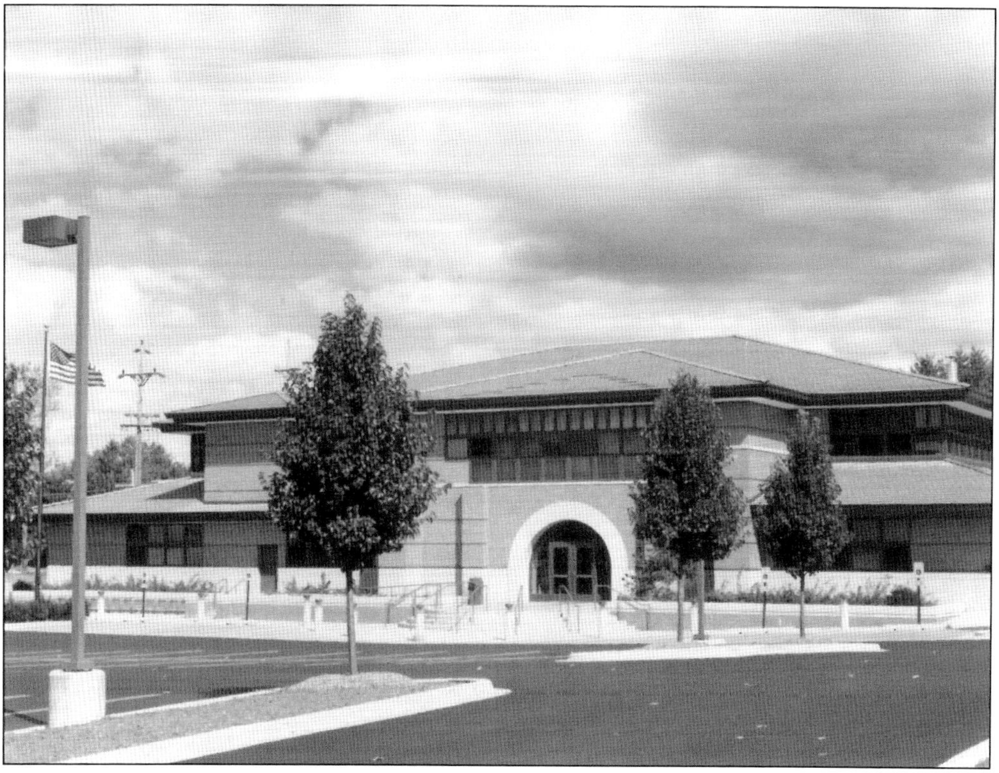

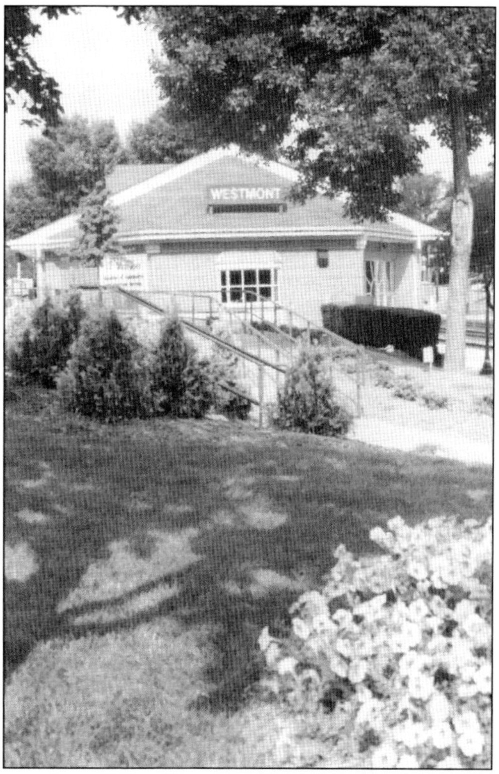

On January 27, 1993, the new Westmont Public Library opened near the former site of the North Acres School. This location moved the library from its previous home south of the tracks to a new facility north of the train tracks near Ogden Avenue. Today, the library serves the public through its large collection of books, e-books, audiobooks, makery space, and programming for all ages. (Courtesy of the Westmont Area Historical Society.)

As Westmont grew as a commuter suburb, a new train station was built to better accommodate the residents who commuted in and out of the city each day. An office for the chamber of commerce was also built and served as the home of the chamber until its new office opened in 2000. (Courtesy of the Village of Westmont.)

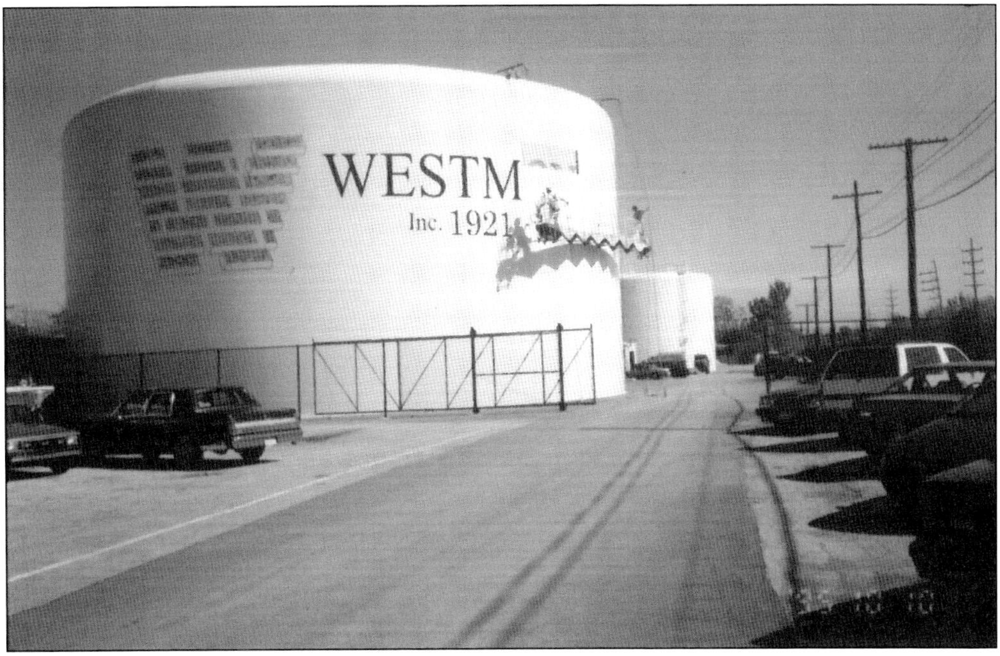

A new water tower was built near the village's public works facility. This water tower features the village's logo of a letter "W" made up of red bricks, as well as the year of the village's incorporation. This marked the beginning of a larger consistent branding campaign across the village. (Courtesy of the Village of Westmont.)

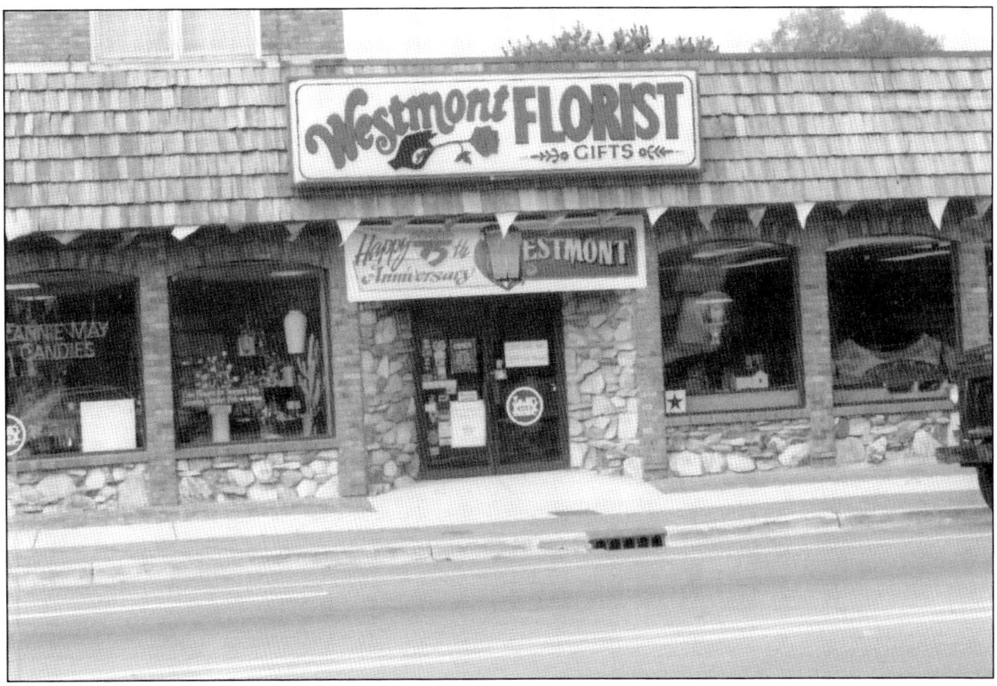

Longtime business Westmont Florist displays a banner for the 75th anniversary of the village's incorporation. As the village continues to grow, local businesses still support village events and celebrations. (Courtesy of the Westmont Area Historical Society.)

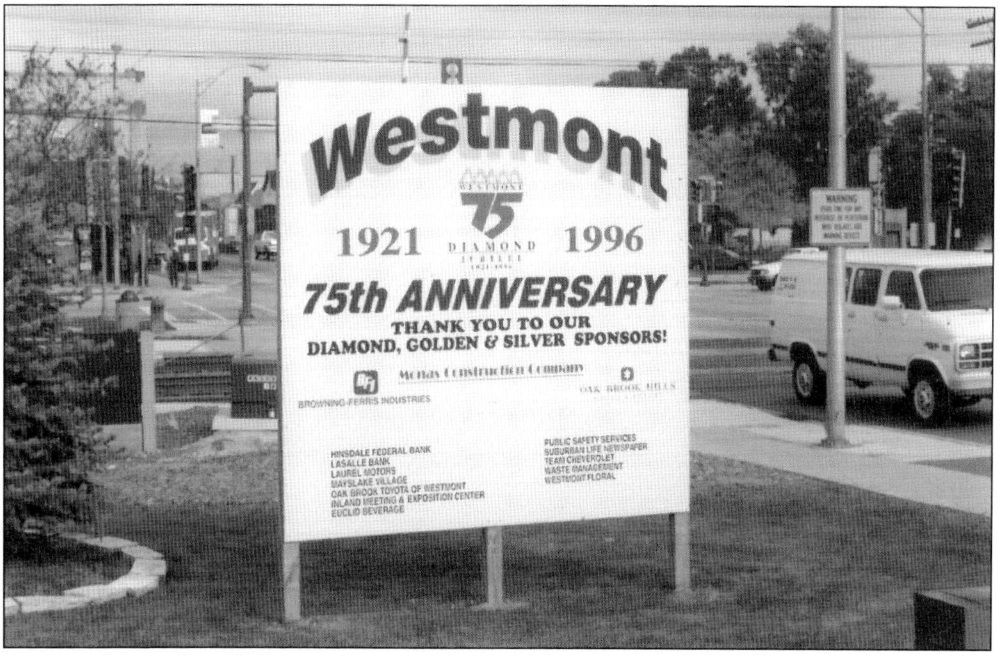

In 1996, the village celebrated its 75th anniversary with as much pomp and circumstance as it had its 50th. Pageants, parades, and community gatherings helped showcase Westmont's pride in its history. The town that had started as prairie and farmland was now a bustling commuter suburb. (Courtesy of the Village of Westmont.)

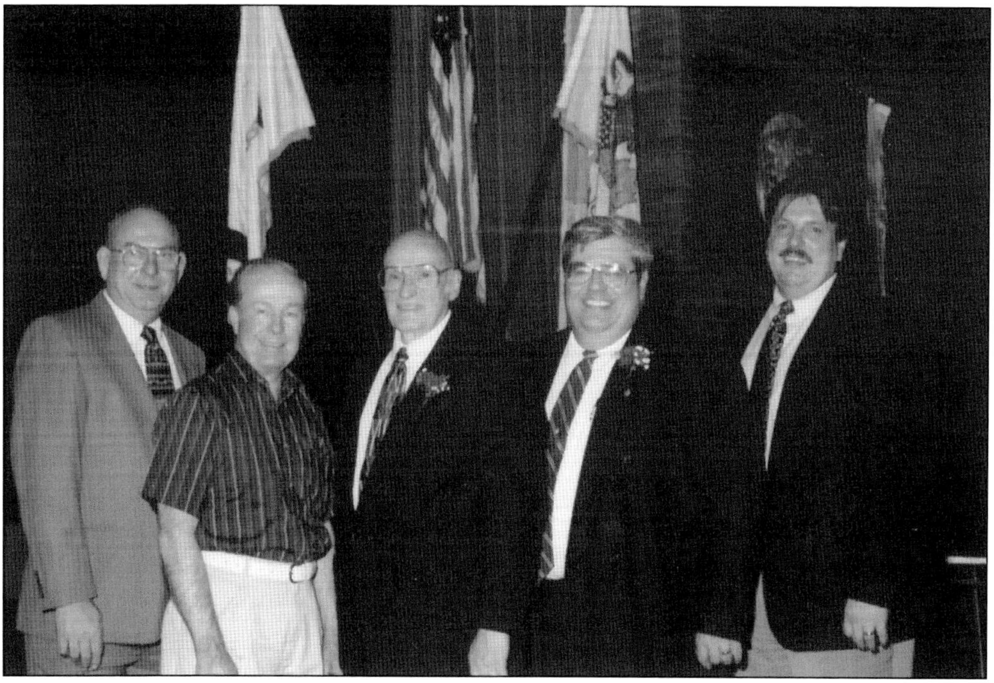

Several of Westmont's former mayors pose in this photograph. From left to right are Robert Maciejewski (1977–1981), Frank Bellerive (1985–1993), Edwin Burke (1997–1999), James Addington (1993–1997), and Gregory Szymski (1981–1985). (Courtesy of the Village of Westmont.)

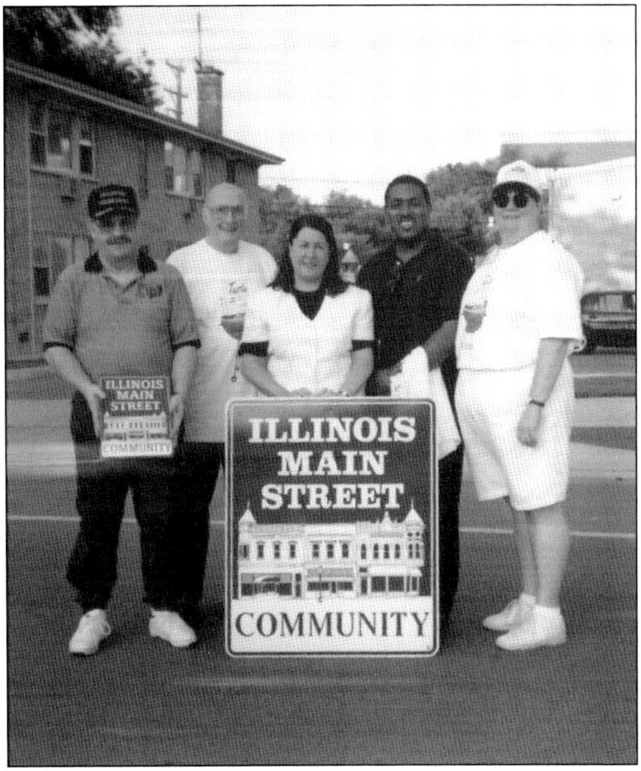

The Westmont Main Street organization was formed in the late 1990s and began to facilitate events such as the Taste of Westmont. It won several Governor's Hometown Awards before ultimately dissolving in the new millennium. (Both, courtesy of the Village of Westmont.)

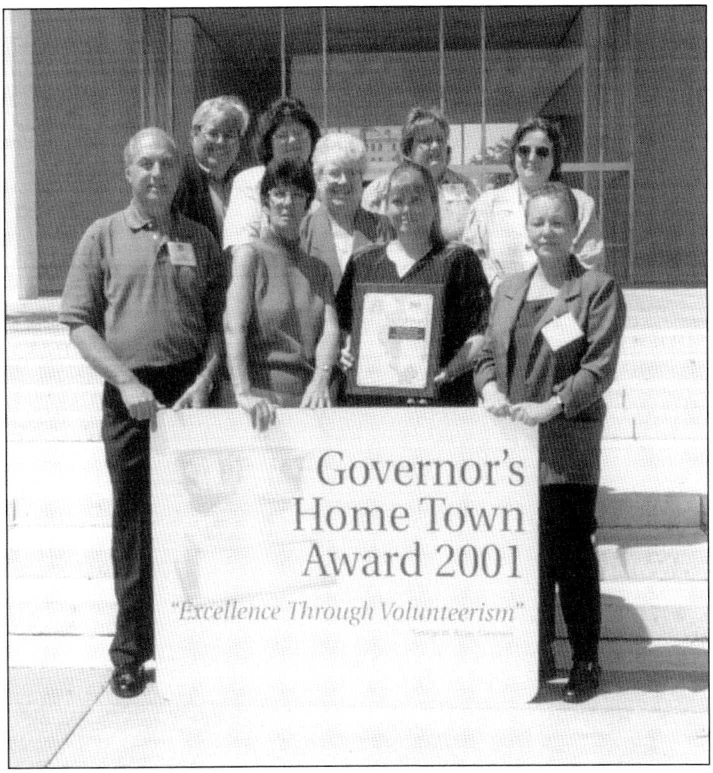

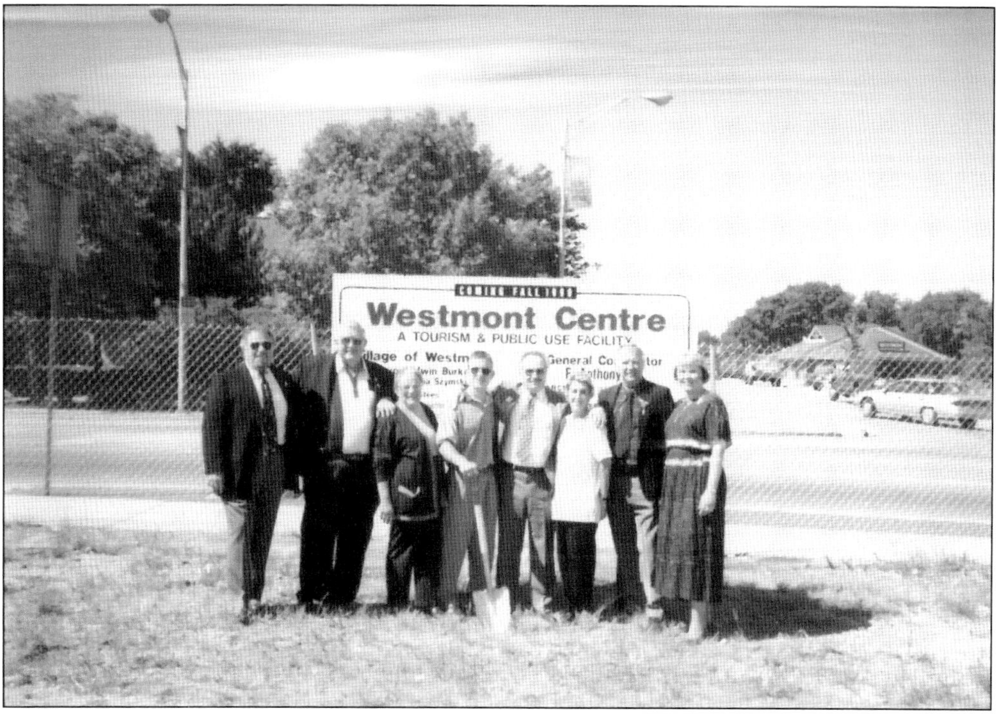

As part of Project 2000, a new office structure was planned to stand at 1 South Cass Avenue. This building, known as Westmont Centre, became the home of the chamber of commerce, Westmont Special Events Corporation, School District 201 administration, and the office of Westmont's member of the state House of Representatives. (Both, courtesy of the Village of Westmont.)

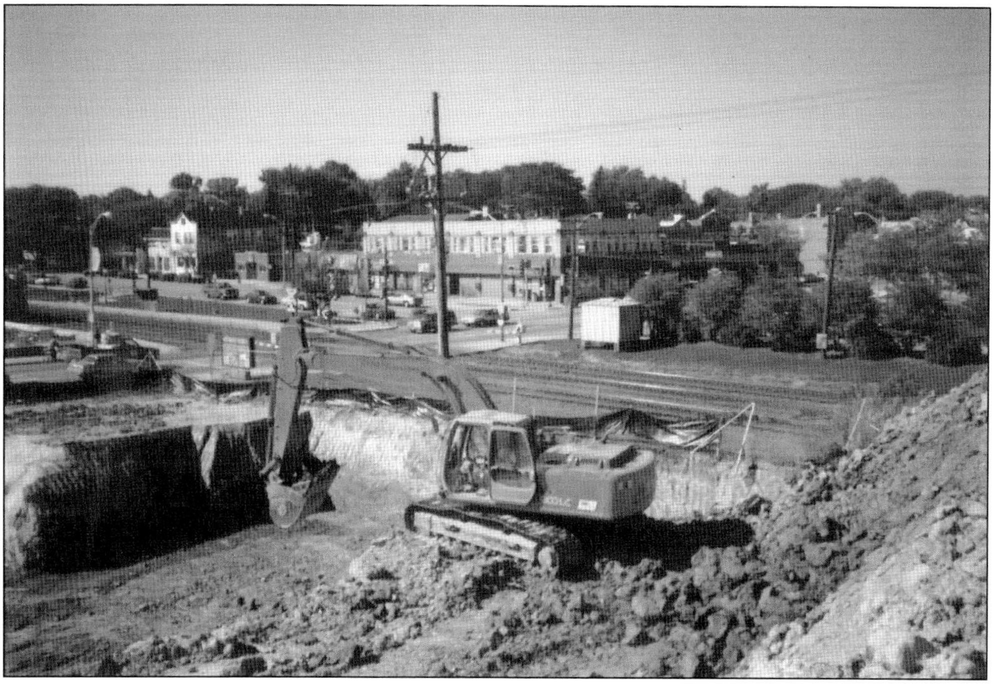

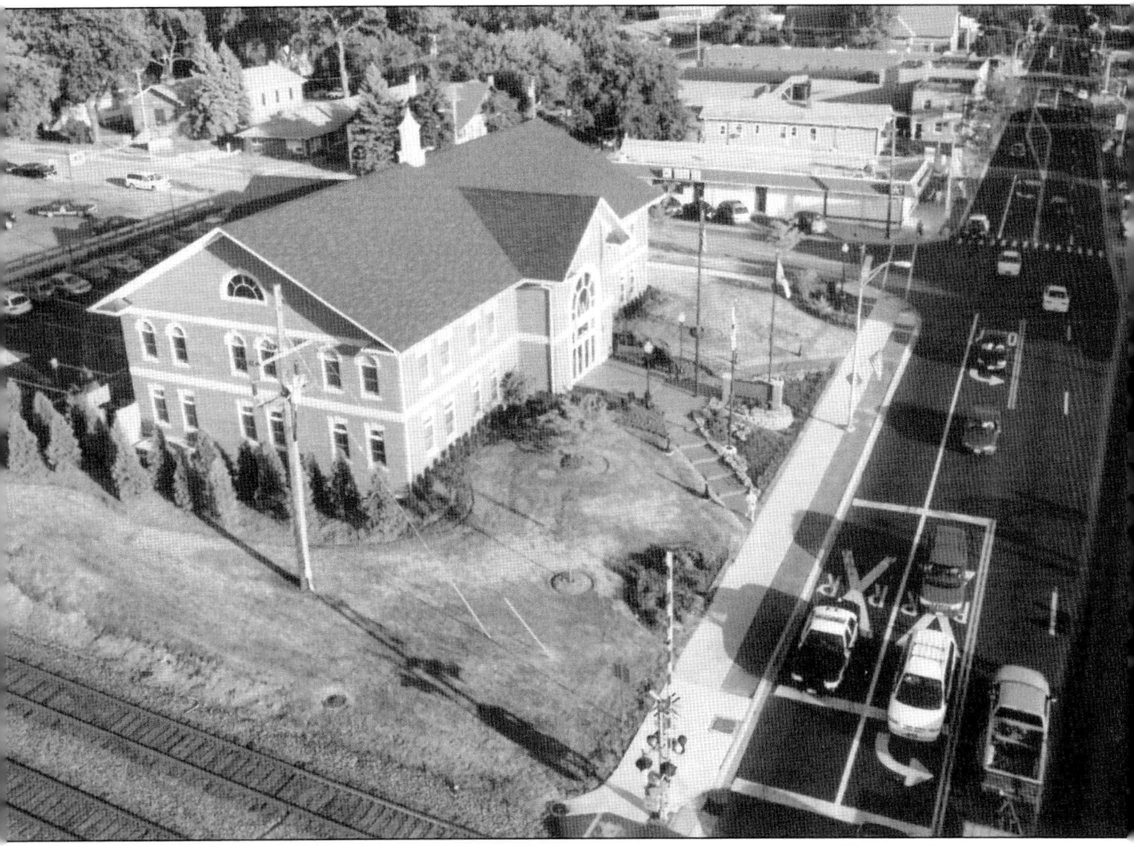

This aerial photograph shows the completed Westmont Centre structure. The building is the site of the aforementioned organizations, as well as a museum honoring Muddy Waters. During the holiday season, Westmont Centre is also the hub of holiday cheer in Westmont. Children can come to the building to meet Santa and Mrs. Claus following the annual Frosty and Friends Parade. (Courtesy of the Village of Westmont.)

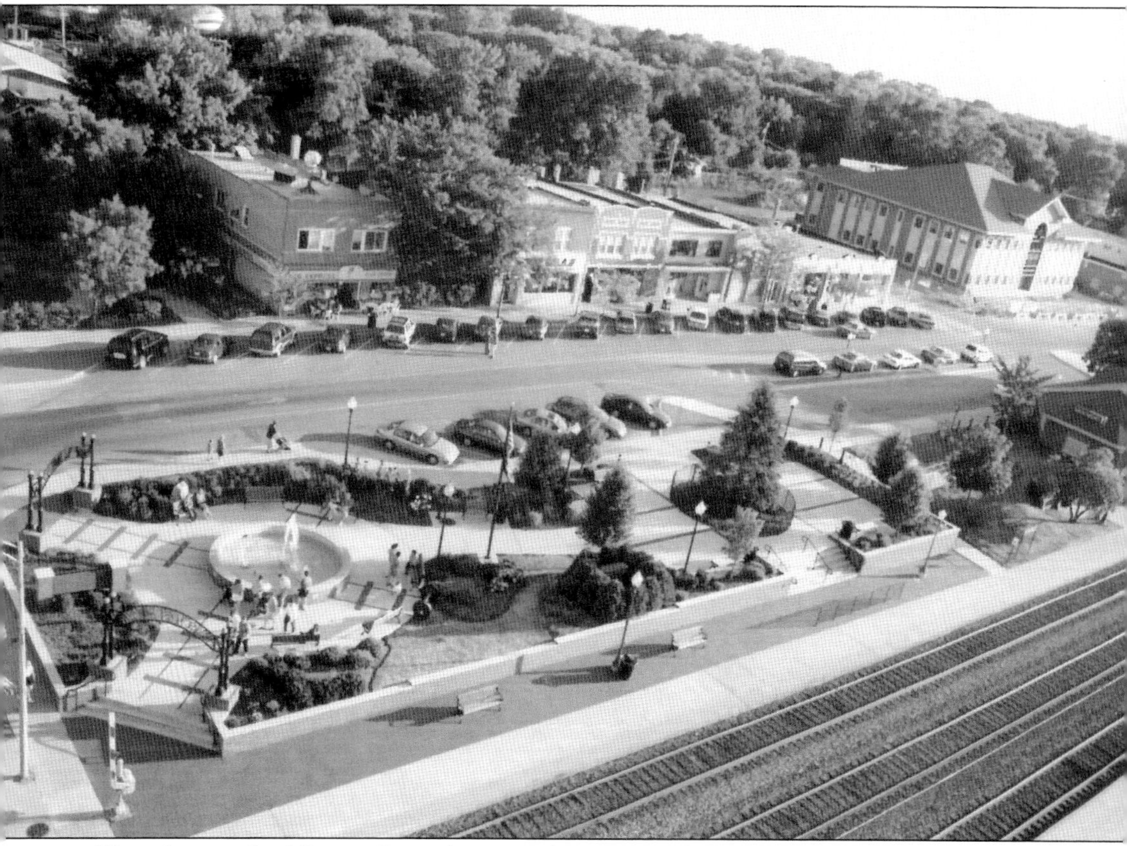

This photograph of Quincy Street features other aspects of Project 2000. A beautifully landscaped fountain and park harken back to the WPA fountain. In the distance, the new village hall can be seen. (Courtesy of the Village of Westmont.)

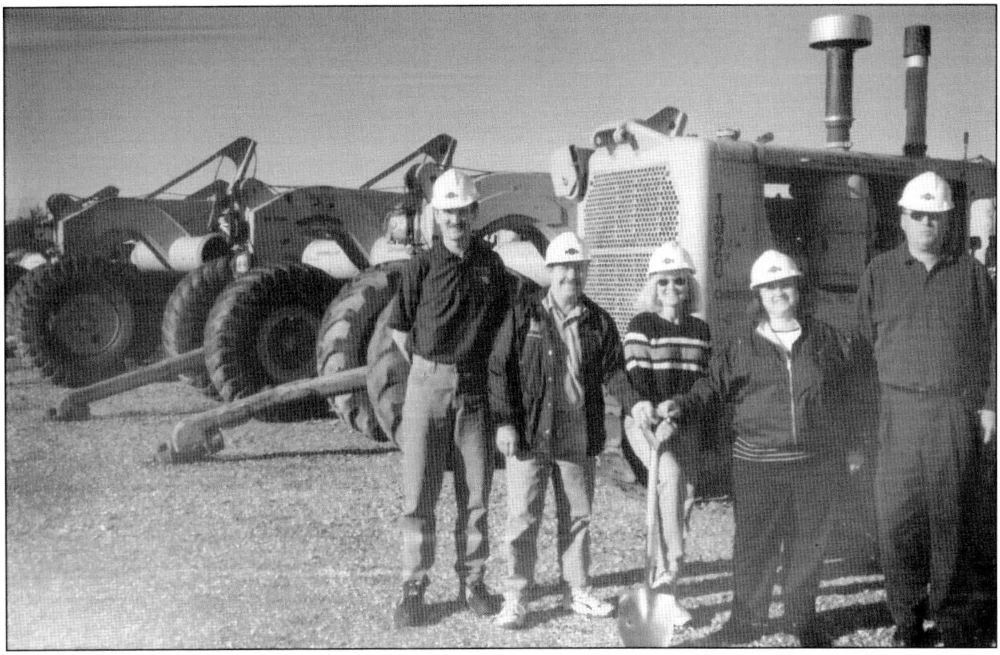

Members of the park district board of commissioners and staff break ground at the site of Ty Warner Park. From left to right are Ronald Gunter, Frank Bellerive, Diane Main, Sandra Smith, and James Long. The development of this park was made possible through close collaboration between the park district and Ty Inc. Ty is best known as the creator of the popular Beanie Baby line of stuffed toys, which once dominated the toy landscape. (Both, courtesy of the Westmont Area Historical Society.)

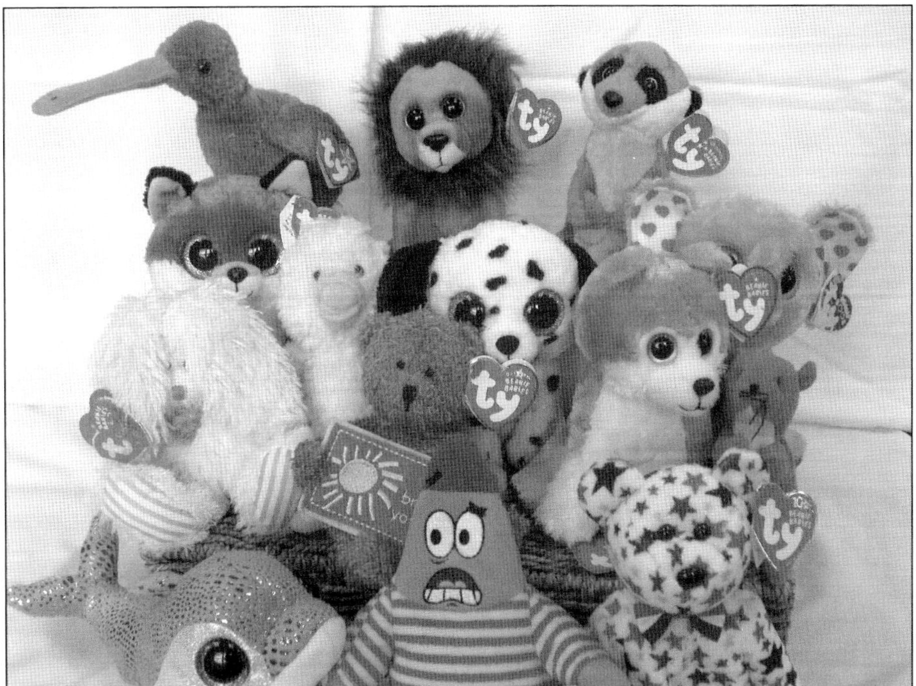

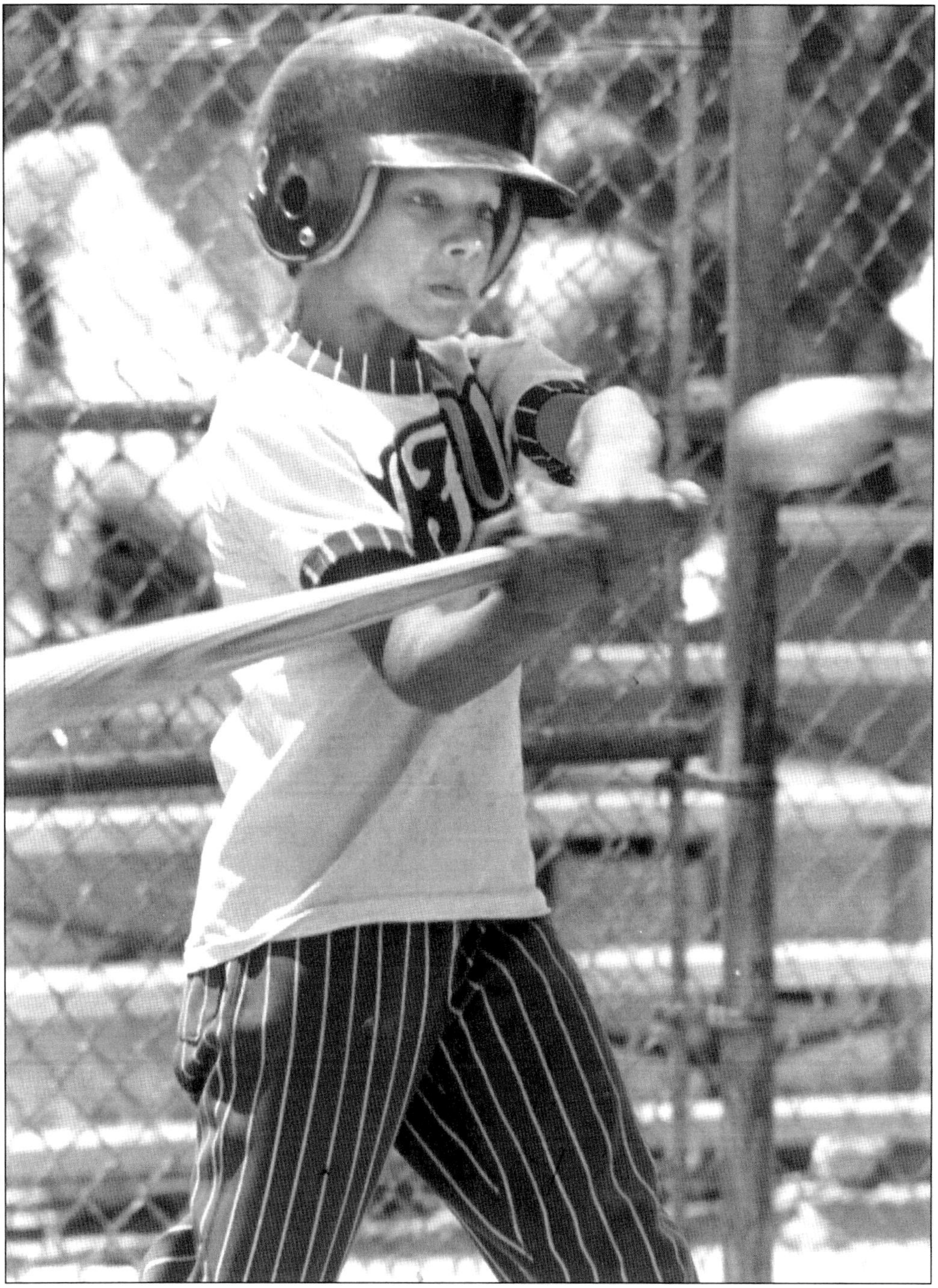

Westmont's Little League was established by Warren Lebeck. In the beginning, the uniforms were paid for by the Chicago White Sox. Later, local businesses and organizations paid to sponsor a team and pay for their uniforms. Games were played on the fields adjacent to the Park District Community Center. Children had to try out to secure a spot on a team, so not everyone was able to participate. Today, the Westmont Youth Baseball Association administers the program. The 1993 movie *Rookie of the Year* was filmed on Westmont's Little League field.

Five

A Century of Progress

2000 to Present

Since the year 2000, Westmont has continued to grow. Project 2000 created a newly landscaped park near the BNSF train tracks, a new village hall, and Westmont Centre, which serves as the home of Westmont Special Events Corporation and the Westmont Chamber of Commerce. On July 4, 2000, Ty Warner Park opened on the village's north side. The park was made possible through the collaboration of the Westmont Park District and Ty Inc., creator of the popular Beanie Baby toys.

Today, the Westmont Park District operates 155 acres of recreational space in the village, including the community center, administration staff and senior center, Westmont Park District Fitness Club, and Twin Lakes Golf Club. A natatorium has been constructed at the south end of Ty Warner Park, with Olympic-quality aquatic facilities.

Over the past 20 years, the village of Westmont has grown its relationship with the Taiwanese community, both locally and abroad. In 2017, Westmont entered into a sister city relationship with Hsinchu County, Taiwan, in order to build municipal, economic, cultural, and educational ties between the two communities.

In 2021, the village will celebrate 100 years since its incorporation. In 100 years, Westmont has grown from a rural, prairie community to a bustling, thriving suburb of Chicago.

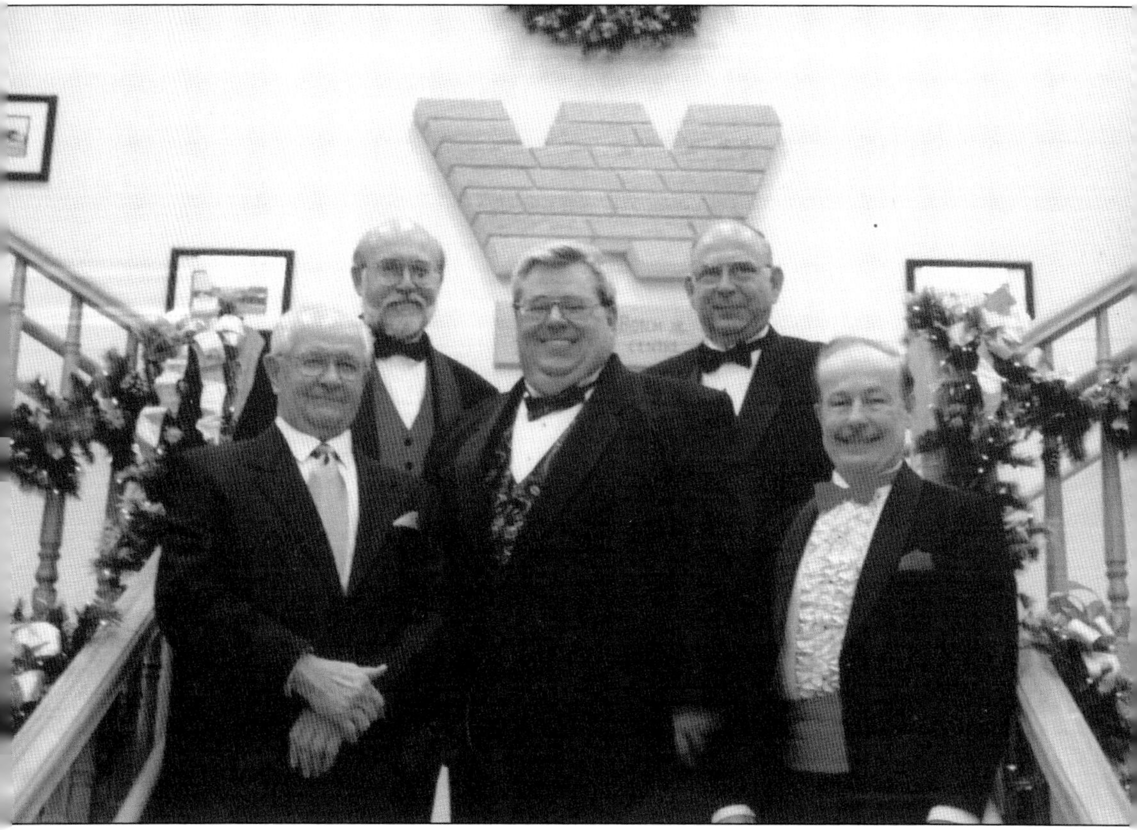

Westmont Centre was unveiled as the new millennium began with a black-tie event. Here, some of Westmont's mayors pose in their formal wear. From left to right are Joseph Johanik (1961–1965), William Rahn (1999–2013), James Addington (1993–1997), Robert Maciejewski (1977–1981), and Frank Bellerive (1985–1993). (Courtesy of the Village of Westmont.)

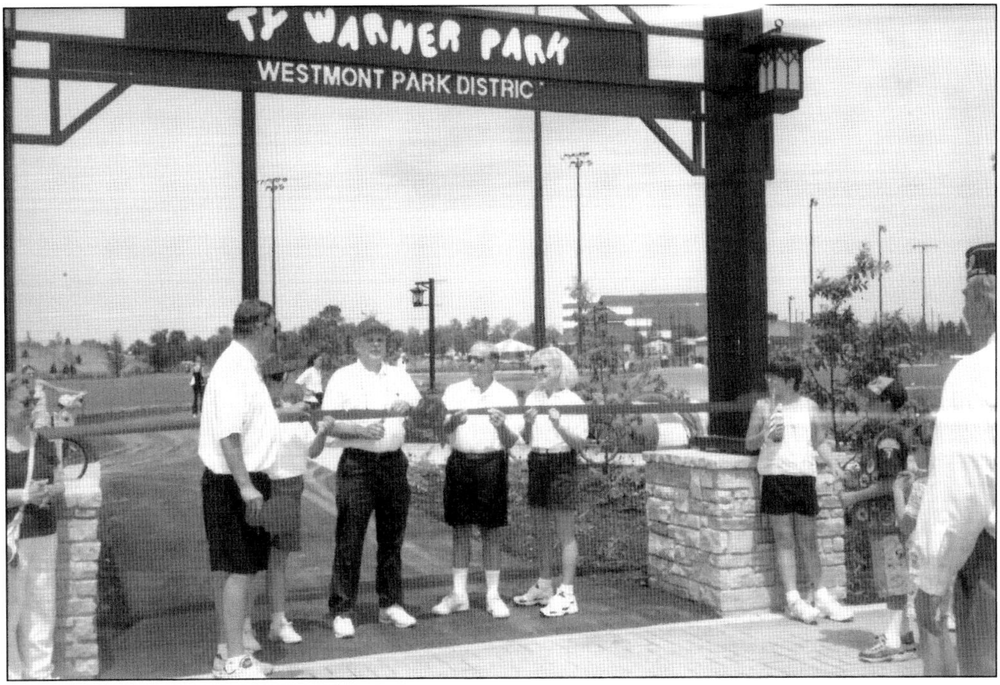

On July 4, 2000, Ty Warner Park was opened to the public. The park, which was designed by Robert Fleck, features a zero-depth splash pad, three covered pavilions, baseball and softball fields, a sledding hill, two playgrounds, tennis courts, and walking paths as well as natural prairie and wetlands. (Courtesy of the Westmont Area Historical Society.)

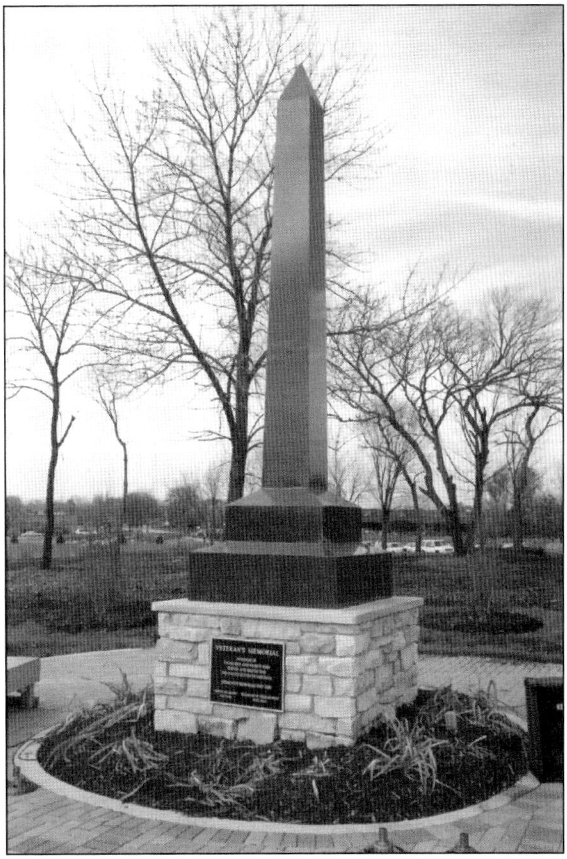

To honor Westmont's long and proud history of military service, a memorial to its veterans was dedicated at Ty Warner Park. The memorial obelisk overlooks an area with memorial bricks and benches for moments of reflection. (Courtesy of the Village of Westmont.)

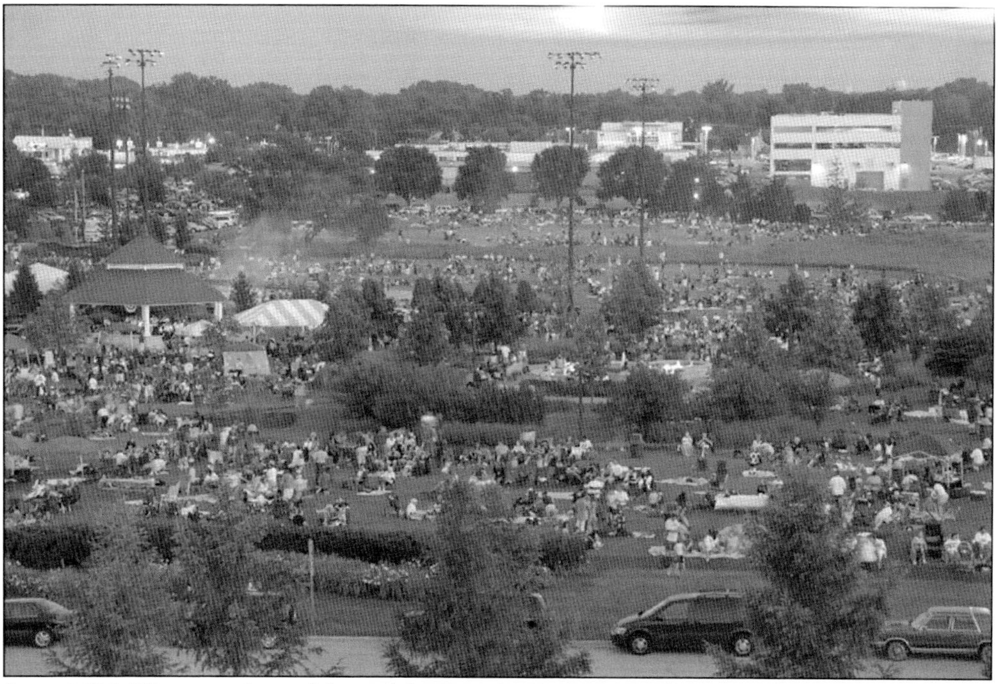

Since 2000, Westmont has celebrated the Fourth of July at Ty Warner Park. The event features petting zoos, live music, food, and—of course—a fireworks spectacular. (Courtesy of the Village of Westmont.)

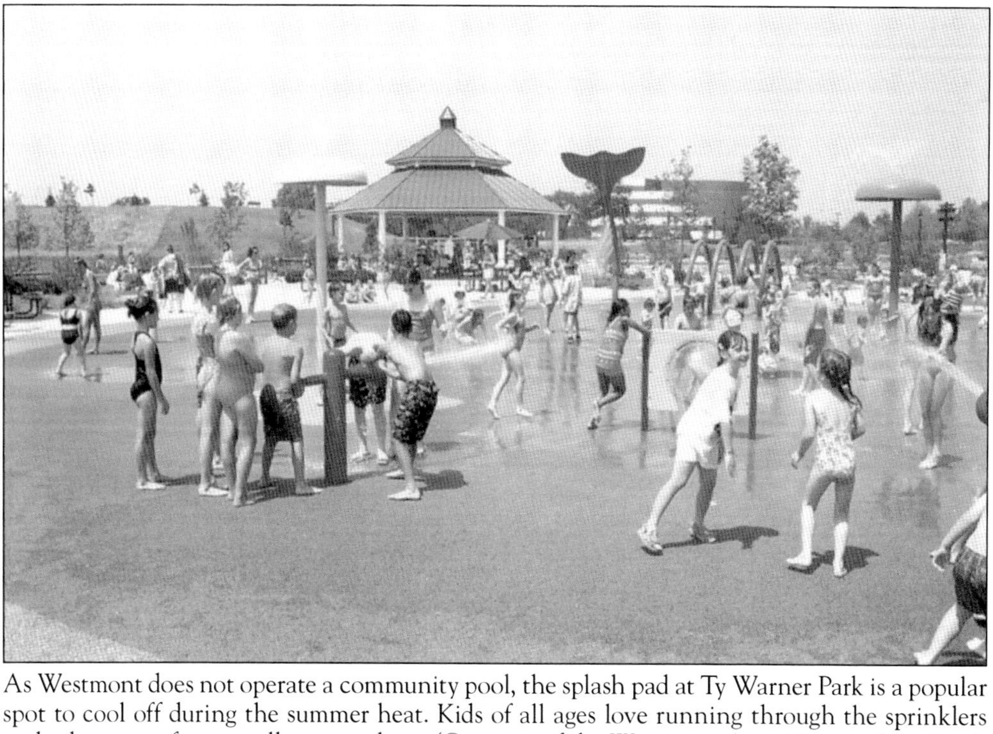

As Westmont does not operate a community pool, the splash pad at Ty Warner Park is a popular spot to cool off during the summer heat. Kids of all ages love running through the sprinklers and other water features all summer long. (Courtesy of the Westmont Area Historical Society.)

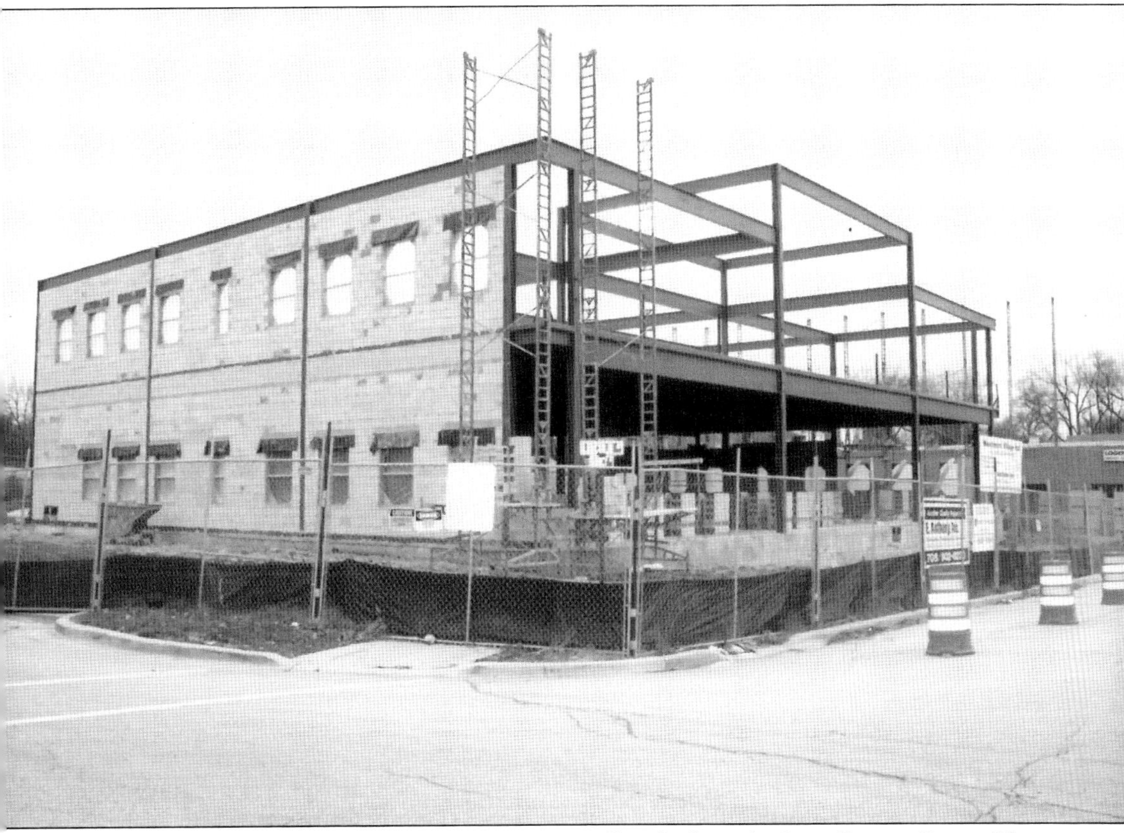

Following construction of Westmont Centre, a new village hall was built on Quincy Street. This village hall marks the first time in the village's history that the administration has not shared offices with the police or fire departments. (Courtesy of the Village of Westmont.)

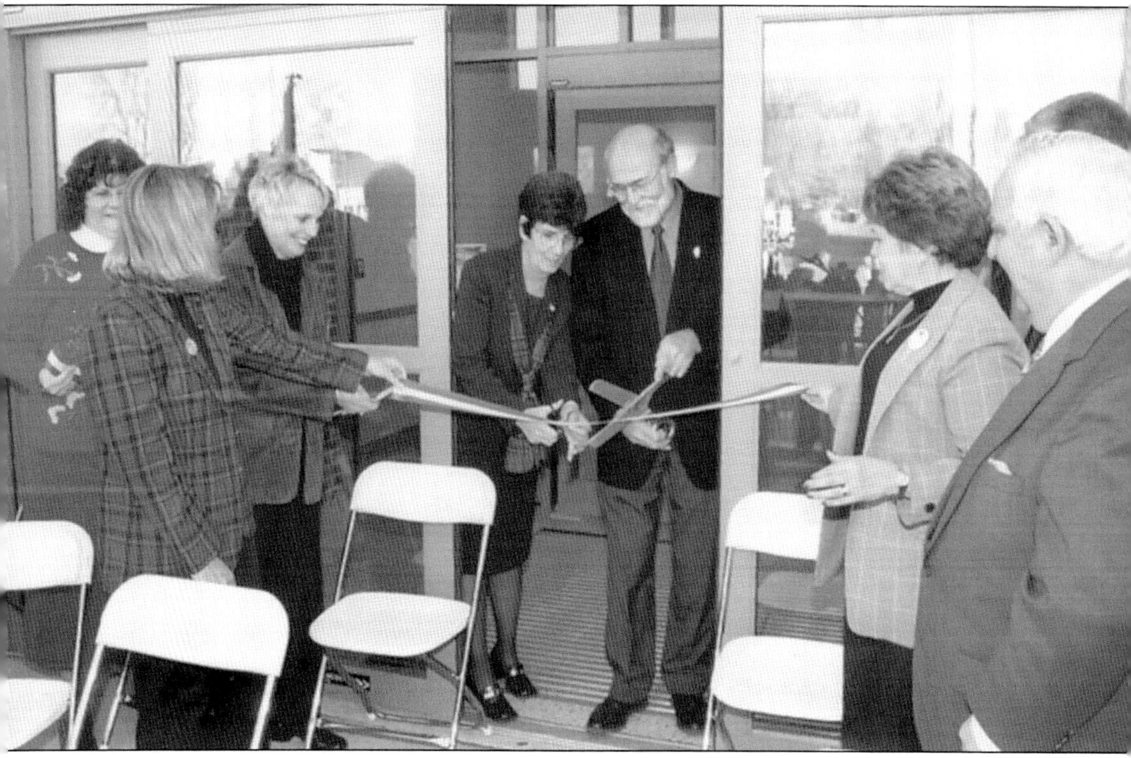

Mayor William Rahn and village clerk Virginia Szymski cut the ribbon to the new village hall. The updated building provides adequate space for all of the departments of a village that was undergoing tremendous growth. (Courtesy of the Village of Westmont.)

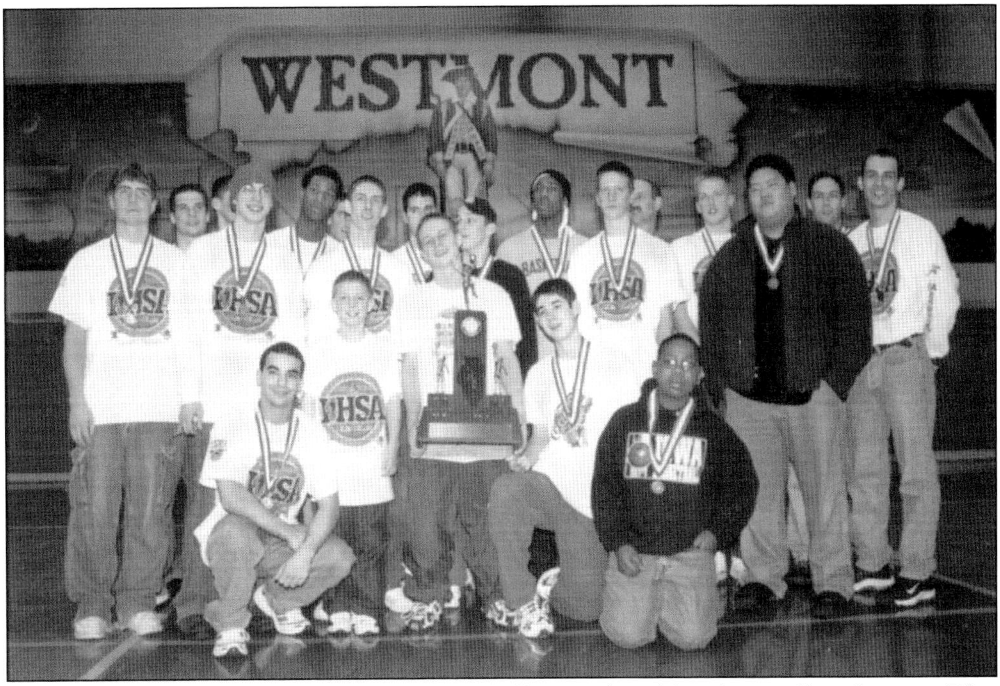

In 2001, Westmont High School's boys' basketball team placed fourth overall in the state. This was a major achievement for the team and the village as a whole. Here, members of the team pose with their trophy. (Courtesy of the Village of Westmont.)

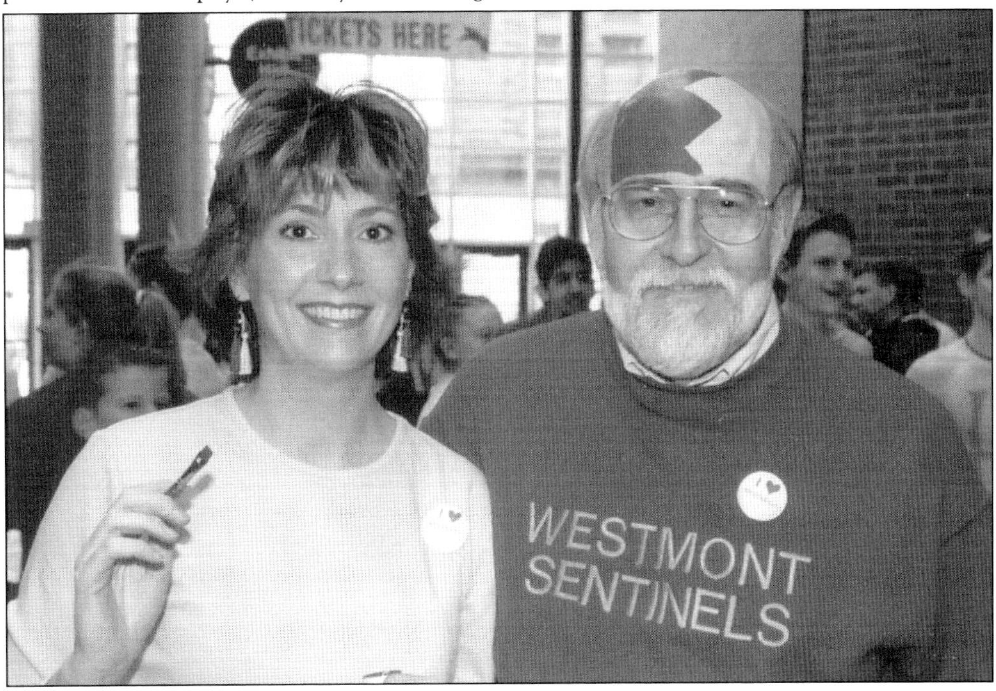

Resident Sharon Macak and former mayor William Rahn get into the spirit before game day. Pride in Westmont athletics at all levels has always been strong in the village. (Courtesy of the Village of Westmont.)

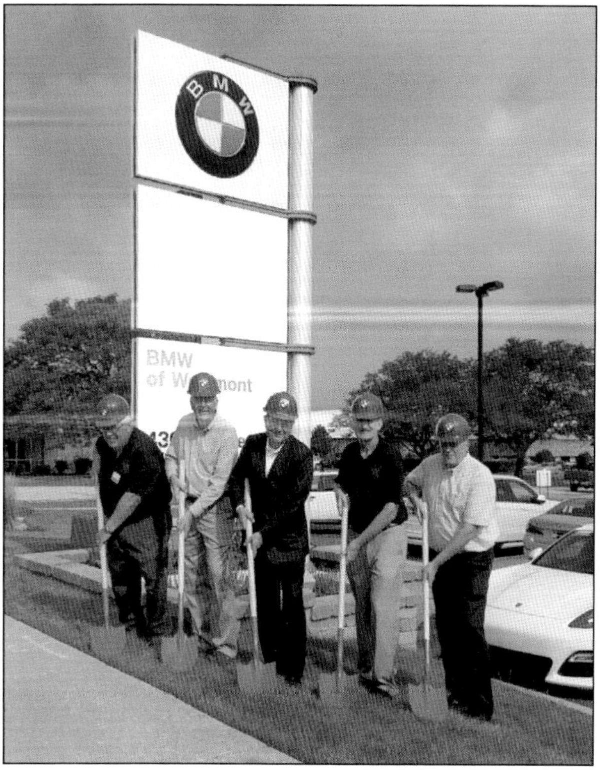

One of Westmont's major industries is auto sales. The Westmont Auto Mile is a collection of dealerships on Ogden Avenue. The auto mile sponsors special events in the village, such as Taste of Westmont, the Fourth of July, and Holly Days. The original members of the auto mile were Laurel BMW, Audi of Westmont, McGrath Lexus, McGrath Acura, and Infiniti of Clarendon Hills. (Courtesy of the Village of Westmont.)

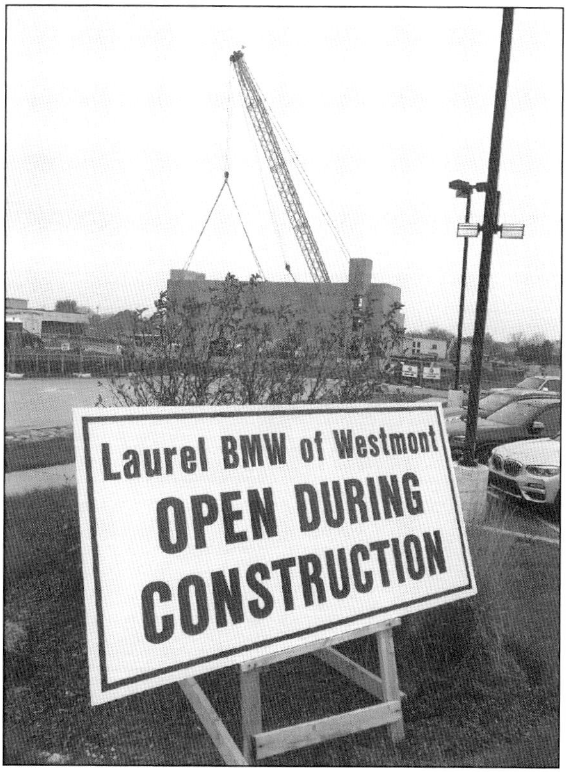

Even today, growth in the auto mile continues. Dealerships continue to build new showrooms and remodel and expand existing spaces to continue serving customers from all across Chicagoland. (Courtesy of the Village of Westmont.)

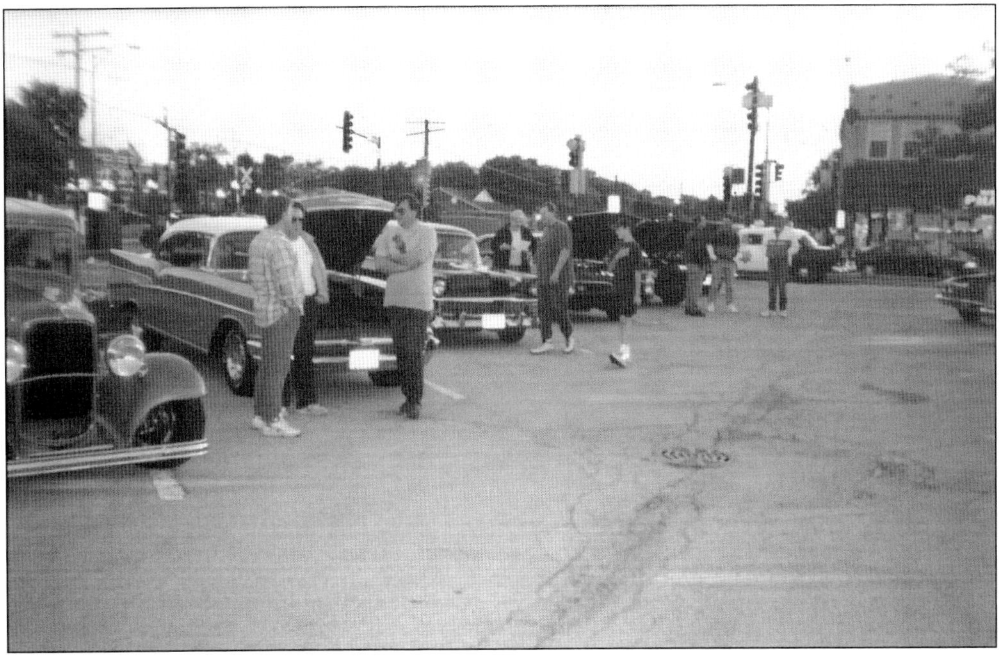

One of Westmont's most popular summer events is Cruisin' Nights. This car show features live music and a chance for any kind of auto lover to come out on Thursday nights during the summer and enjoy downtown Westmont. What began as a small parking lot full of vintage cars has grown to the point that Cass Avenue is now shut down to accommodate three blocks of vintage cars, municipal vehicles, and a live band. (Both, courtesy of the Village of Westmont.)

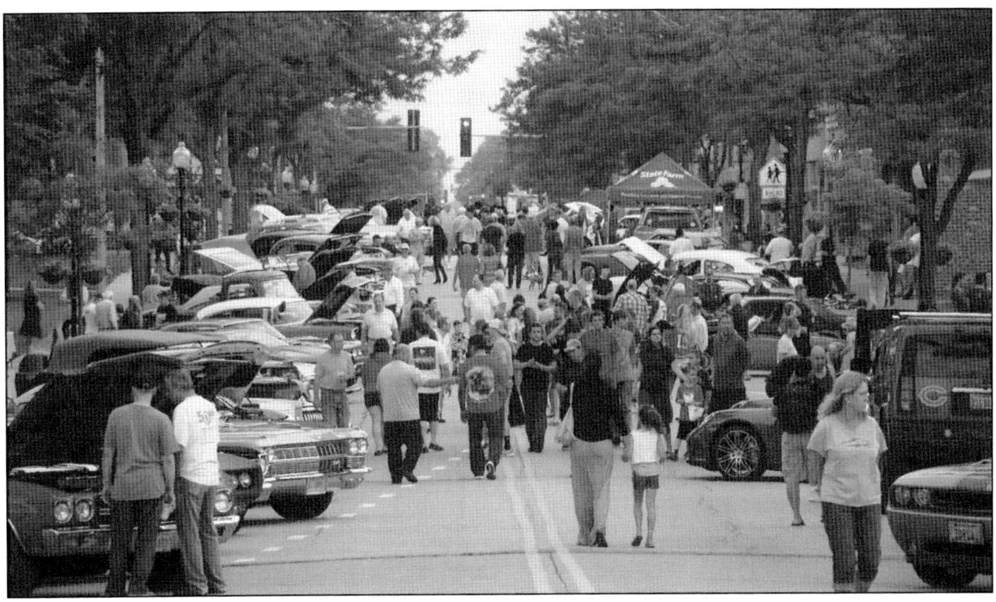

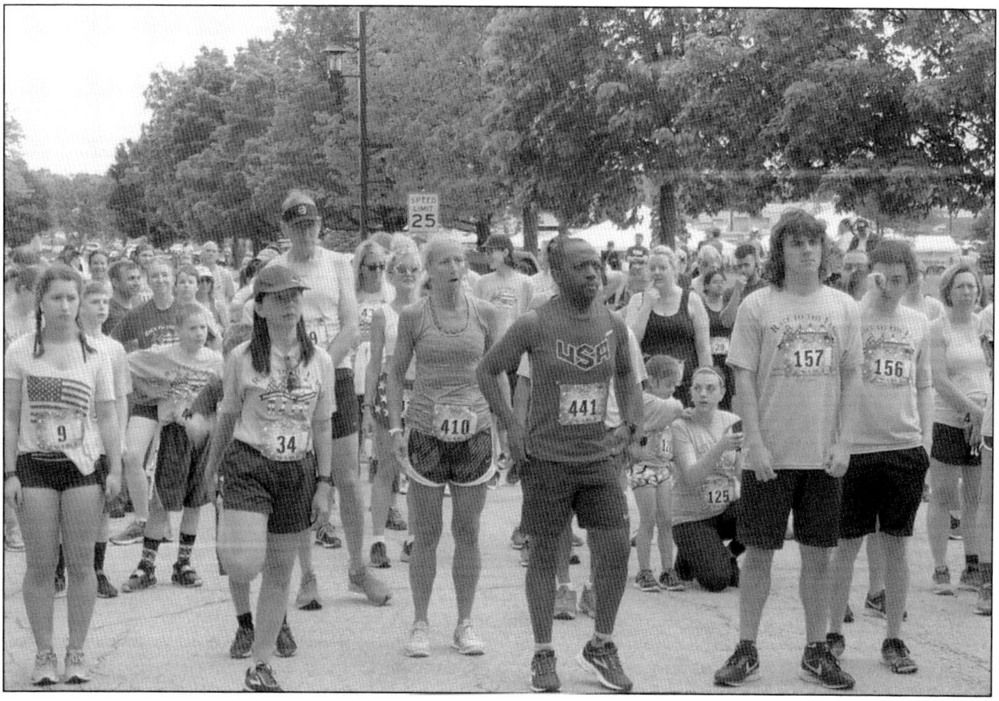

Race to the Flag is one of two annual 5K races in the village. The race previously benefitted St. Jude's Research Hospital and now benefits the People's Resource Center (PRC). PRC helps to connect people in need with resources to help in their situation. It operates a food pantry and clothes closet, and holds various professional workshops. (Both, courtesy of the Village of Westmont.)

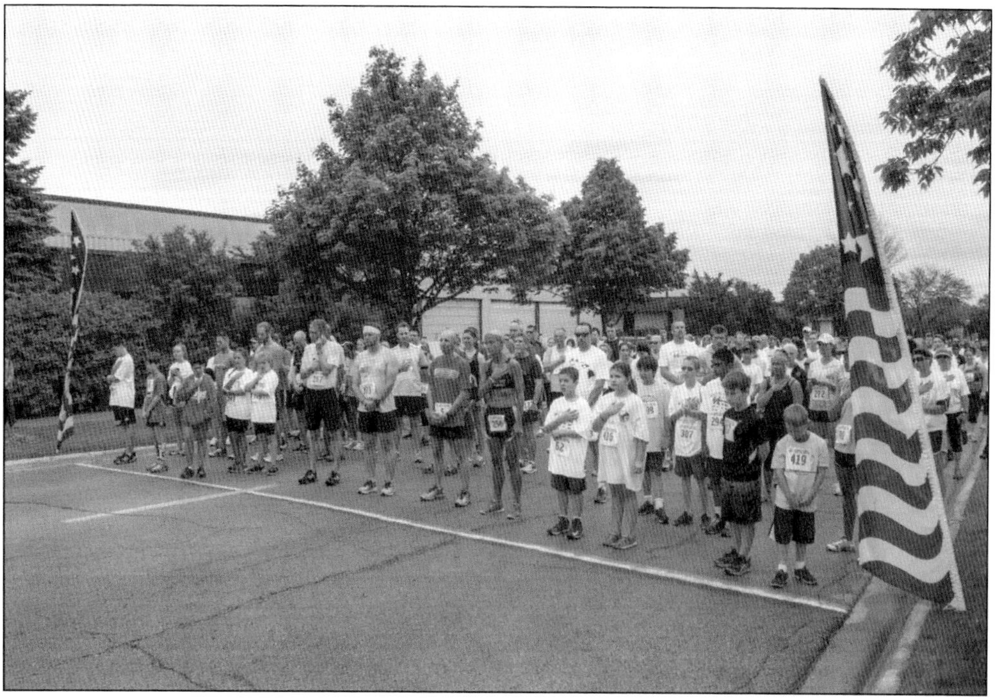

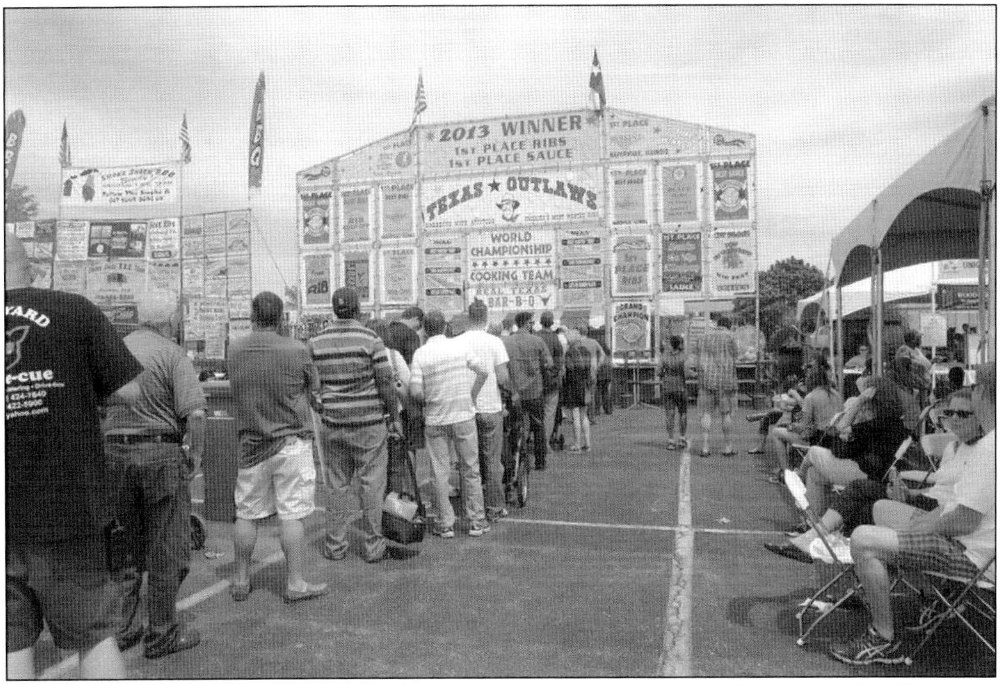

Red, White & BBQ is an annual barbecue competition and festival hosted by the Westmont Lions Club at Ty Warner Park. The event features different barbecue competitions, music, and a carnival and is a Memorial Day weekend tradition in the area. (Above, courtesy of the Village of Westmont; below, courtesy of Westmont Lions Club.)

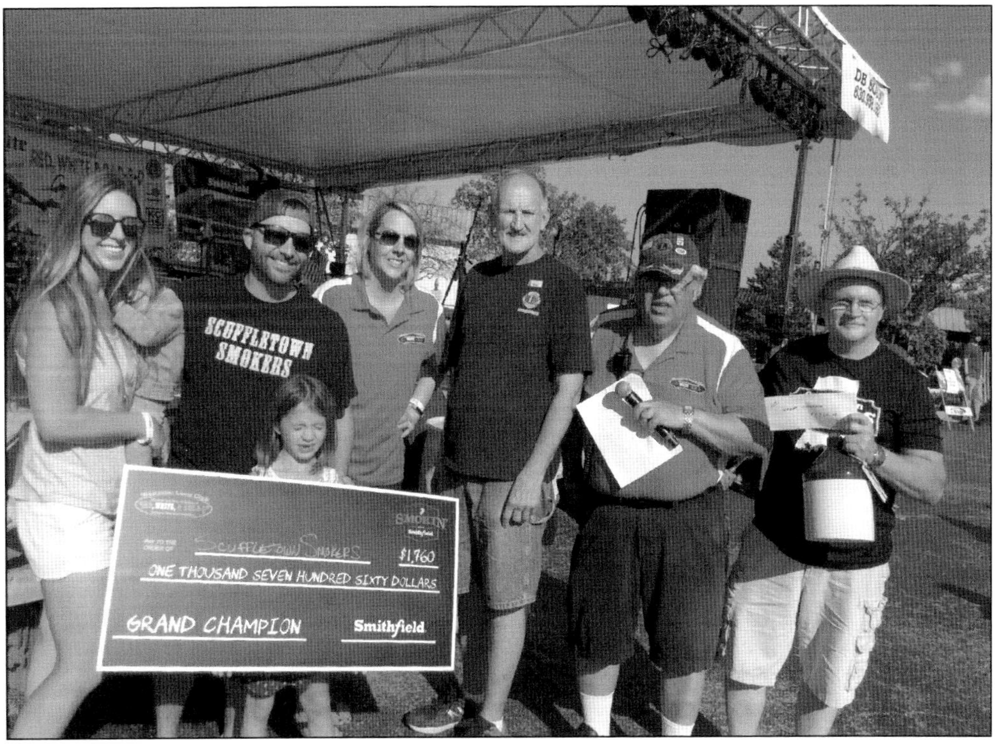

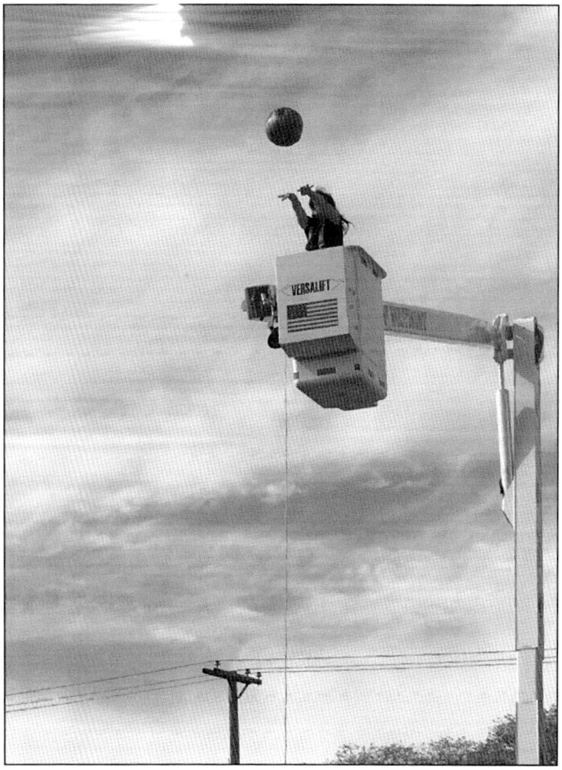

To celebrate Halloween, the Westmont Special Events Corporation has begun hosting Wicked West Fest on Cass Avenue. Traditionally held the weekend before Halloween, residents and community groups can take part in a pumpkin smash—the person whose pumpkin makes the biggest splat on the target is Westmont's pumpkin king or queen! (Courtesy of the Village of Westmont.)

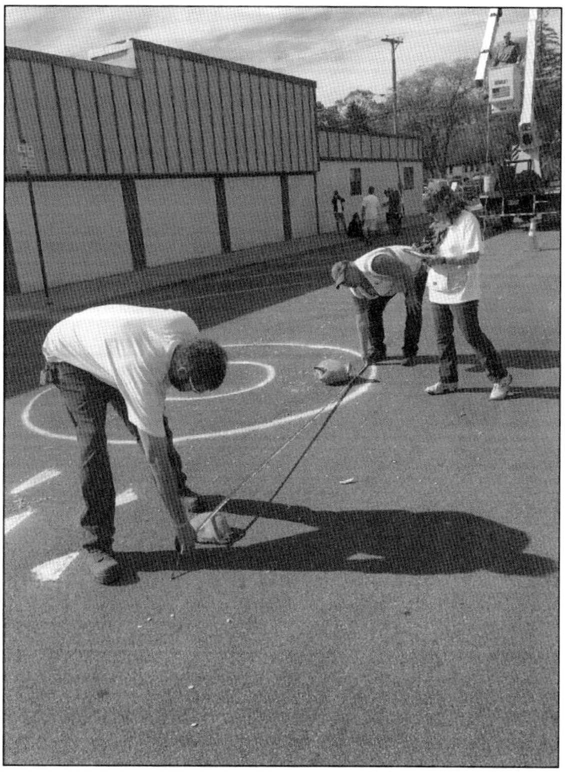

A member of the Public Works department measures the splat from a pumpkin. To chuck a pumpkin, participants have to be comfortable being lifted in a bucket truck, which is not for the faint of heart! (Courtesy of the Village of Westmont.)

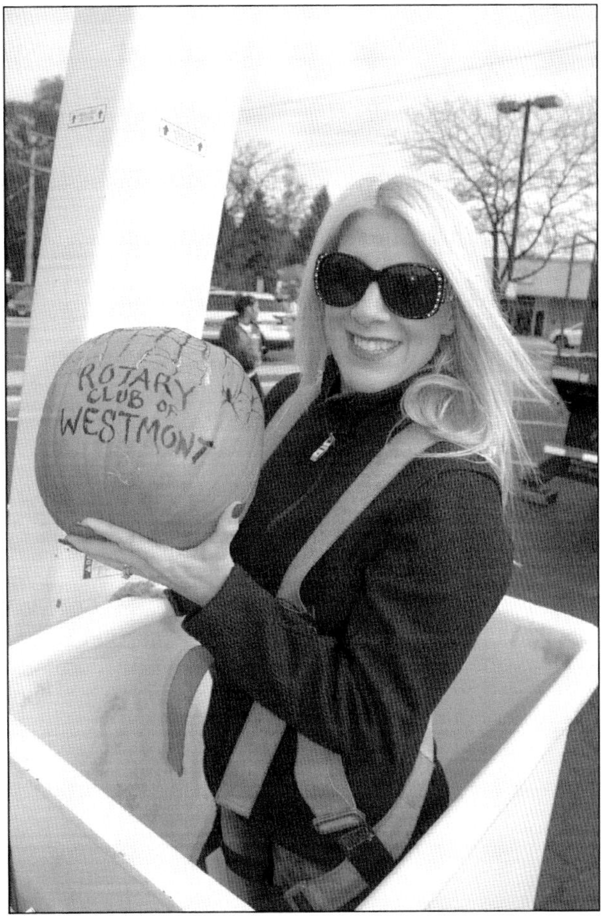

Before taking flight to launch her pumpkin, Tracy Valerio poses with her creation. Pumpkins are judged on appearance, how close they come to the target painted on the ground, and the size of their splat. This event raises awareness of pumpkin-composting opportunities in the area. (Courtesy of the Village of Westmont.)

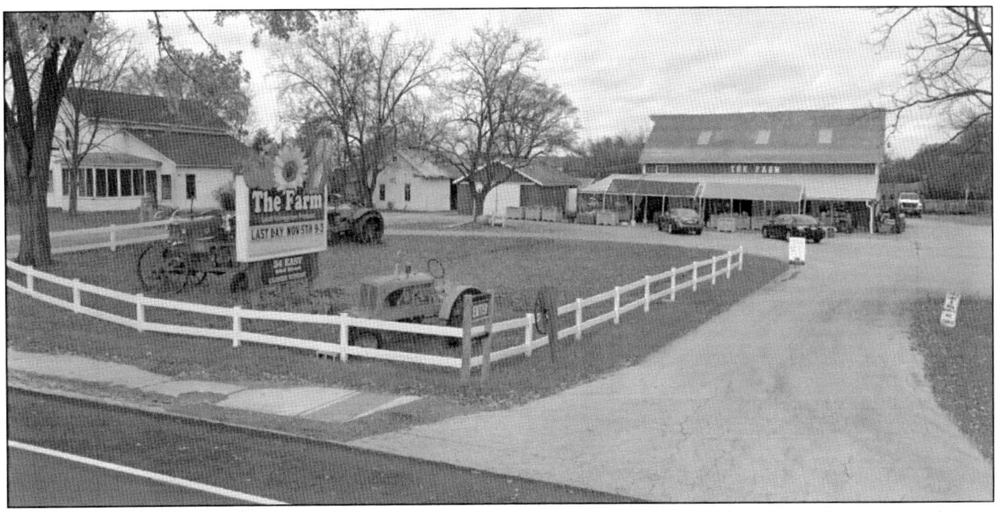

The Farm stands on the site of the former Oestmann farm. It sells fresh produce and plants, harkening back to when the Oestmann dairy herds wandered the surrounding area and the farmers held their threshing bees. The white house at left is the Oestmann farmhouse. (Courtesy of the Village of Westmont.)

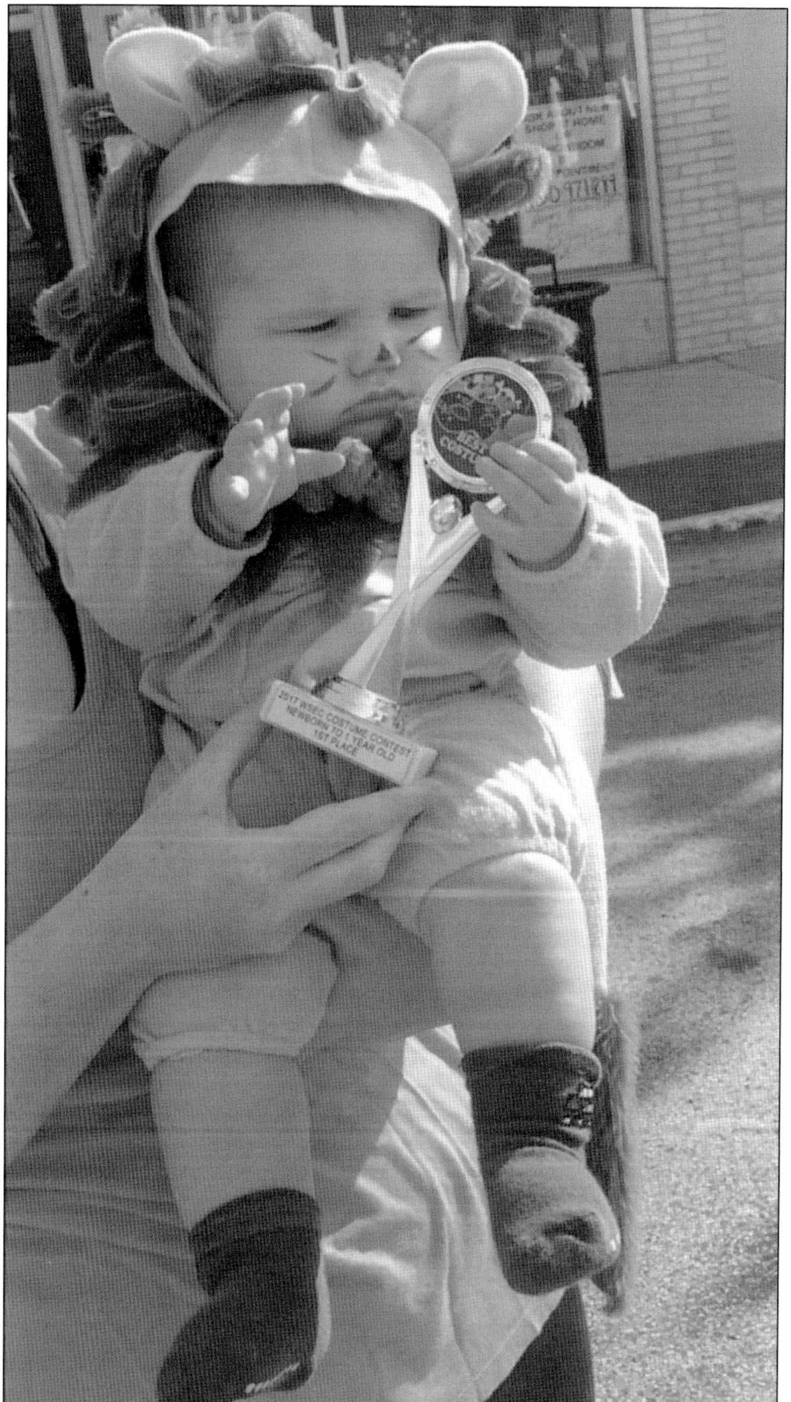

Families and individuals can take a break from trick or treating and enter a costume contest. This little lion won in his age group! Attendees can make their way up and down Cass Avenue to trick or treat at local businesses while enjoying autumn festivities in downtown Westmont. (Courtesy of the Village of Westmont.)

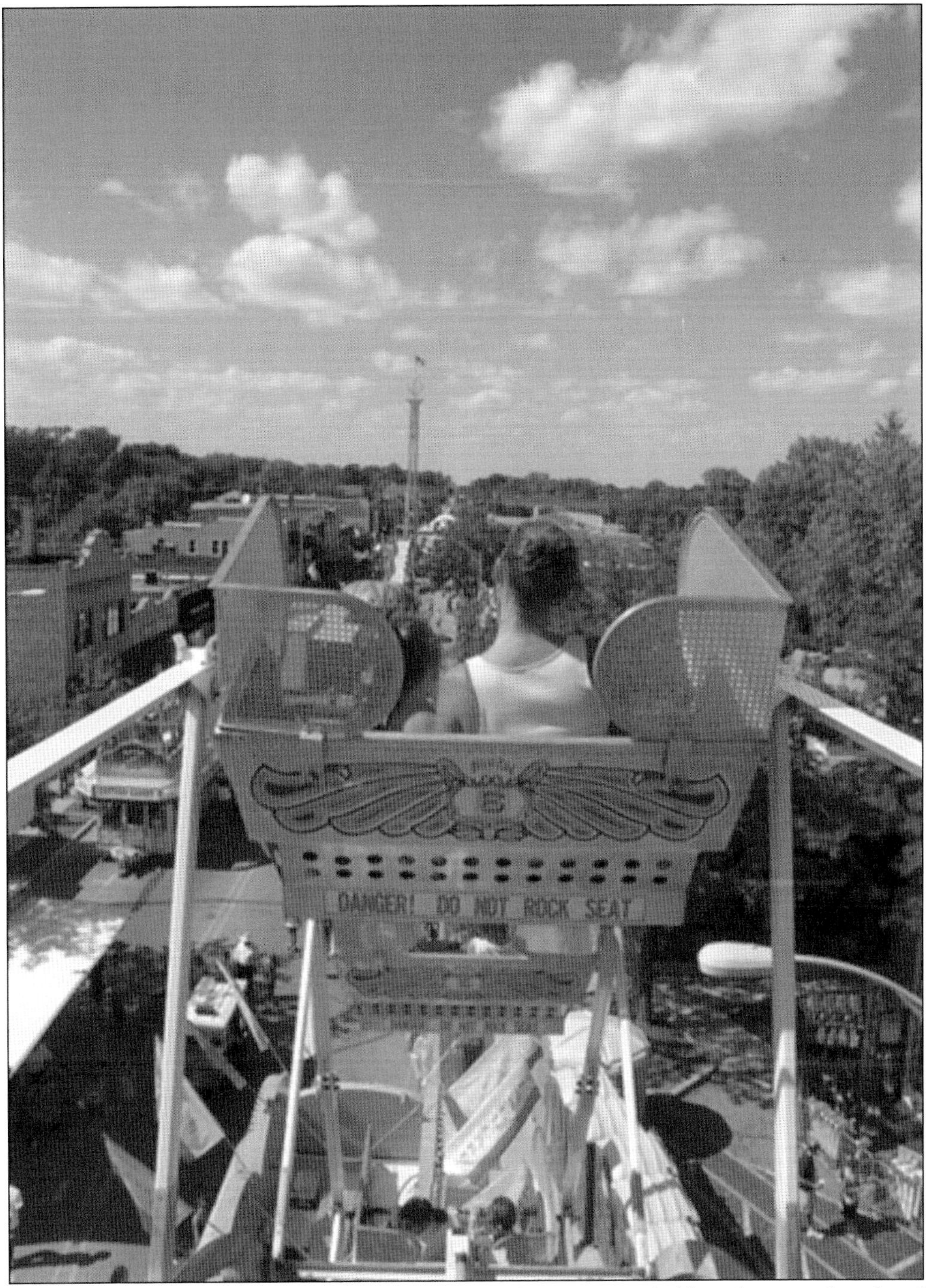

Perhaps Westmont's most popular event, the Taste of Westmont is held on the second weekend of July each year. Since its creation in 1996, it has brought thousands of visitors to the village, offering a taste of what Westmont has to offer in food and talent. The weekend is also full of music, featuring local and national artists, as well as a blues jam in honor of Muddy Waters. Kids of all ages enjoy the carnival rides and games that fill Cass Avenue. (Courtesy of the Village of Westmont.)

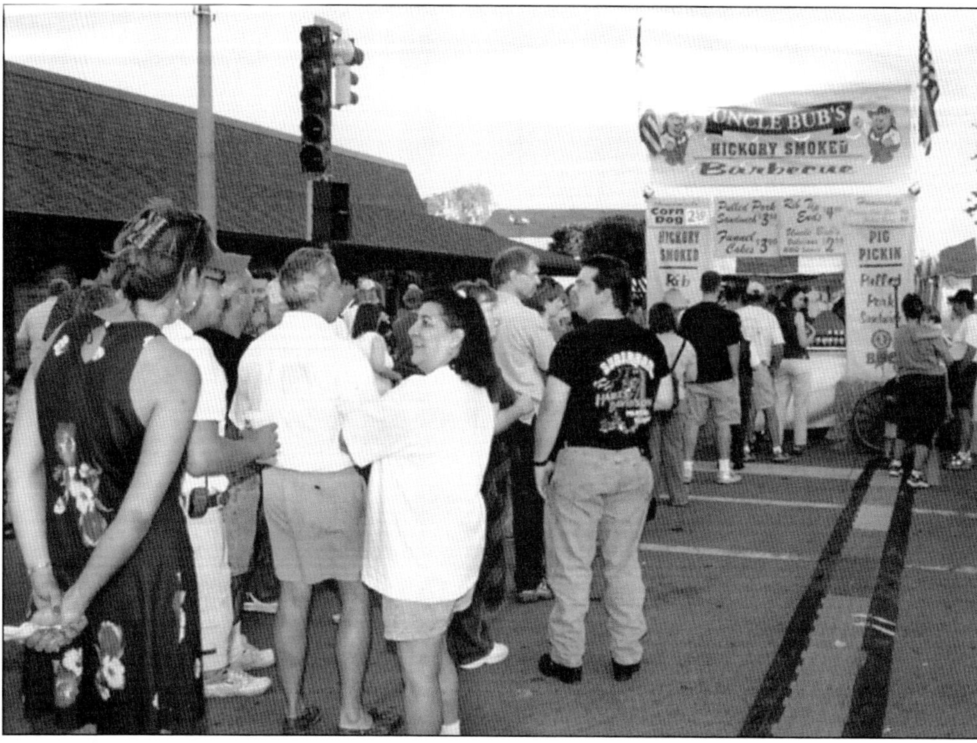

Patrons line up to sample offerings from Uncle Bub's at the Taste of Westmont. Westmont's restaurants take part and offer specials to visitors from across the state at this popular summer event. (Courtesy of the Village of Westmont.)

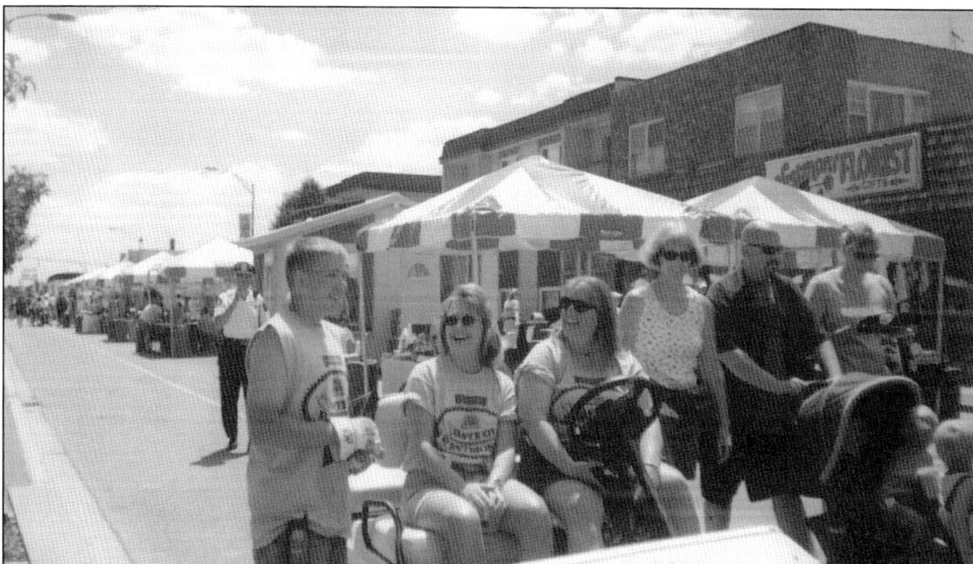

Westmont Special Events Corporation was founded in 2004 to manage the village's many special events. Today, it manages Cruisin' Nights, the Taste of Westmont, several pub crawls, Holly Days, and more. It brings thousands of visitors to the area each year to take part in what Westmont has to offer—spectacular events during all seasons. (Courtesy of the Village of Westmont.)

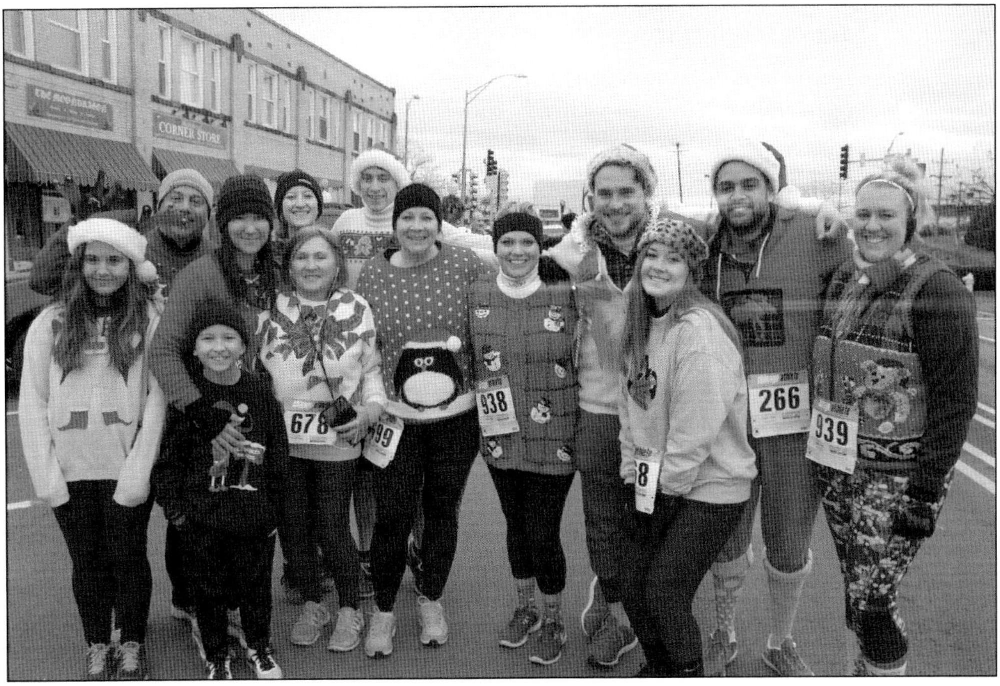

The Rotary Club of Westmont hosts its Ugly Sweater 5K race each year during the Holly Days season. The run is typically kicked off by Frosty the Snowman, who will sometimes run the entire 3.1 miles with the racers! The race benefits the Rotary Club of Westmont. (Courtesy of the Village of Westmont.)

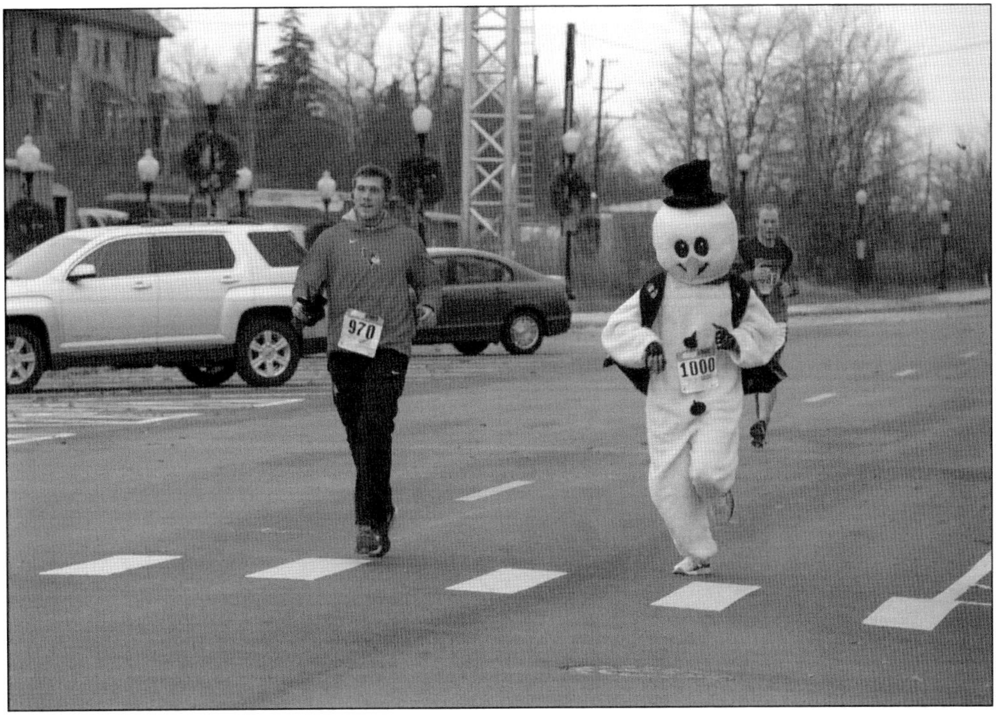

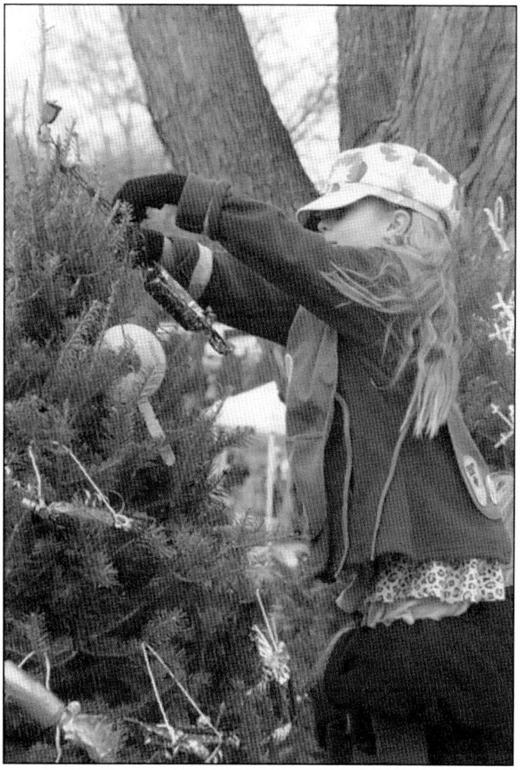

The week of Thanksgiving kicks off the village's Holly Days celebration. Community groups, Scout troops, and local businesses can sponsor and decorate the Christmas trees that line the paths outside of the Westmont Park District Community Center. This scout is putting the finishing touches on her troop's tree before heading into the gymnasium to do some Christmas shopping at the Holly Days Craft Bazaar. The Lions Club also serves up a warm pancake breakfast for those participating in the festivities. (Courtesy of the Village of Westmont.)

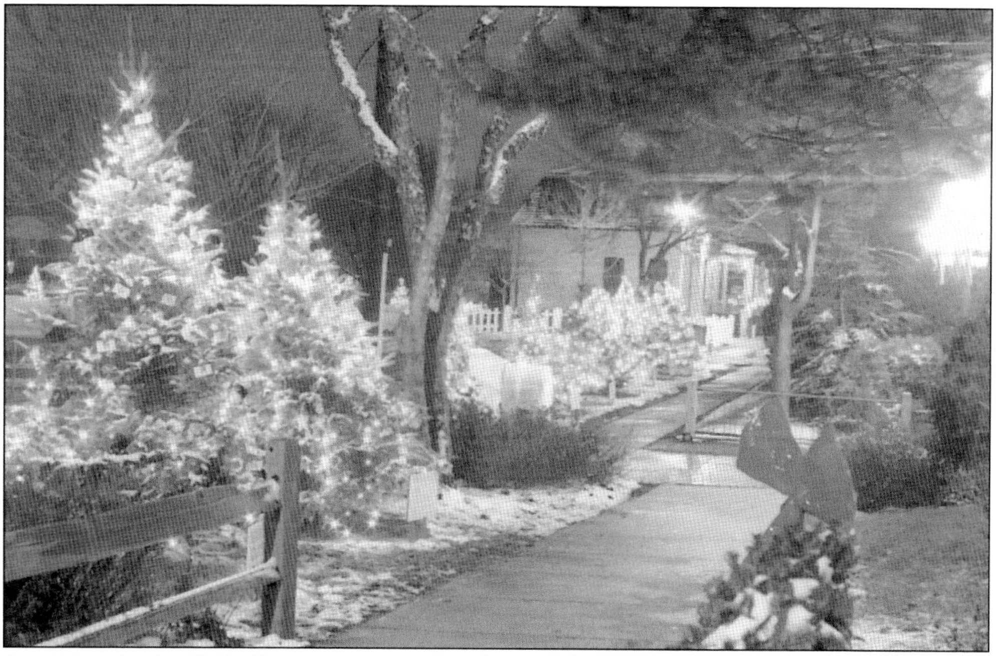

At night, the lit Holly Days trees provide a beautiful winter walk for families. Each tree is decorated with love by the students, Scout troops, businesses, and community groups, and each tree is different. Decorating the trees has become an annual tradition for Westmont families. (Courtesy of the Westmont Park District.)

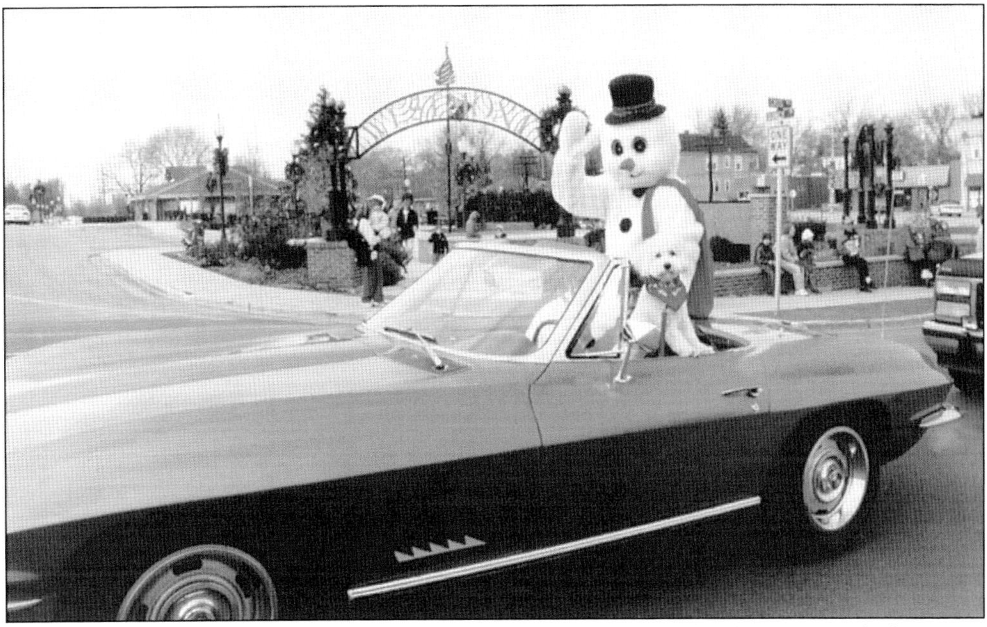

The official kickoff to Holly Days takes place the Saturday after Thanksgiving with the Frosty and Friends Parade. Featuring Frosty the Snowman, marching bands, Scout troops, and other entertainment, the evening parade is a great way to start the Holly Days season. (Courtesy of the Village of Westmont.)

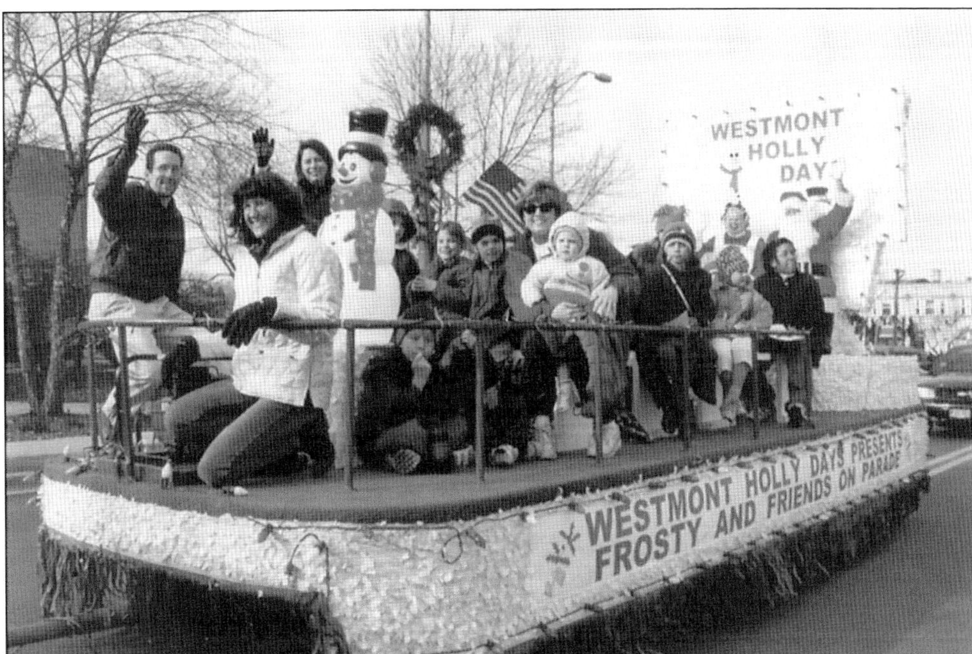

Of course, the parade would not be complete without a visit from Santa and Mrs. Claus. After the parade, Westmont's children can meet them and take photographs while enjoying hot cocoa and carolers at Westmont Centre. (Courtesy of the Village of Westmont.)

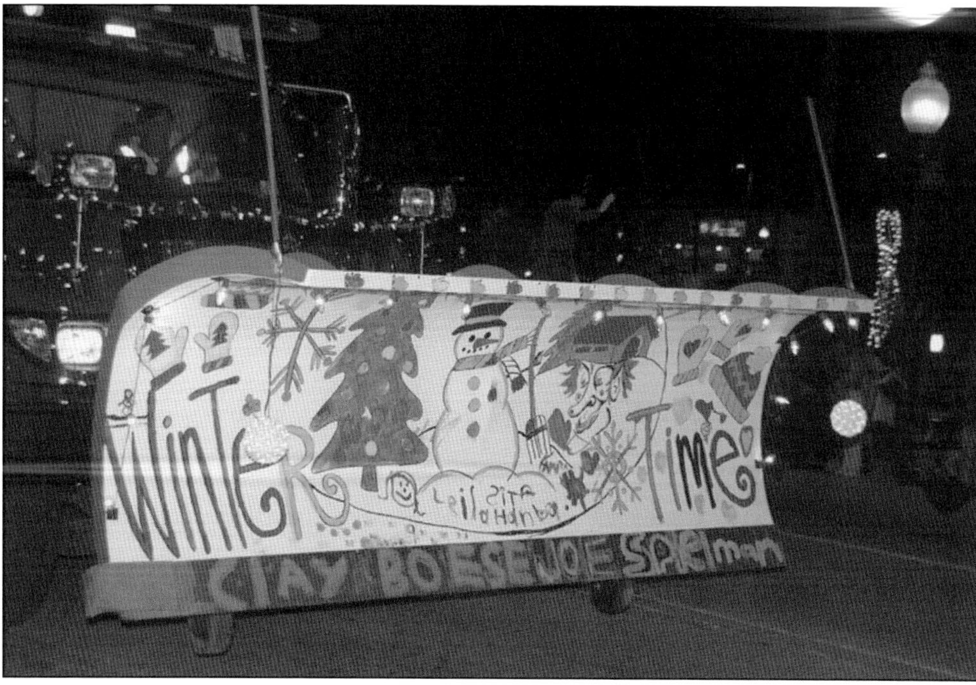

For years, Westmont's students have painted the village's snowplows with images of holiday cheer. This plow had a place of pride in the Frosty and Friends Parade, leading a decorated truck down Cass Avenue. (Courtesy of the Village of Westmont.)

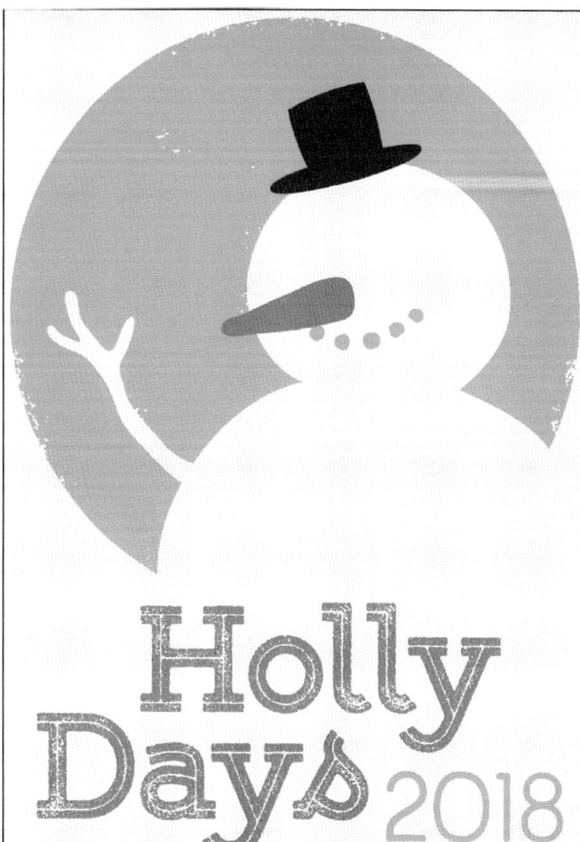

Holly Days started in 1995 and was modelled after East Peoria's Festival of Lights. The parade began in 2002. To offer more consistent branding for its events, the village introduced new logos for Holly Days and Wicked West Fest. The logo for Wicked West Fest, also known as "the Nightmare Before Holly Days," is rendered in shades of orange and purple and features a witch's hat and gnarled hands. The Holly Days logo is a decidedly brighter affair, featuring Frosty the Snowman in shades of light blue. (Courtesy of the Village of Westmont.)

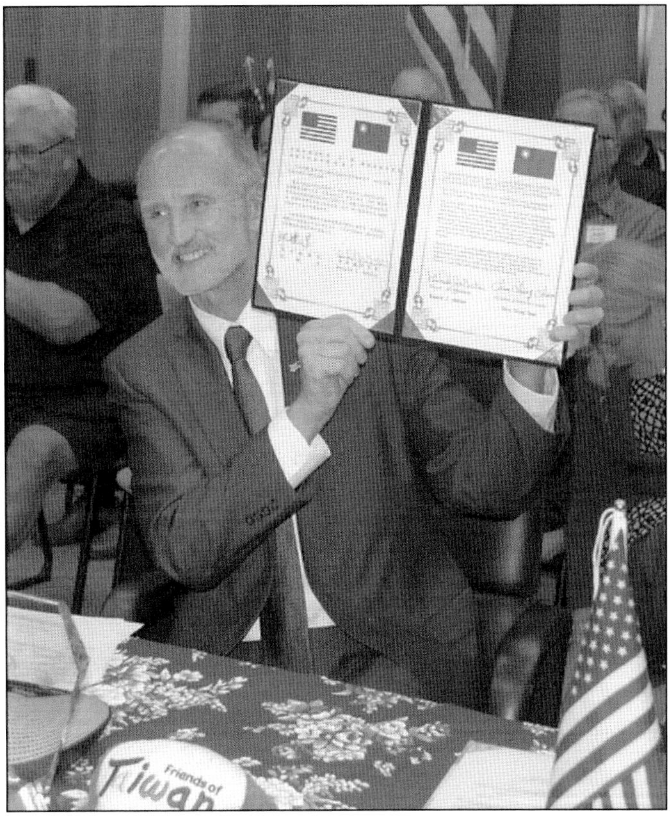

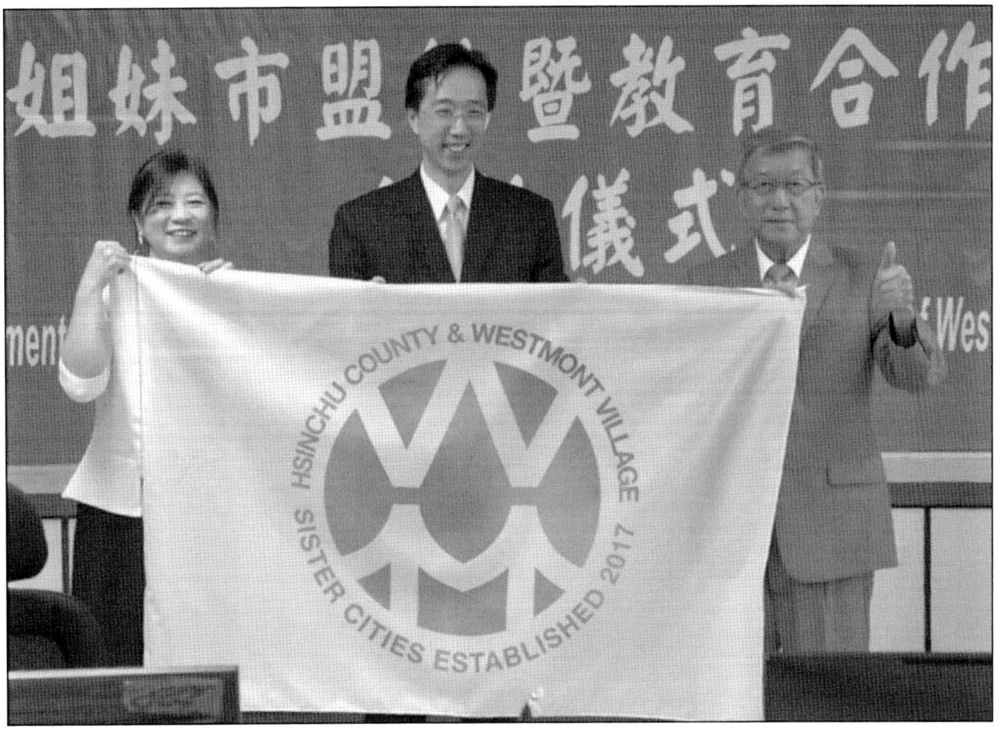

Over the past several decades, Westmont has grown its relationship with its local Taiwanese population. In 2017, Mayor Ron Gunter signed a sister city agreement with officials from Hsinchu County, Taiwan. This agreement will build cultural and economic ties between the two villages. (Both, courtesy of the Village of Westmont.)

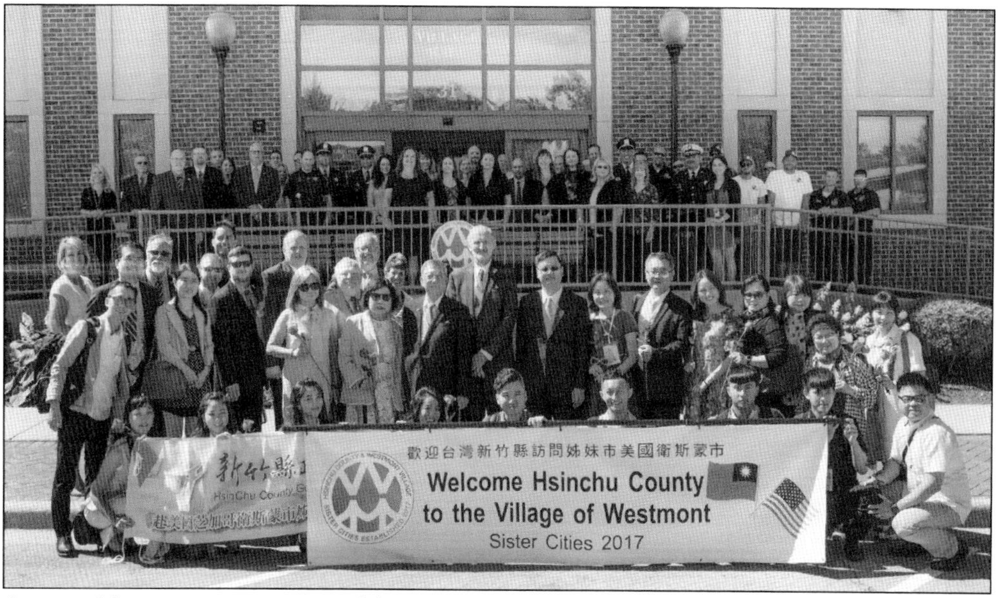

As part of the sister city program, a delegation from Hsinchu County visited Westmont in July 2018. The delegation, led by Magistrate Ching Chun Chiu, included officials from Hsinchu County's cultural and education departments, an eight-person dance troupe, and a master gourmet chef, who participated in the Taste of Westmont. (Courtesy of the Village of Westmont.)

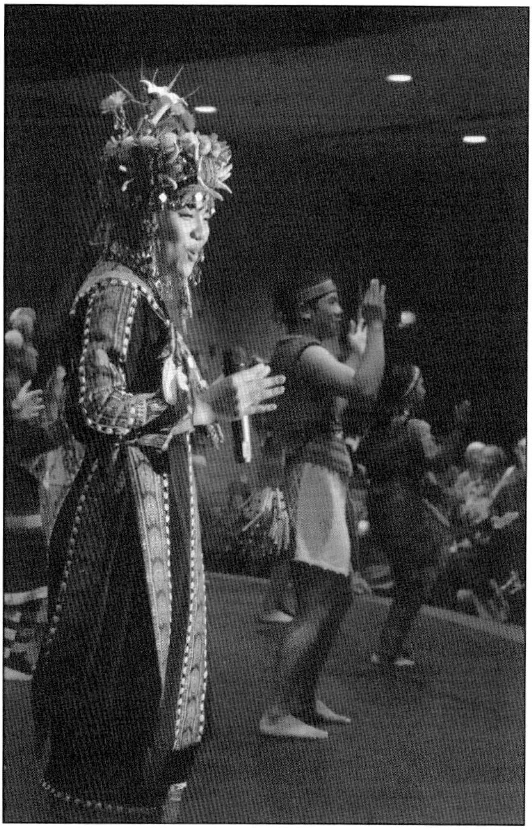

As part of the cultural exchange between the communities, a dance troupe from Taiwan has visited Westmont several times. Here, a dancer performs at the Taiwanese Cultural Center at 55 East Sixty-Third Street. (Courtesy of the Village of Westmont.)

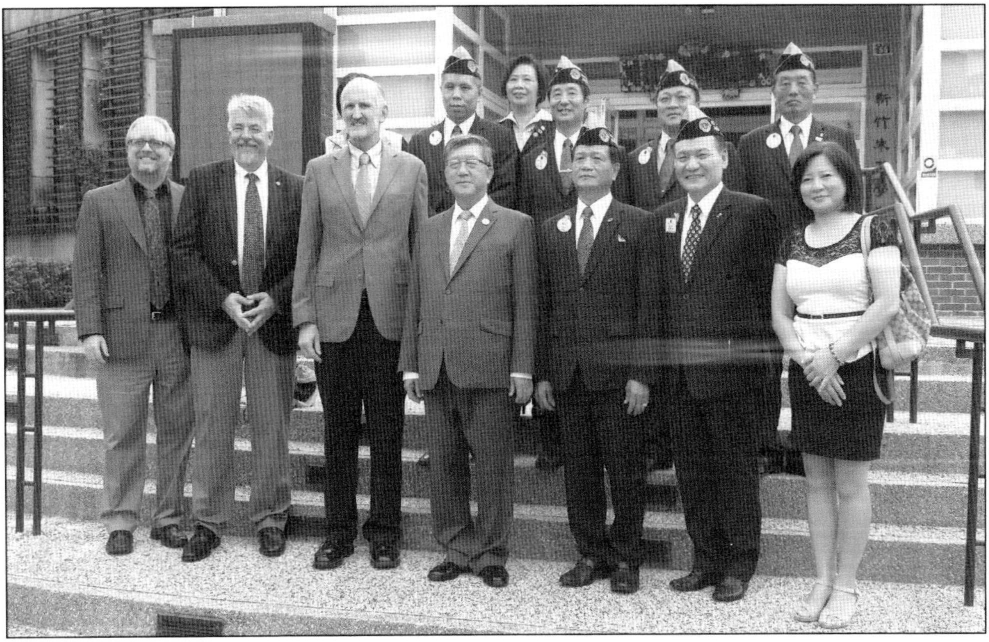

Delegates from Westmont visited Hsinchu County to propose a sister city connection. From left to right, Larry McIntyre (communications director), Larry Forssberg (chamber of commerce executive director), and Mayor Ron Gunter pose with some of the officials from Hsinchu County. (Courtesy of the Village of Westmont.)

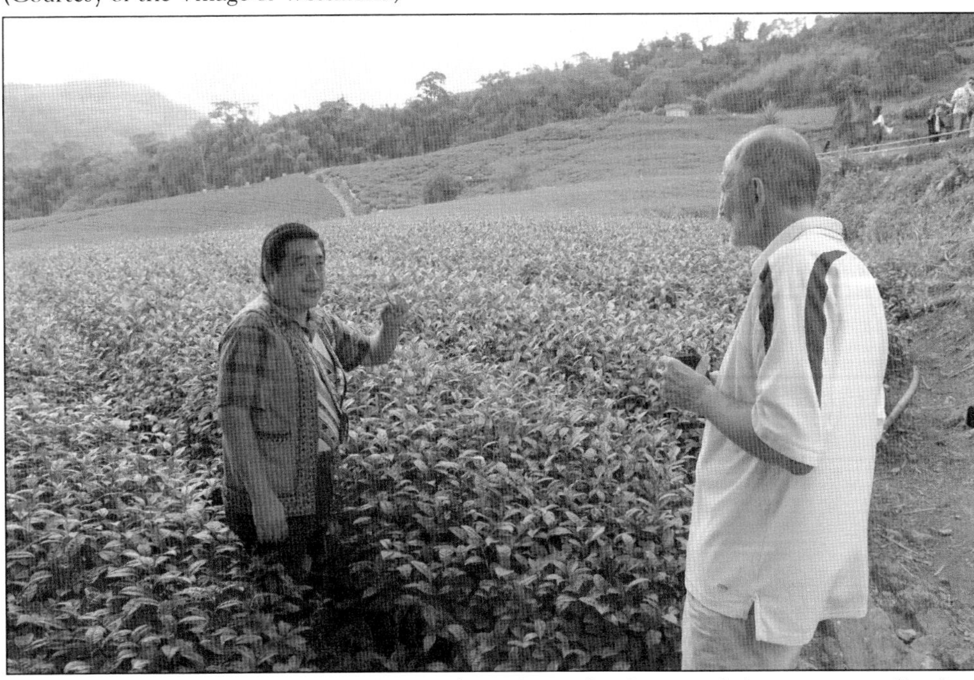

Mayor Ron Gunter stops to chat with a resident of Hsinchu County while visiting a coffee farm on Alishan Mountain. Officials from the different village organizations, including the Lions Club and Rotary Club, have visited Taiwan several times. Westmont High School also hosts several Taiwanese exchange students each year. (Courtesy of the Village of Westmont.)

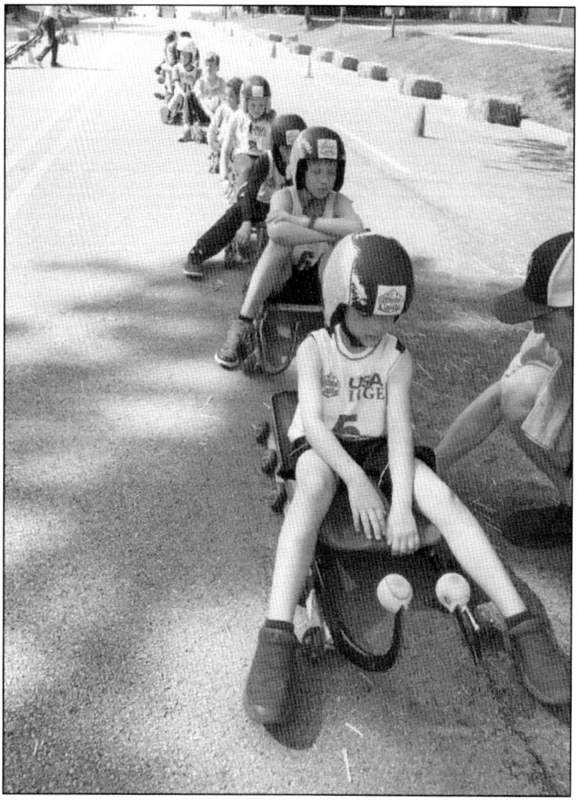

For the past several years, the US Olympic luge team has conducted tryouts in Westmont. These "slider searches" take place on Cass Avenue between Fifty-Fifth and Dallas Streets. Hundreds of Olympic hopefuls have taken part in these tryouts. (Both, courtesy of the Village of Westmont.)

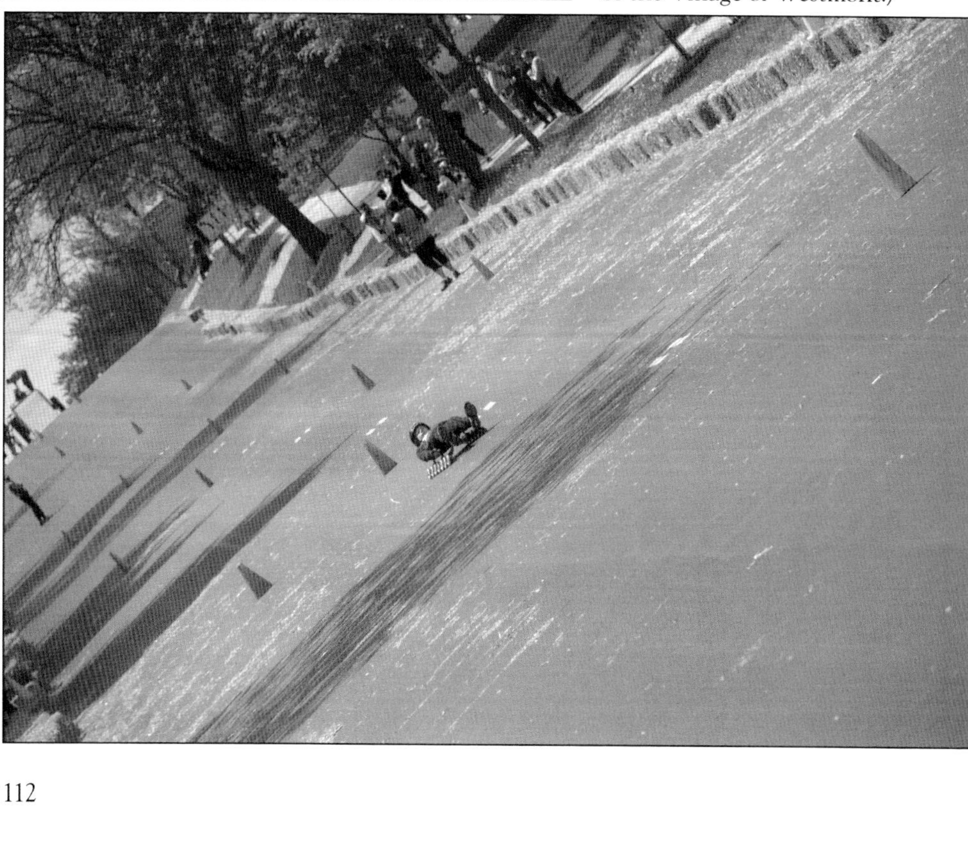

Part of the Taste of Westmont is the annual Blues Jam, which is held in the afternoon. Here, Blues legends John Primer and Koko Taylor perform for the crowds. (Courtesy of the Village of Westmont.)

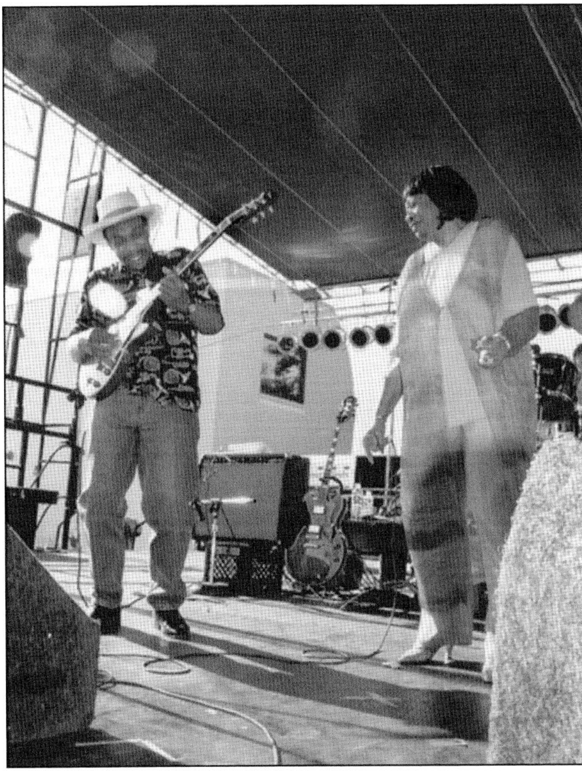

Cass Avenue is also Honorary Muddy Waters Way. From left to right, Ron Gunter, Joe Morganfield, Keith Reich, and Larry McIntyre pose with an autographed version of the street sign currently on loan to the Muddy Waters Museum. The sign has been autographed by numerous Blues performers. (Courtesy of the Village of Westmont.)

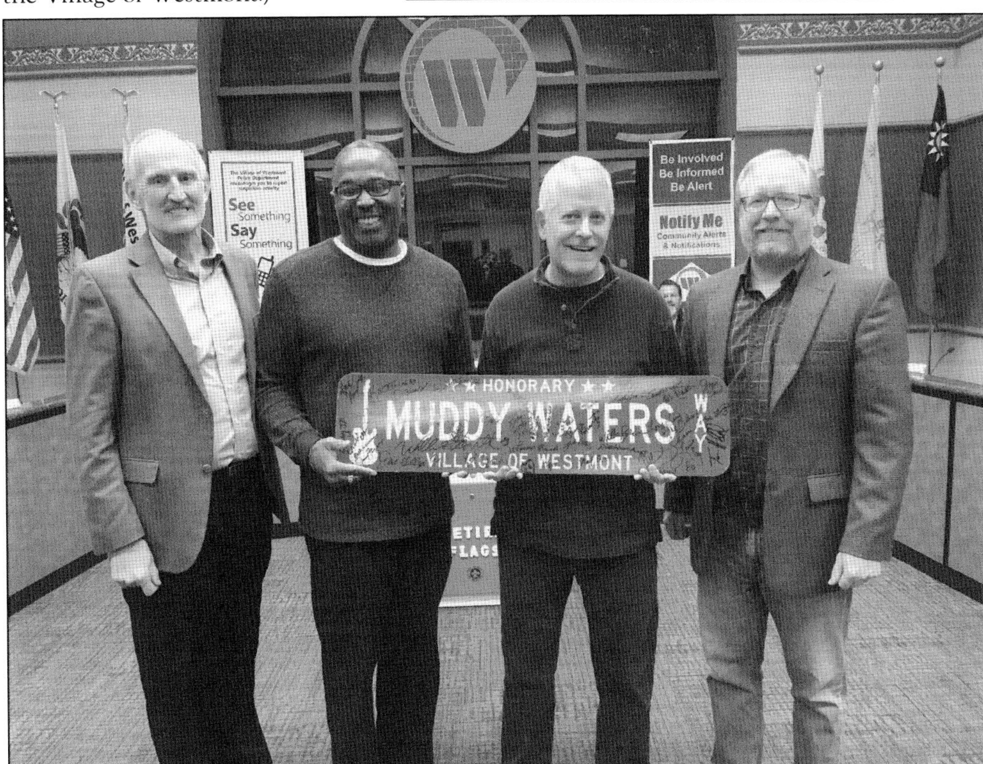

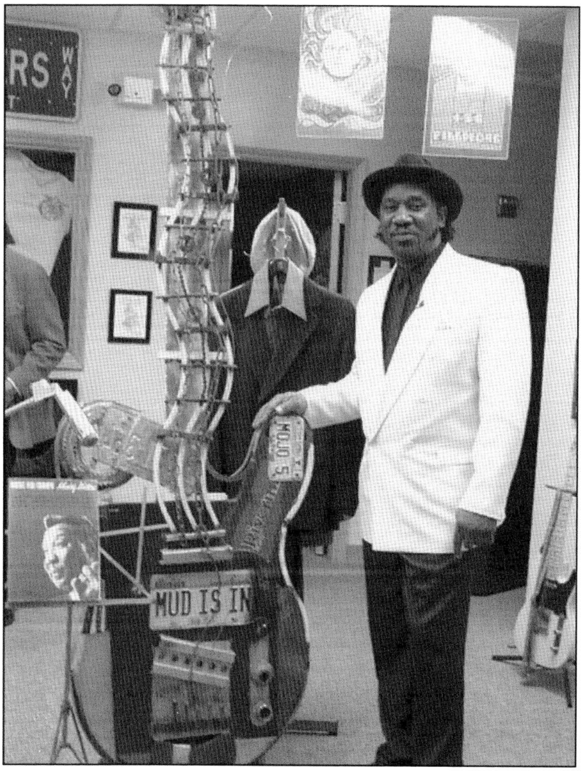

The Muddy Waters Museum was formed in collaboration with the Westmont Area Historical Society and Westmont Special Events Corporation. It is located in Westmont Centre and features memorabilia from and inspired by Muddy Waters's life. Here, his son Larry "Mud" Morganfield poses with a guitar sculpture in the museum. (Courtesy of the Village of Westmont.)

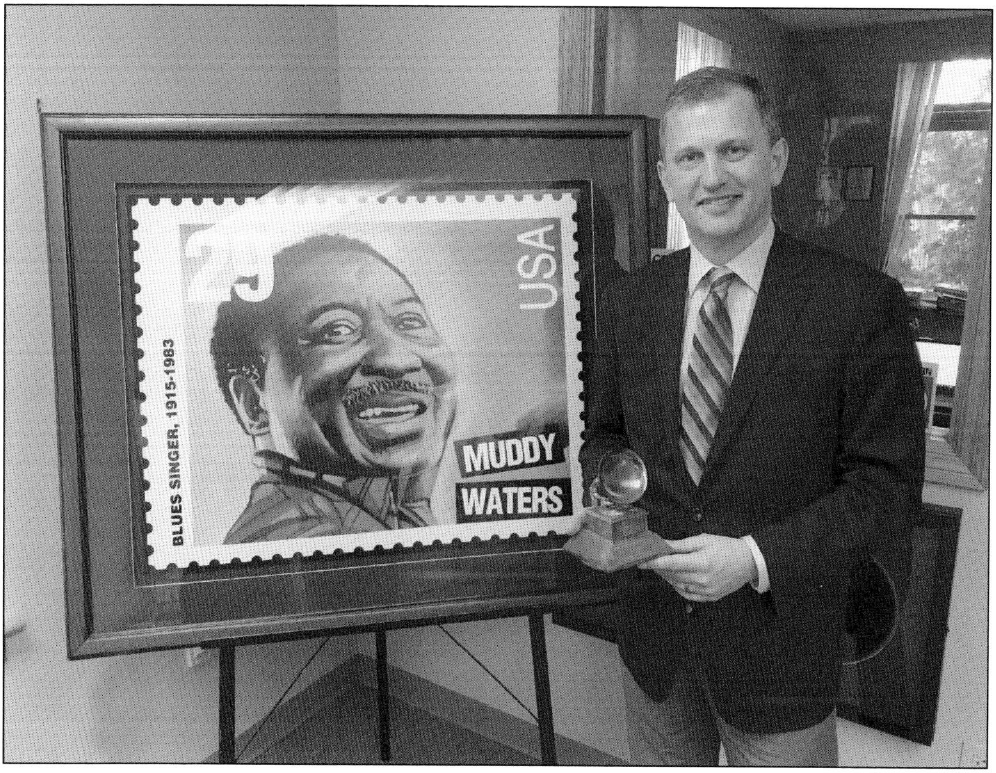

The Muddy Waters Museum attracts many visitors. Congressman Sean Casten visited the museum in 2019 and posed with one of the museum's most popular artifacts—one of Muddy Waters's Grammy awards. (Courtesy of the Village of Westmont.)

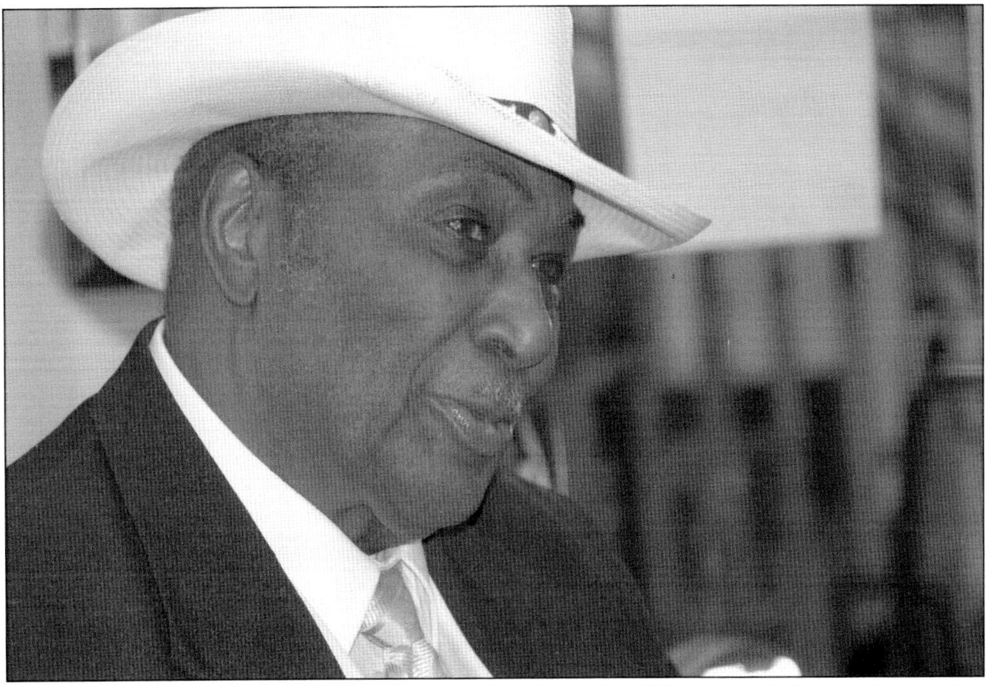

Blues legend Eddy Clearwater often visited and performed in Westmont. Following his passing in 2018, a special tribute performance in his honor was held at the Taste of Westmont, featuring one of his performance outfits. Some of his artifacts are on display in the Muddy Waters Museum. (Both, courtesy of the Village of Westmont.)

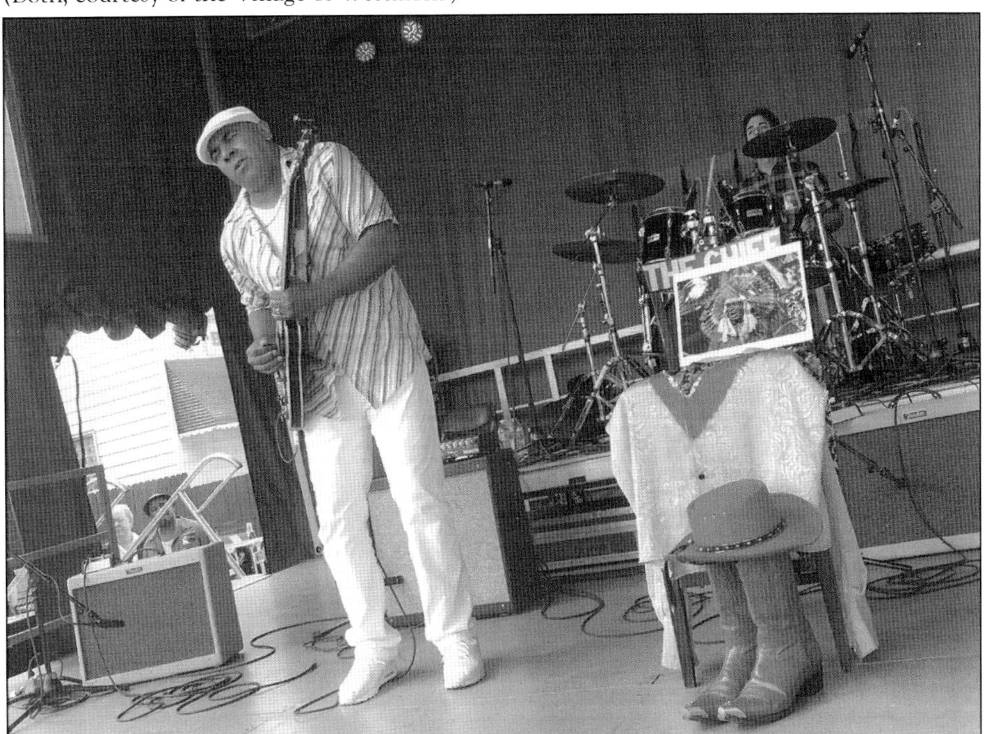

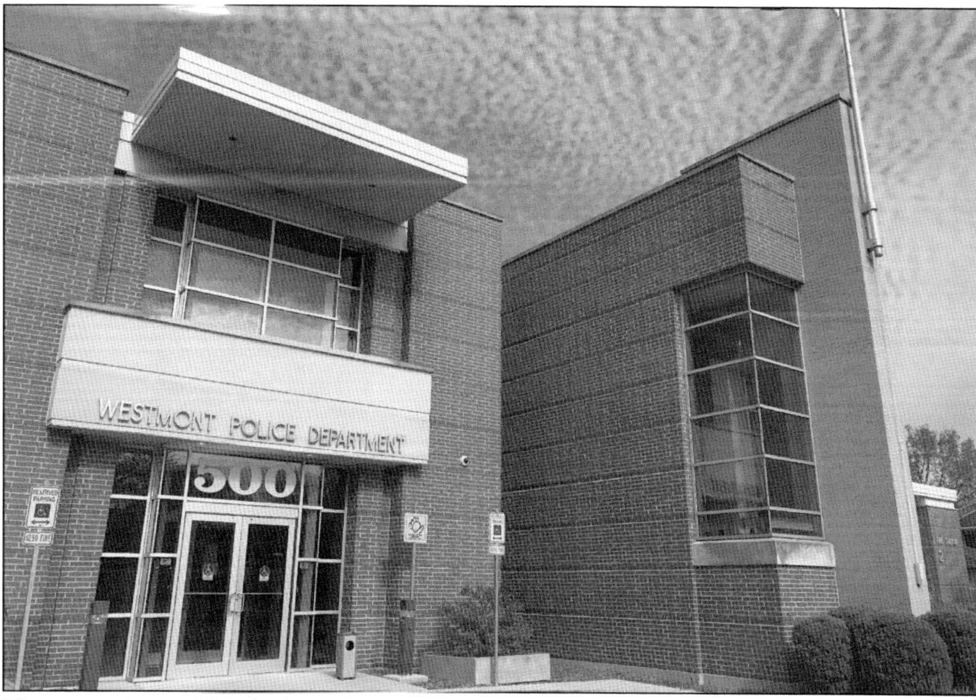

The new police and fire facility, Station No. 182, was built on the north end of town. This facility was constructed near the new library and makes it possible to have emergency response on both sides of the tracks without worrying about trains. (Courtesy of the Village of Westmont.)

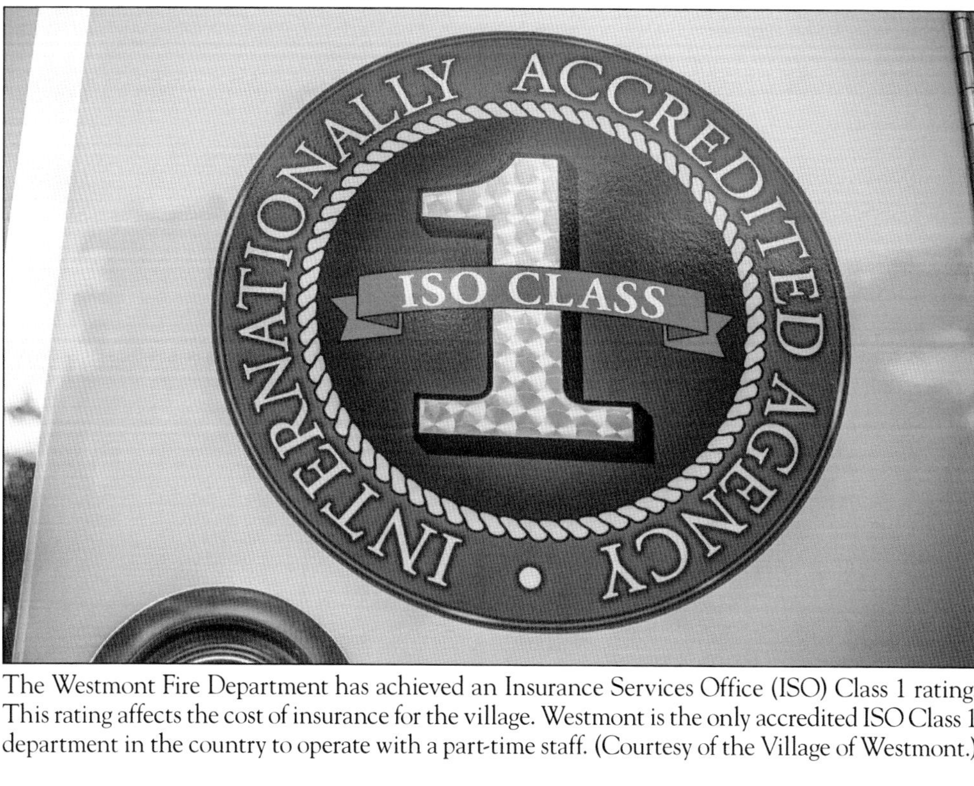

The Westmont Fire Department has achieved an Insurance Services Office (ISO) Class 1 rating. This rating affects the cost of insurance for the village. Westmont is the only accredited ISO Class 1 department in the country to operate with a part-time staff. (Courtesy of the Village of Westmont.)

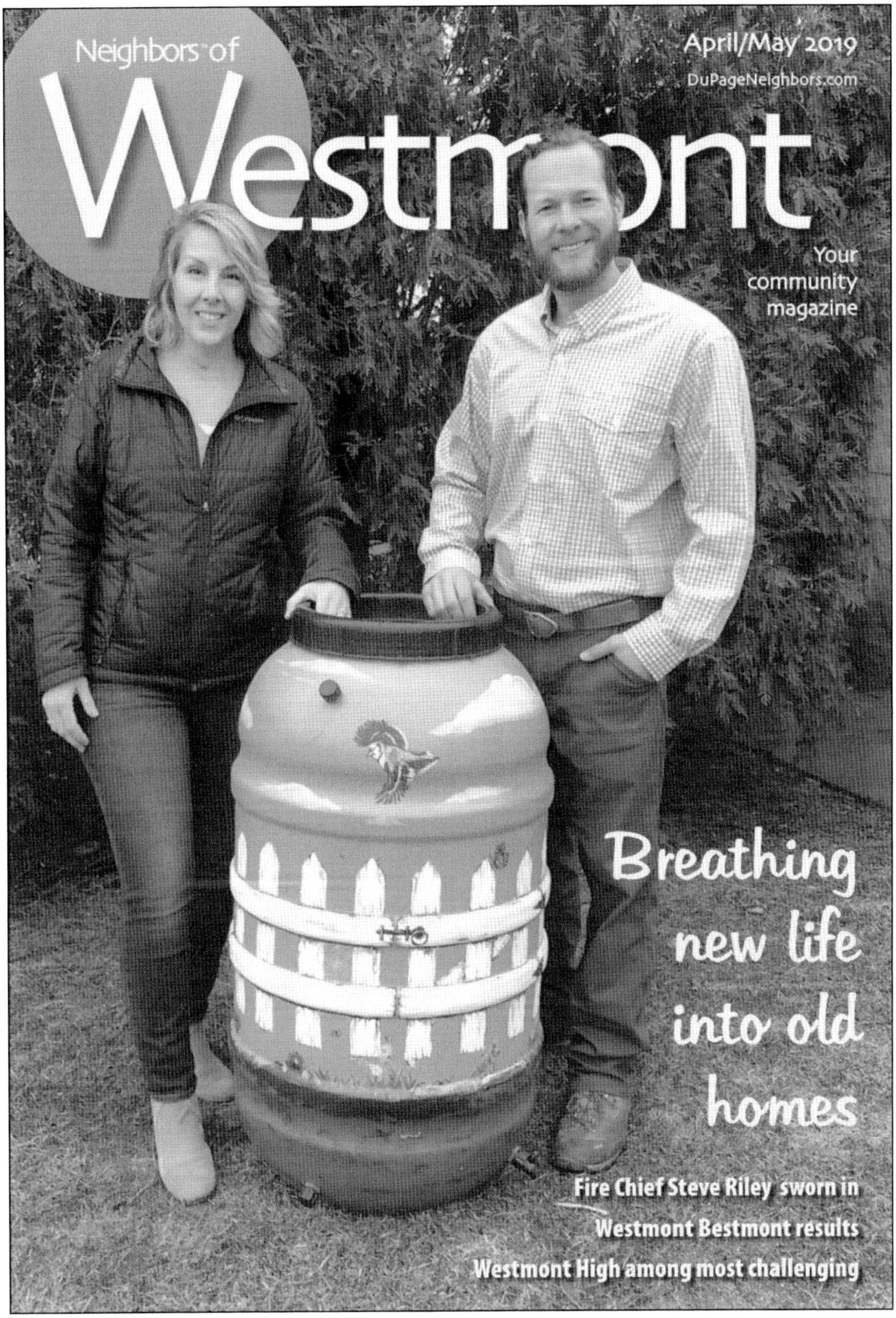

Everett Meservey published the first edition of Westmont's local paper, *The Community Press*, on July 3, 1924. His office was at 22 West Burlington Avenue, where he was also responsible for the community's first library and the first chamber of commerce. This paper was followed by others, including the *Towne Times* and the *Westmont Progress*. Today, residents can get village news and information on events through the bi-monthly magazine *Neighbors of Westmont*. (Courtesy of the Village of Westmont.)

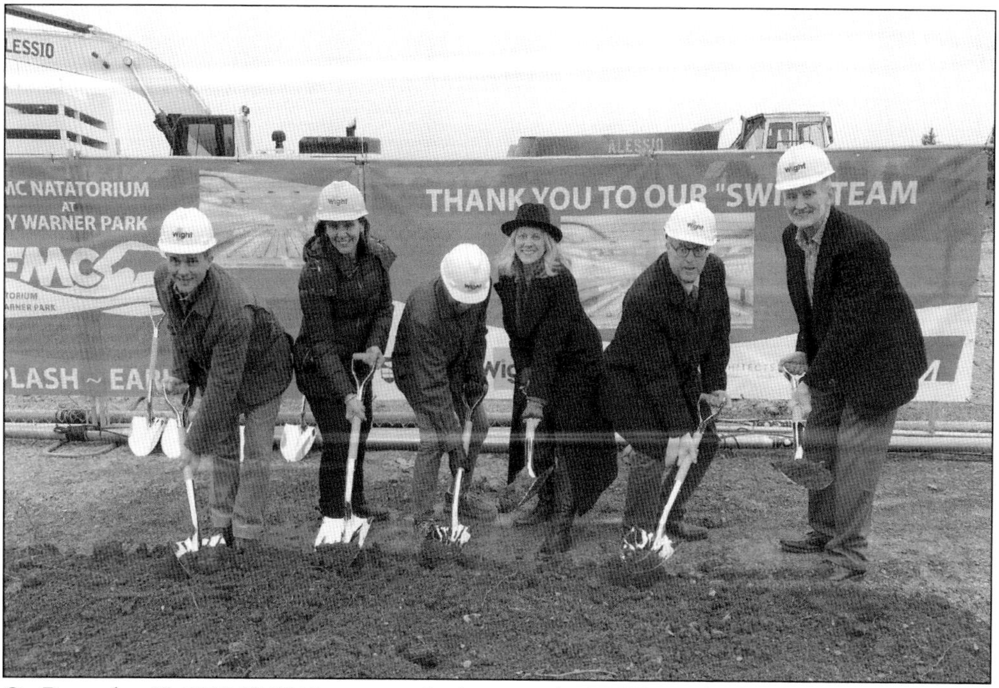

On December 13, 2018, FMC Natatorium broke ground at Ty Warner Park. The project is planned to include a 60,000-square-foot aquatic center including a 9-lane, 50-meter competition pool, and a 25-yard training pool to be used for swim lessons and programming. This project was made possible with close collaboration between the Village of Westmont, the Westmont Park District, and the team at FMC Aquatic Opportunities. (Above, courtesy of the Village of Westmont; below, courtesy of the Westmont Park District.)

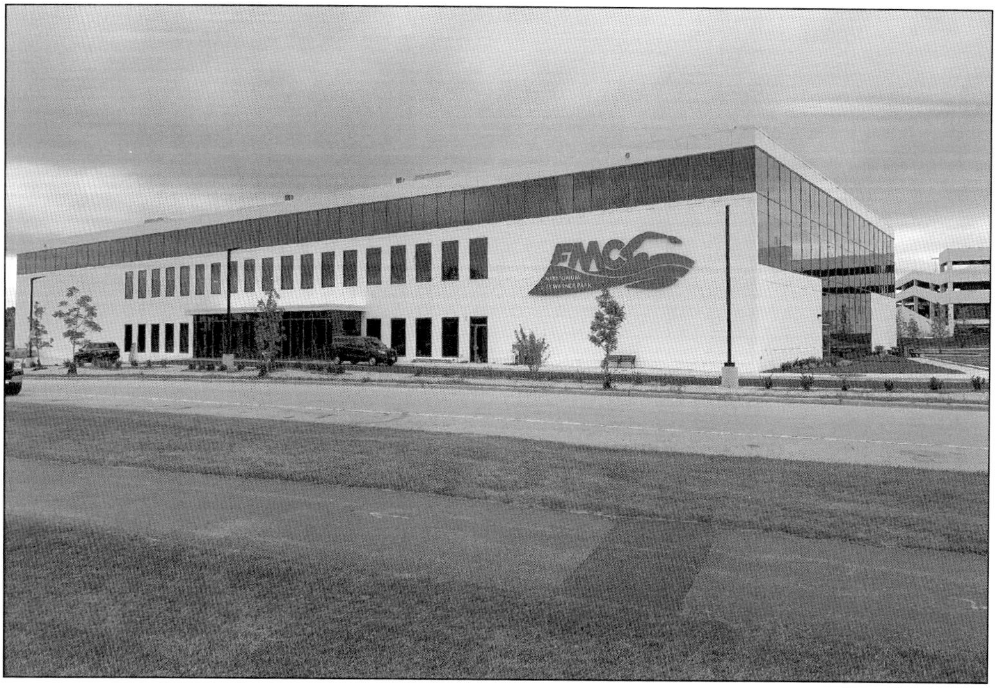

Few local businesses are as popular as Papa Passaro's pizza. The restaurant serves as a culinary anchor on the south end of town, away from the downtown area. Founded in the late 1970s, the pizzeria is popular with families and sports fans in the suburbs. (Courtesy of the Village of Westmont.)

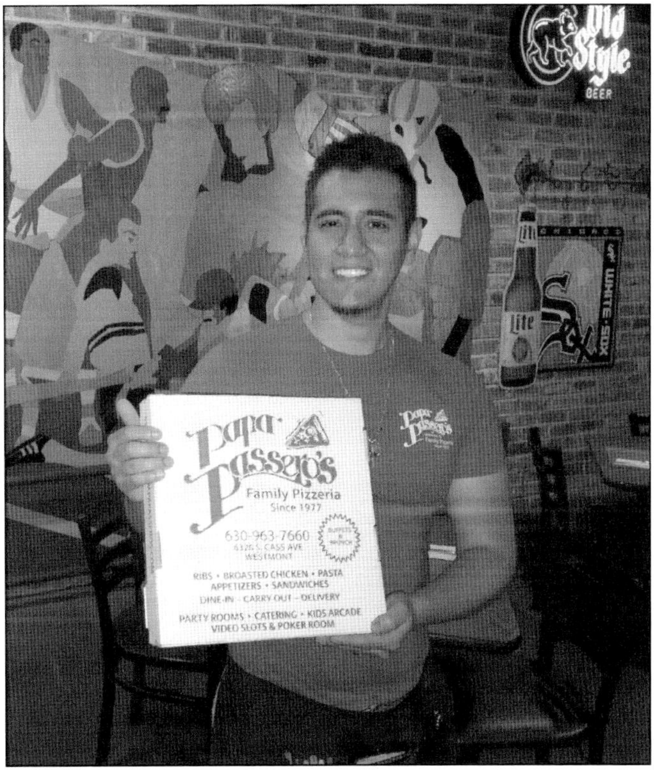

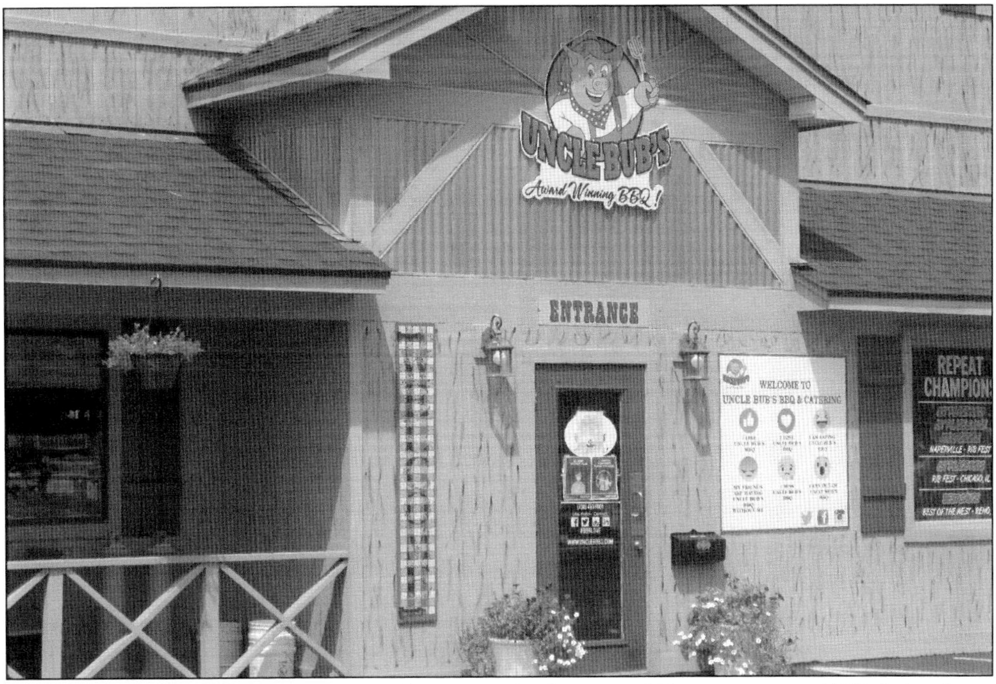

Uncle Bub's has been serving up award-winning barbecue in Westmont since 1997. It has been featured on WGN and the Food Network and in at least one feature film. (Courtesy of the Village of Westmont.)

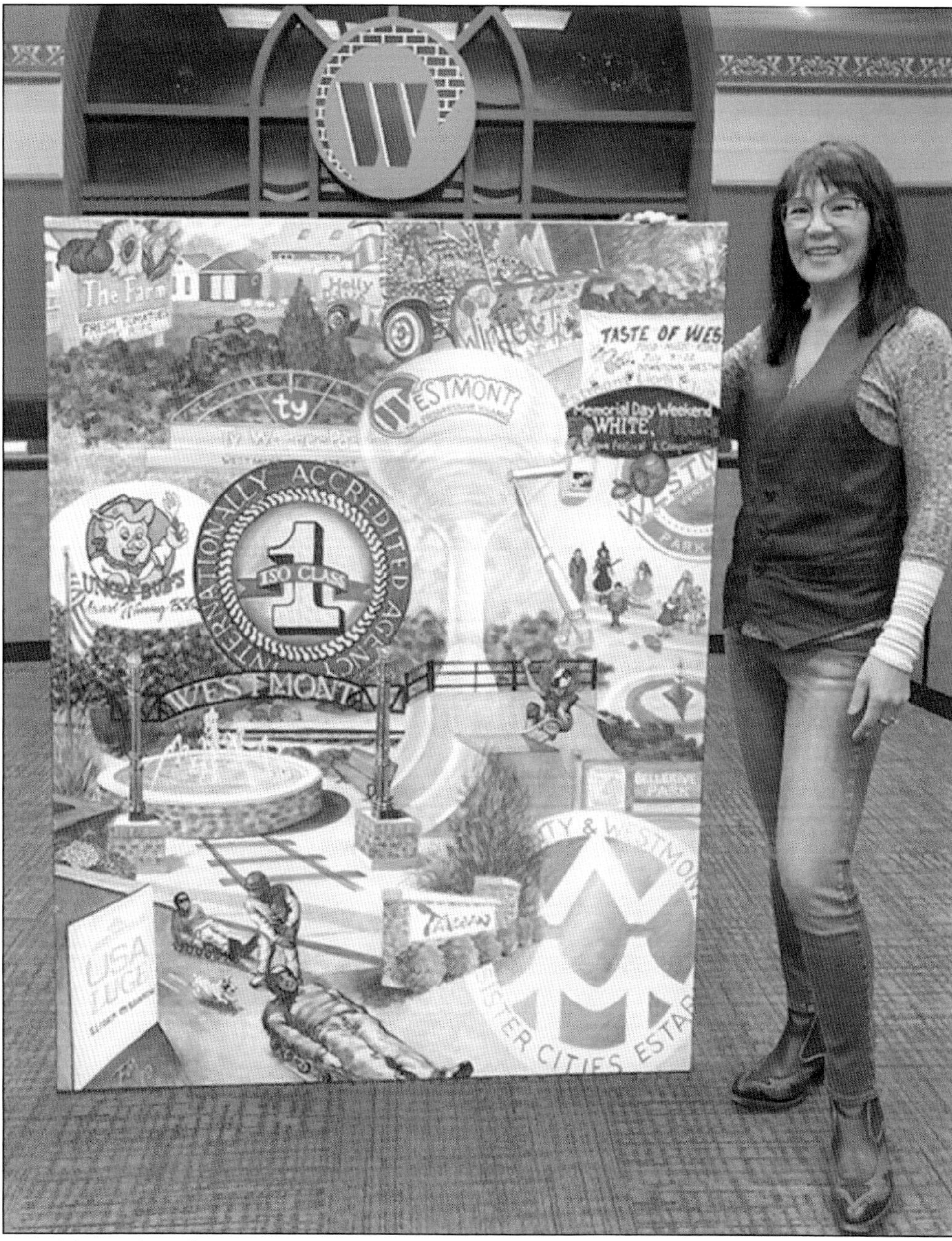

To celebrate the village's 100th anniversary, artist Fanny Moy was tasked with creating murals to depict the area's history. Beginning with preincorporation, she has painted murals that bring to life major events, people, and places that have made Westmont what it is today. The murals are on permanent display at the Westmont Library. (Courtesy of the Village of Westmont.)

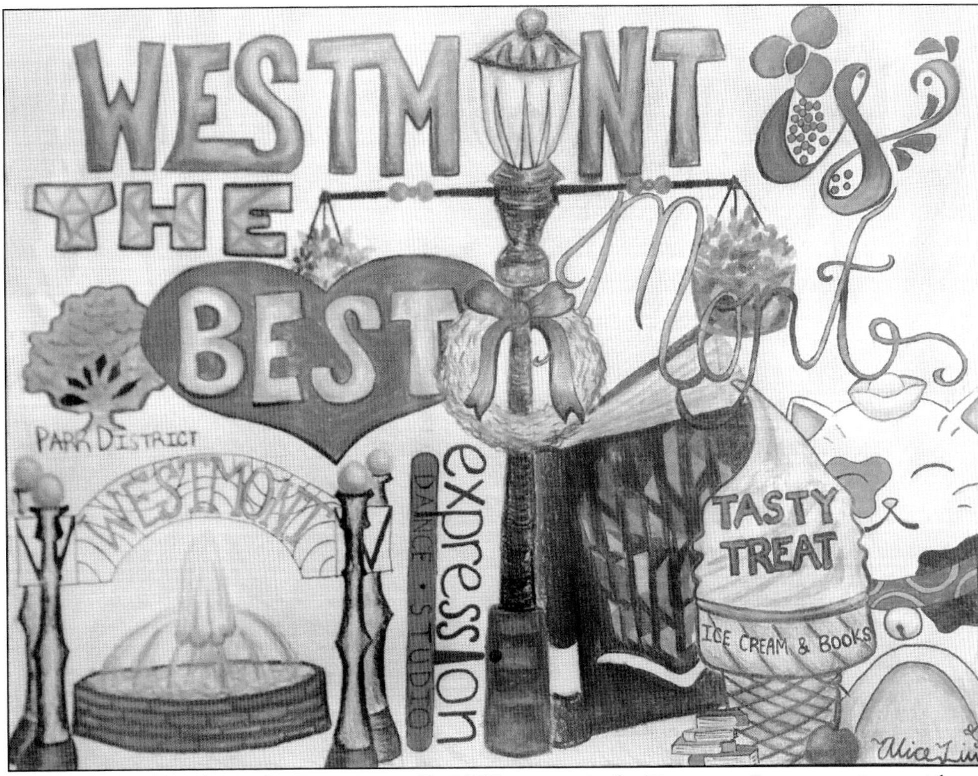

In 2019, the village hosted a campaign called "Westmont is the Bestmont," encouraging residents to share what they thought made the village the best place to live in Illinois. Submissions ranged from art like these drawings, to photography, music, and even a pet or two. (Both, courtesy of the Village of Westmont.)

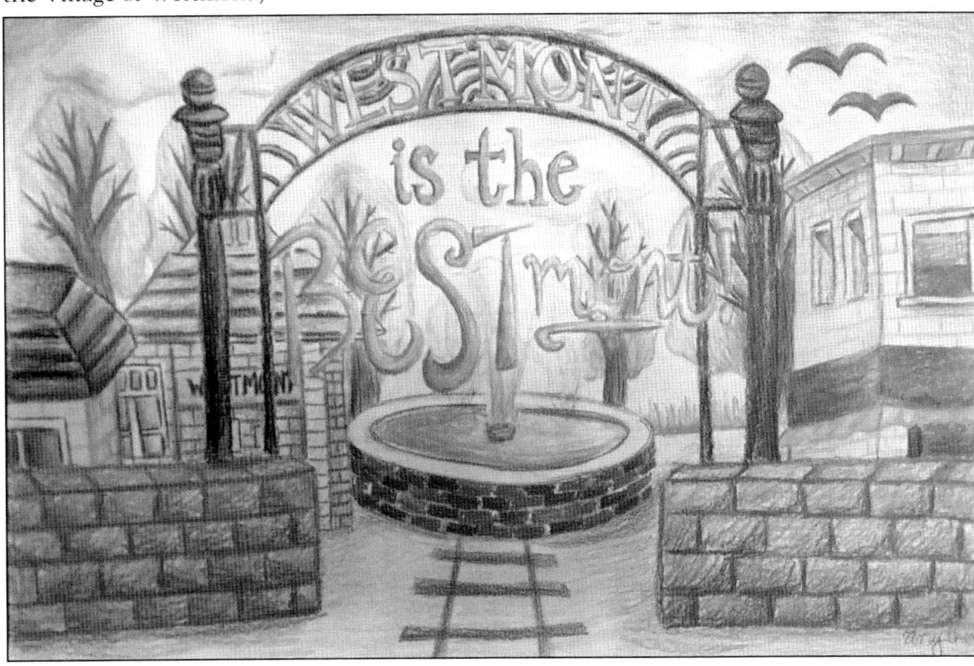

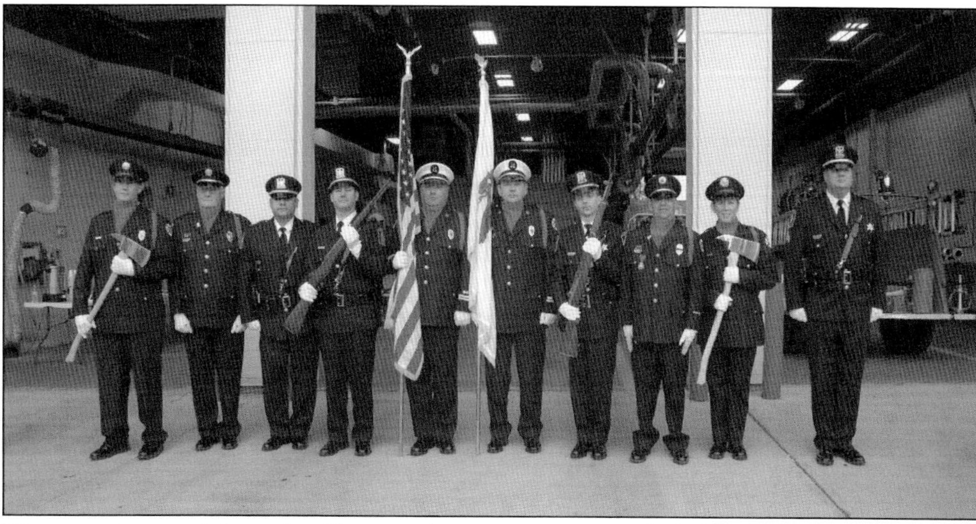

Westmont is one of the only villages in the area to consistently hold a Patriot's Day ceremony each year. This ceremony commemorates the lives lost in the September 11 attacks. (Courtesy of the Village of Westmont.)

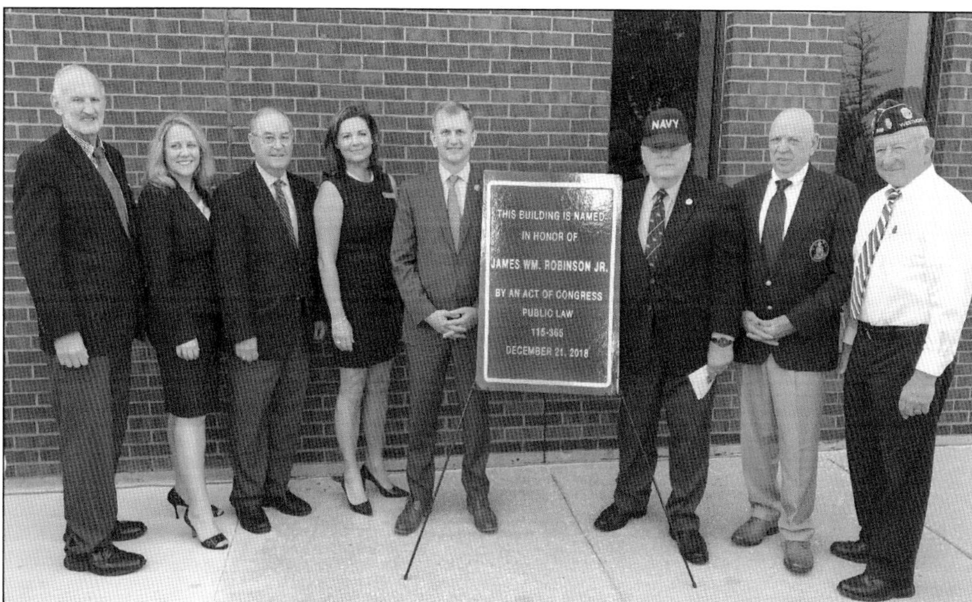

In 2019, Westmont's post office was renamed in honor of James Robinson, a Westmont resident and Medal of Honor recipient who lost his life in the Vietnam War. The American Legion sought to have his sacrifice memorialized in town. (Courtesy of the Village of Westmont.)

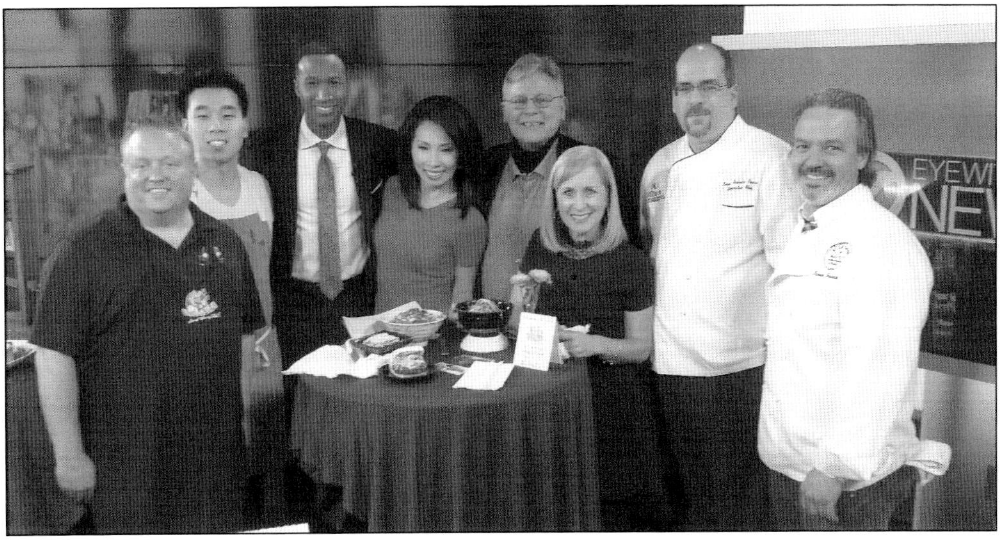

Westmont Restaurant Week offers residents and visitors the opportunity to "dine around the world in Westmont." In 2019, the event organizers were invited on air at ABC 7 to publicize Restaurant Week, which is organized through the chamber of commerce. The event encourages local restaurants to offer prix fixe menus to encourage diners to sample what they have to offer. (Courtesy of the Village of Westmont.)

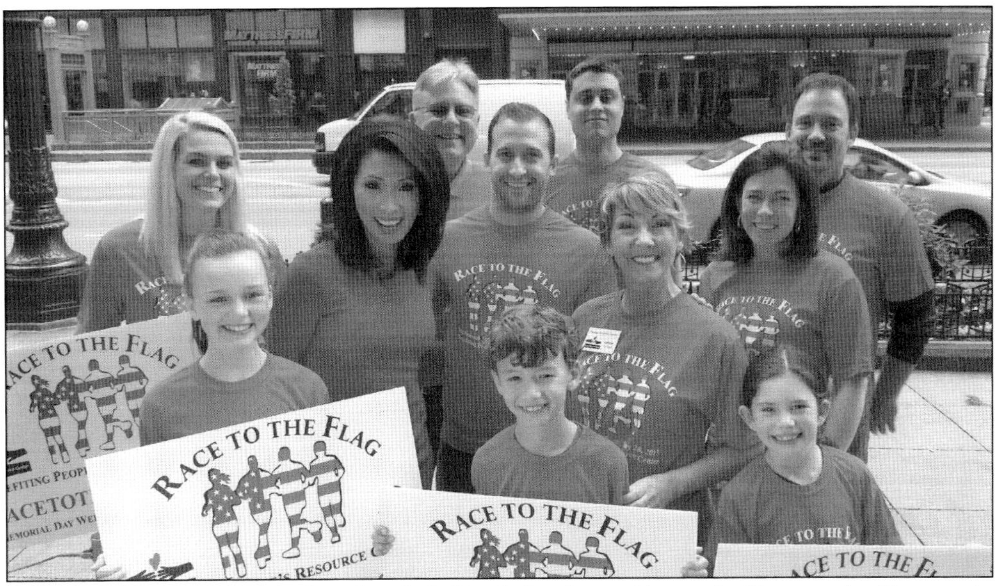

Also on ABC 7, resident and anchor Judy Hsu helped to publicize the Race to the Flag on air. Event organizer Gregg Pill poses with Hsu, volunteers, and staff of the Westmont Park District outside of the ABC 7 studios in Chicago. (Courtesy of the Village of Westmont.)

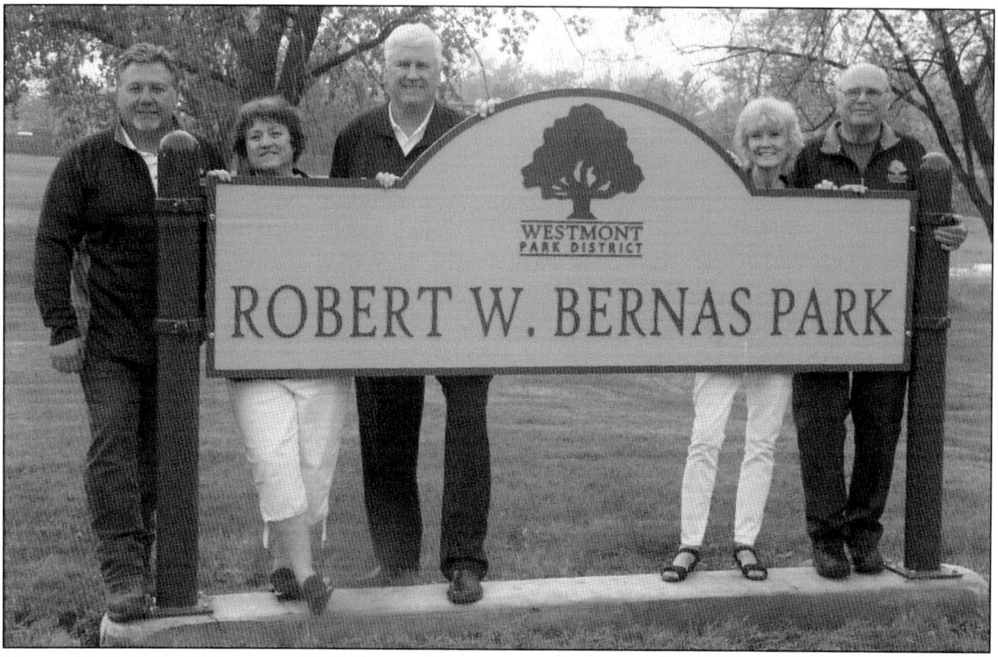

Bernas Park is the Westmont Park District's newest park. Opened in 2018, the park was named in honor of longtime board of commissioners member Robert Bernas. From left to right, commissioners John Karesh, Sandra Smith, James Long, Diane Main, and Robert Bernas pose at the groundbreaking event in 2017. (Courtesy of the Village of Westmont.)

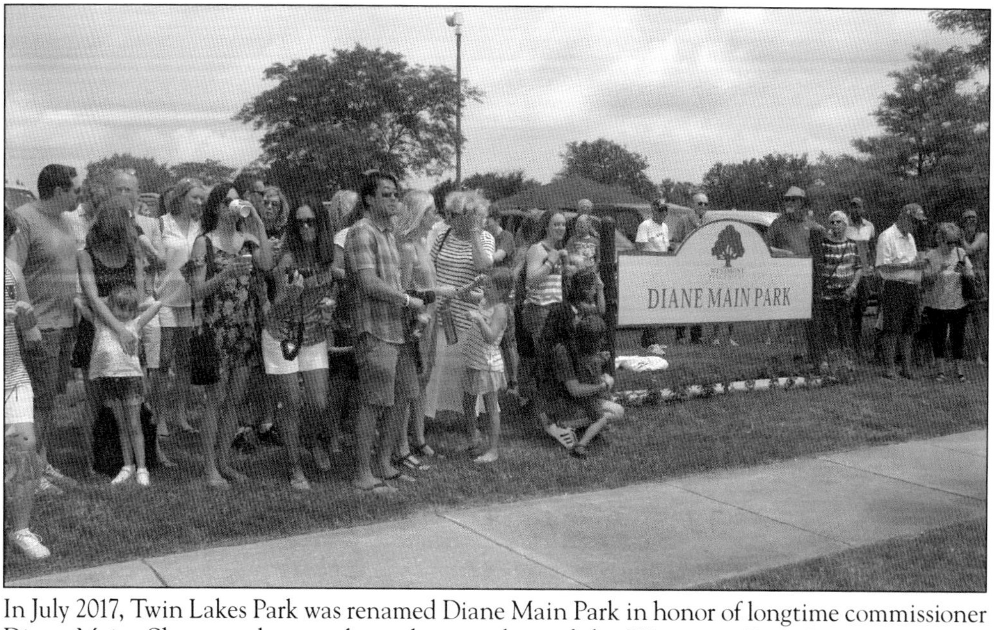

In July 2017, Twin Lakes Park was renamed Diane Main Park in honor of longtime commissioner Diane Main. She served not only as the president of the Westmont Park District Board of Commissioners, but also as the president of the Illinois Association of Park Districts. In addition, she was voted Westmont's Citizen of the Year. The adjoining woodlands were renamed Smith Woods in honor of Sandra Smith's contributions and history of service in 2017. (Courtesy of the Westmont Park District.)

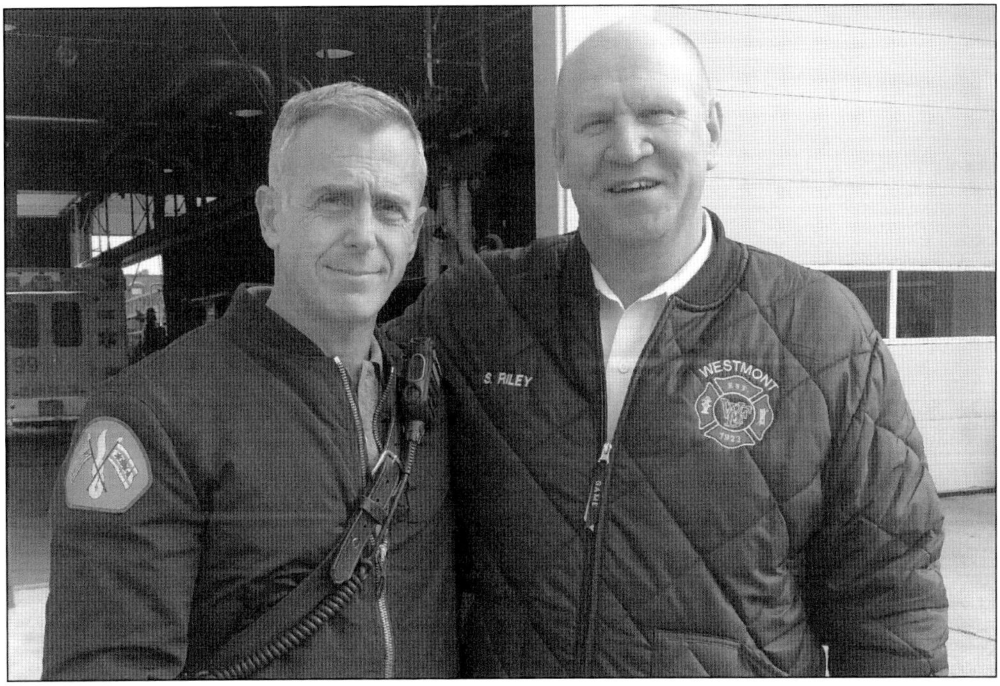

The popular television show *Chicago Fire* has filmed in Westmont several times. Here, actor David Eigenberg poses with fire chief Stave Riley outside of Station No. 182 during filming. (Courtesy of the Village of Westmont.)

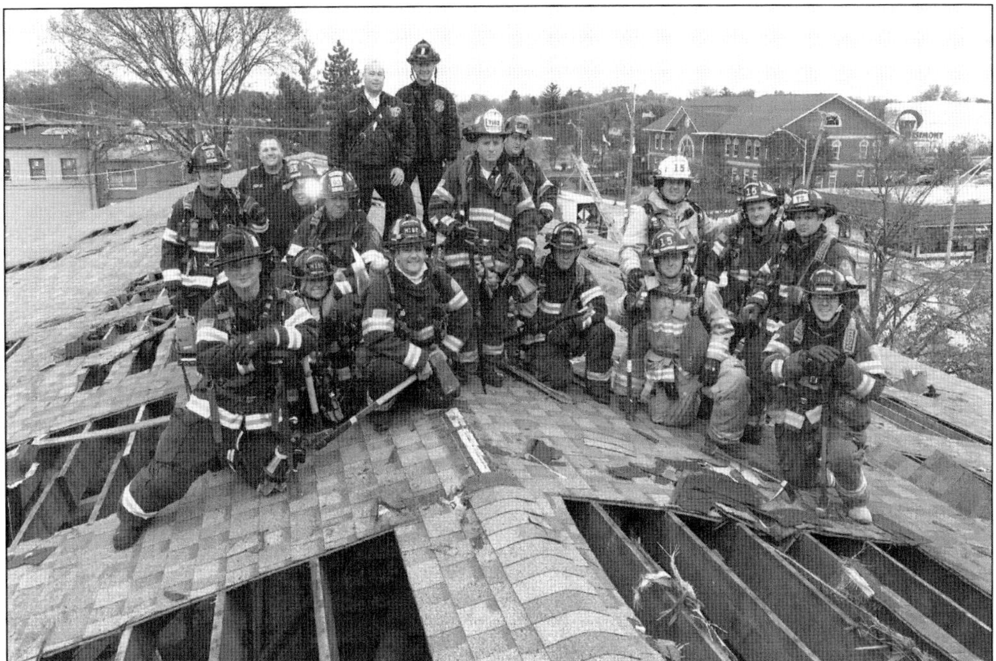

In 2020, the village hosted firefighters from several other communities to conduct training. The training was held in the buildings that formerly occupied the site of the Quincy Station condominiums, Westmont's first high-rise complex. (Courtesy of the Village of Westmont.)

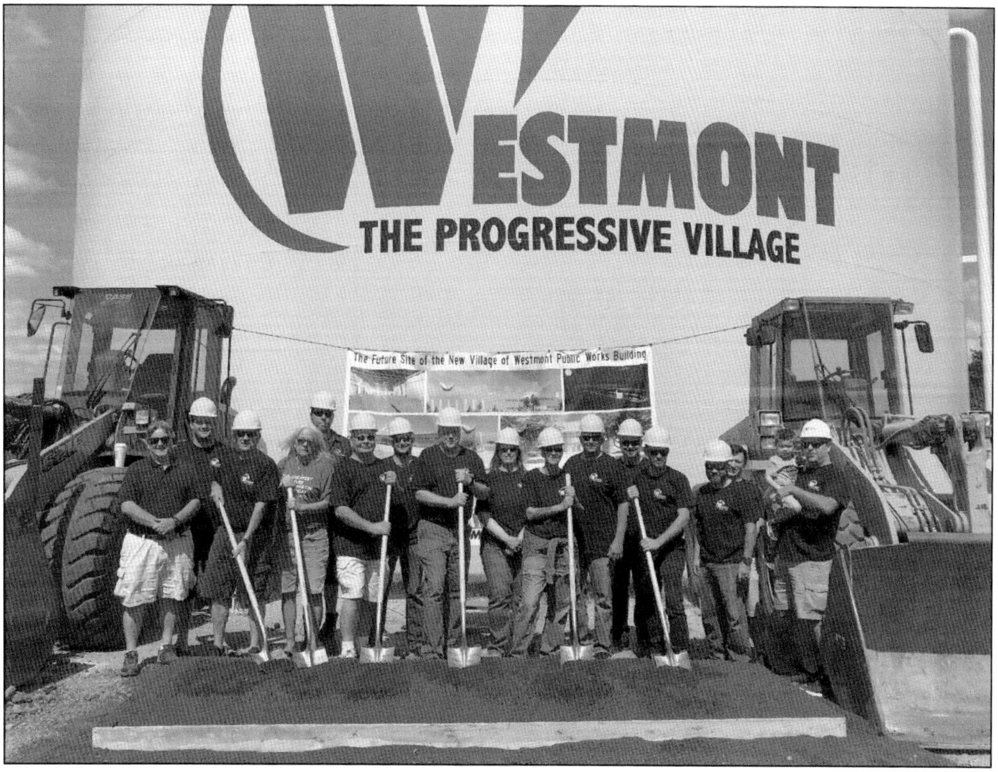

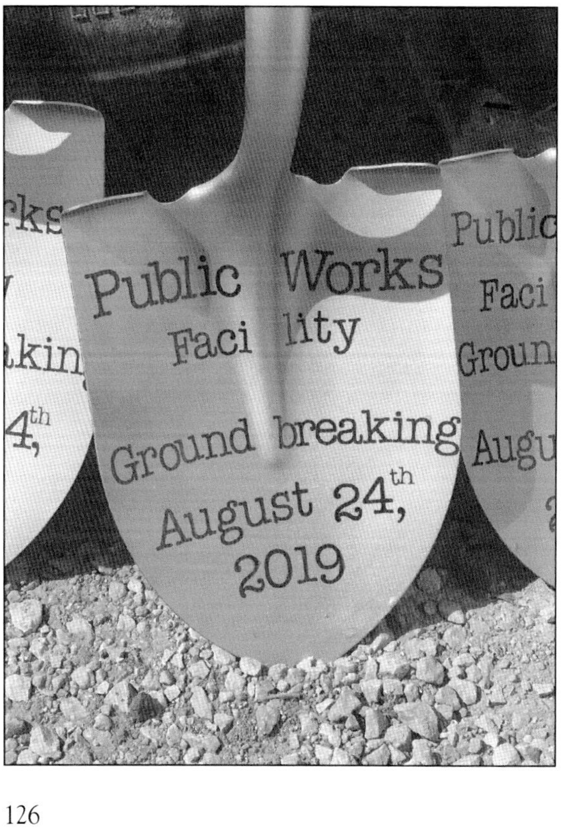

Westmont's public works department is responsible for the maintenance of village infrastructure. By 2019, it had outgrown its previous facility on Burlington Avenue, and ground was broken for a new, larger, state-of-the-art facility. (Both, courtesy of the Village of Westmont.)

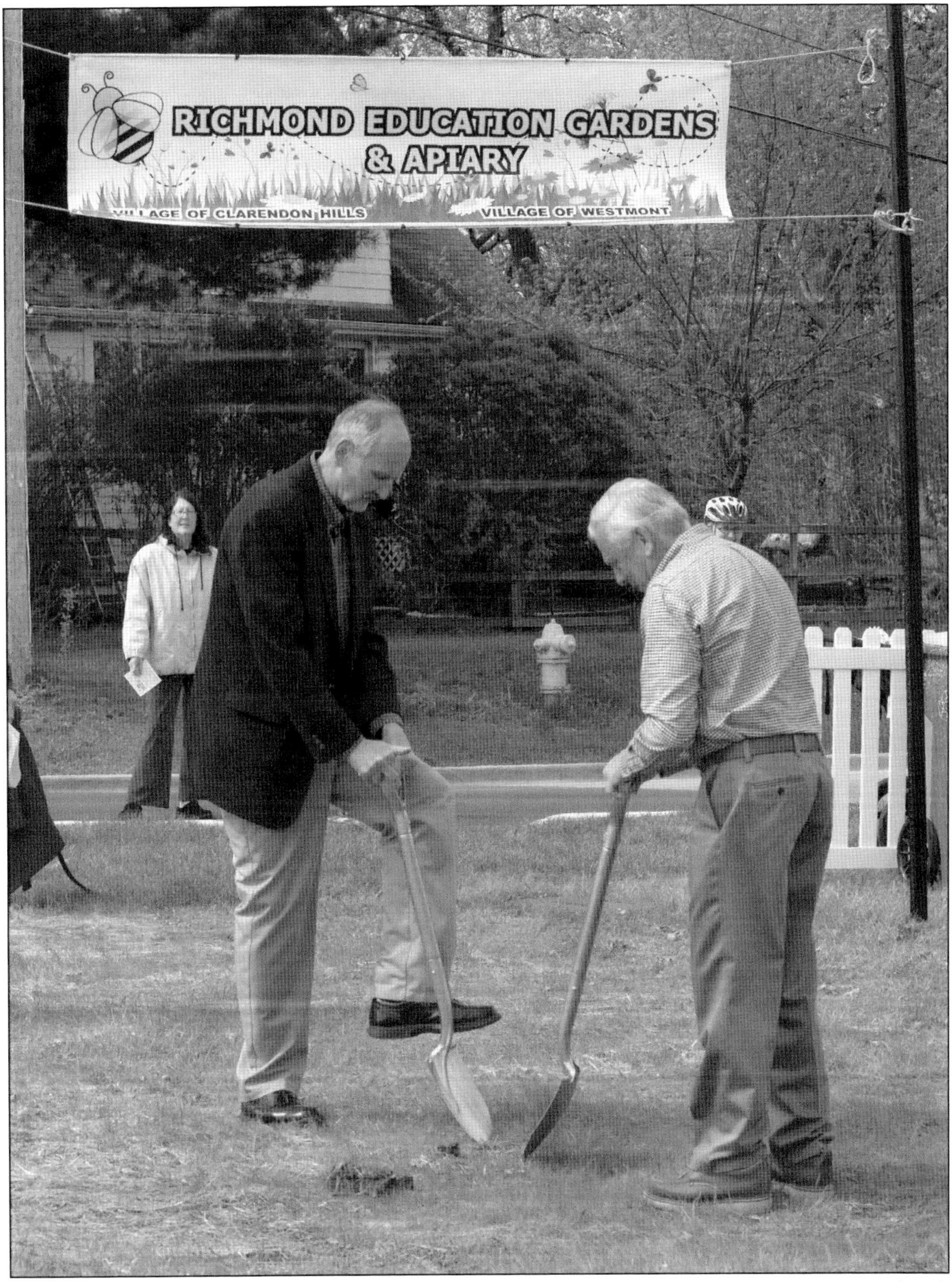

In 2017, Westmont mayor Ron Gunter (left) and Clarendon Hills village president Len Austin break ground for the Richmond Education Gardens and Apiary. The gardens are between Westmont and Clarendon Hills and are designed to include wildflower, vegetable, rain, and wall gardens, as well as beehives. The collaborative project was developed to encourage access to resources, community ownership of process and product, localization, empowerment and collaboration, healthy eating, and organic and environmentally sound gardening and landscaping practices. (Courtesy of the Village of Westmont.)

Consistent with our mission to preserve history on a local level, this book was printed in South Carolina on American-made paper and manufactured entirely in the United States. Products carrying the accredited Forest Stewardship Council (FSC) label are printed on 100 percent FSC-certified paper.